D0104153

RENT-A-(REALLY-SHY!)-GIRLFRIEND

2

REIJI MIYAJIMA
ART ASSISTANCE: YUKA KINAMI

CONTENTS

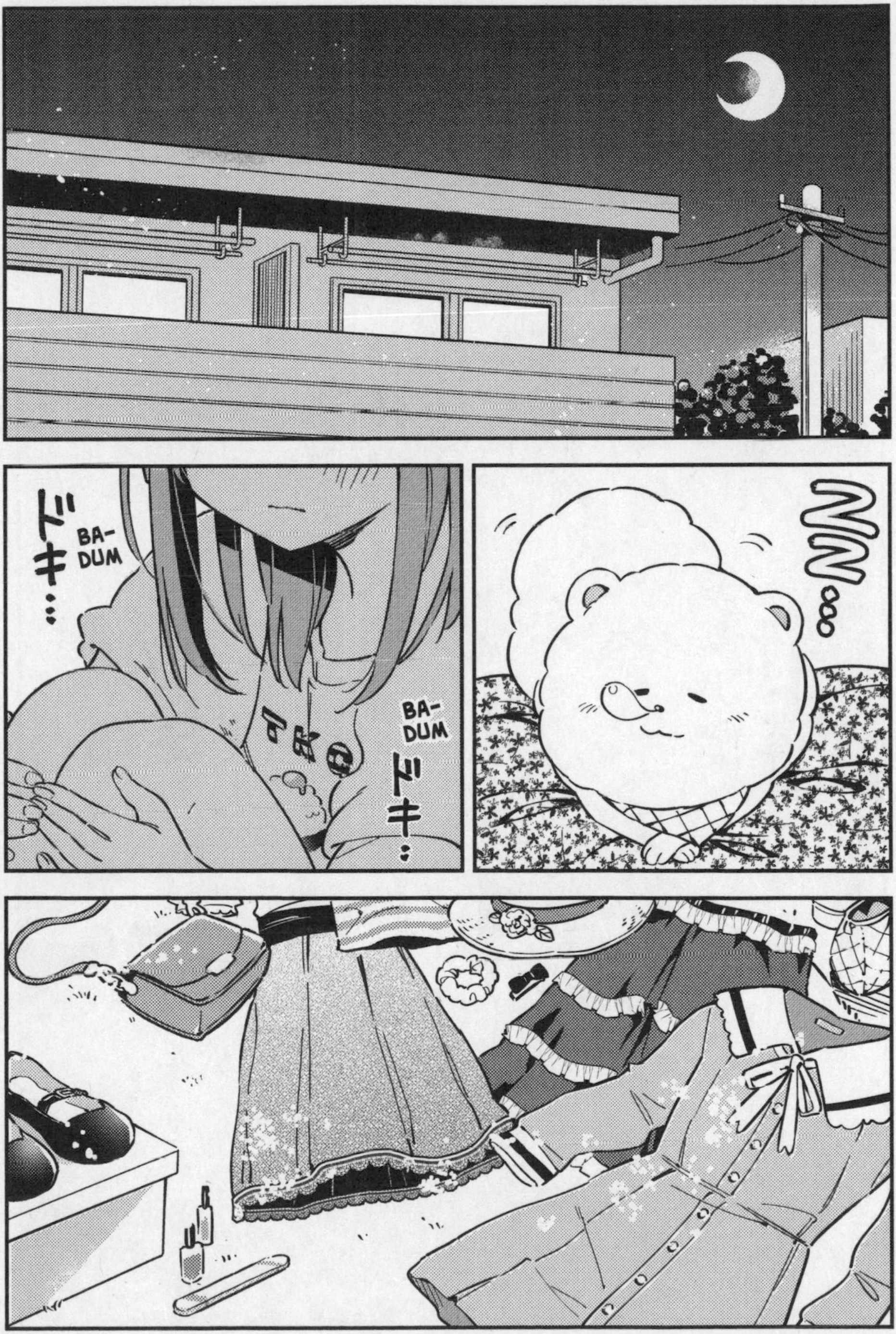
ZZZ
ドキ…
BA-DUM
BA-DUM
ドキ…

RATING 7 SUMI AND KAZUYA-KUN (1)

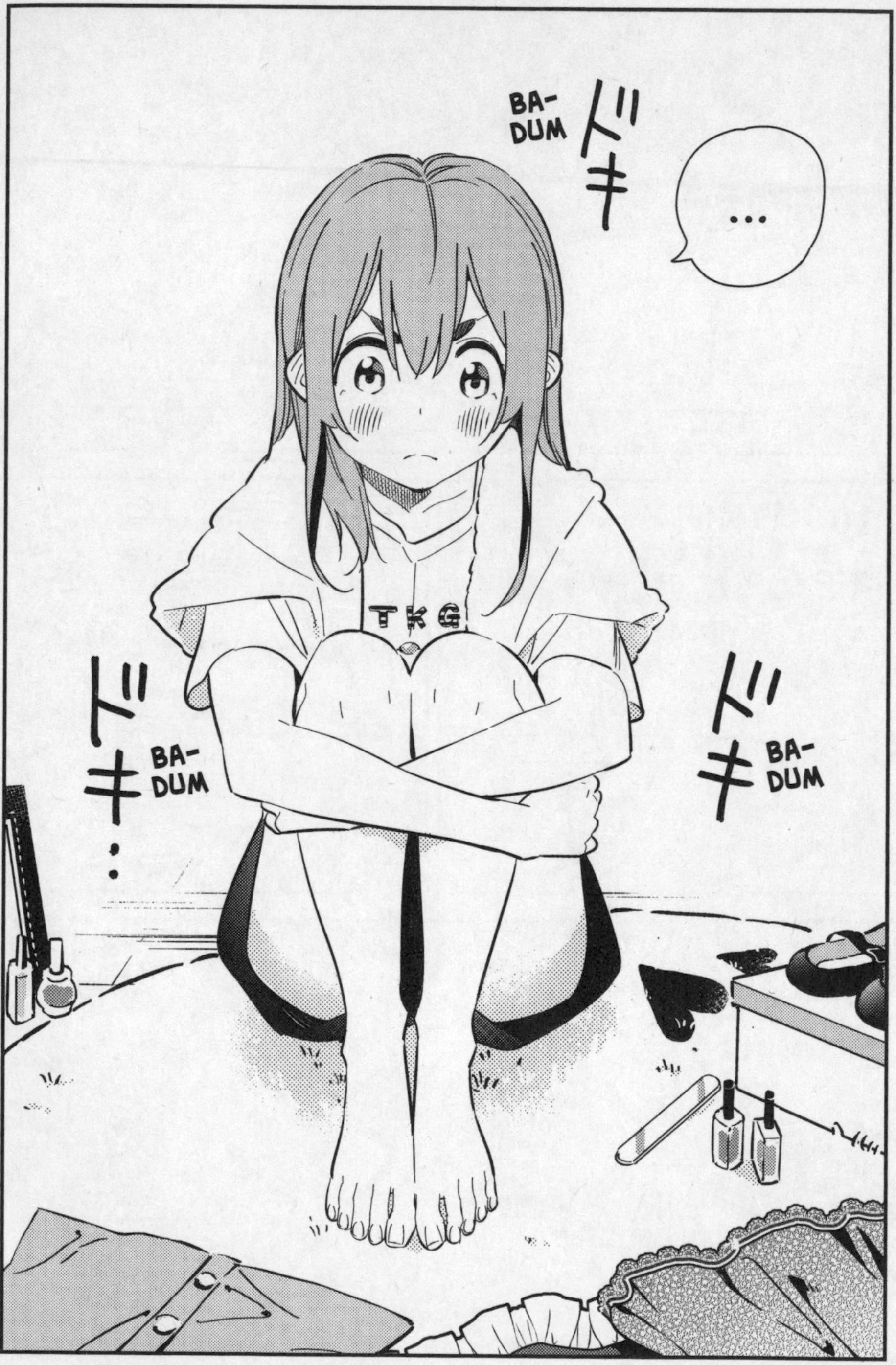
...
ドキ
BA-DUM
TKG
ドキ
BA-DUM
ドキ...
BA-DUM

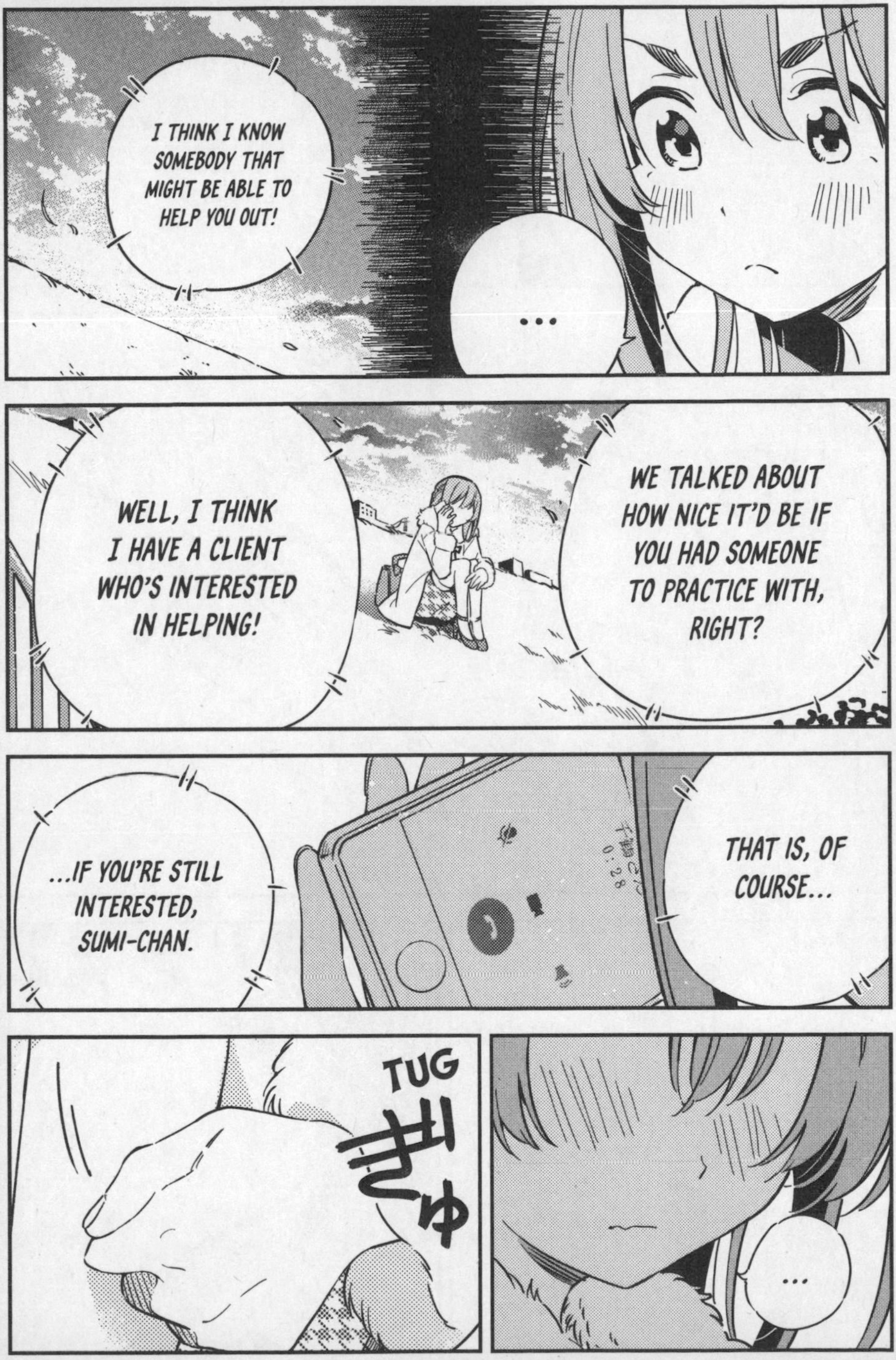
I THINK I KNOW SOMEBODY THAT MIGHT BE ABLE TO HELP YOU OUT!
...
WE TALKED ABOUT HOW NICE IT'D BE IF YOU HAD SOMEONE TO PRACTICE WITH, RIGHT?
WELL, I THINK I HAVE A CLIENT WHO'S INTERESTED IN HELPING!
THAT IS, OF COURSE...
...IF YOU'RE STILL INTERESTED, SUMI-CHAN.
...
TUG

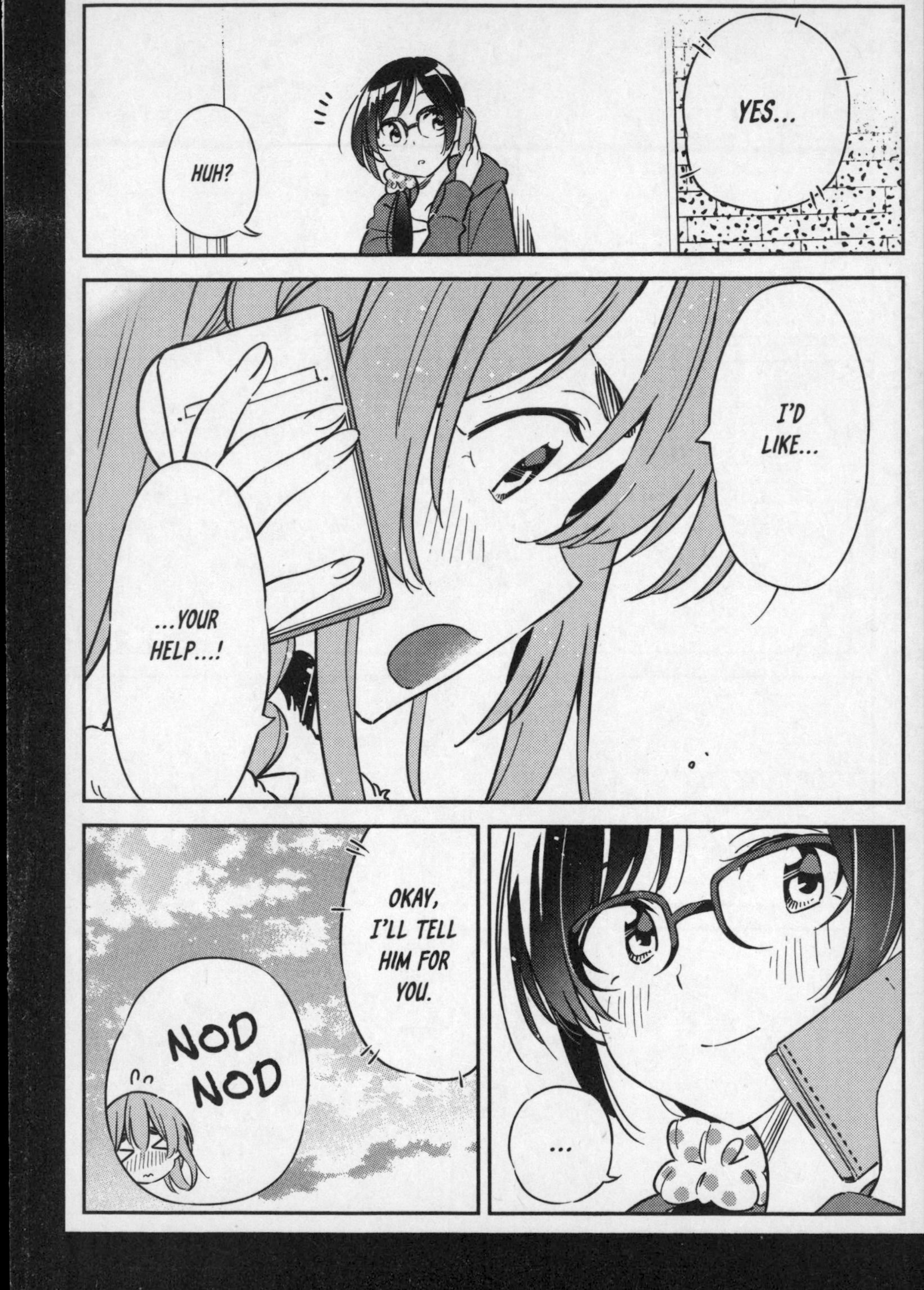
YES...
HUH?
I'D LIKE...
...YOUR HELP...!
...
OKAY, I'LL TELL HIM FOR YOU.
NOD NOD

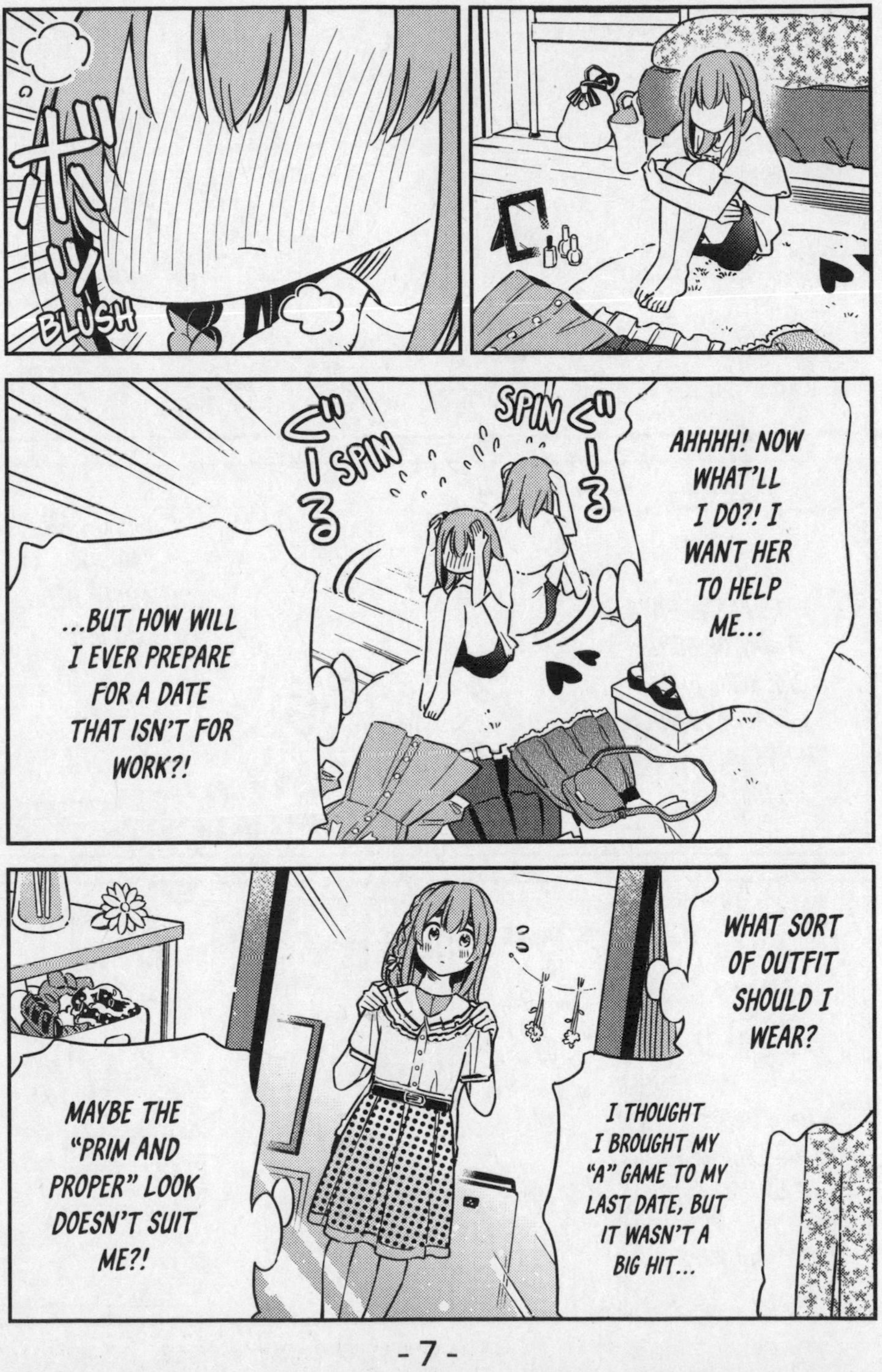
ボッ
BLUSH
AHHHH! NOW WHAT'LL I DO?! I WANT HER TO HELP ME...
SPIN ぐーる
SPIN ぐーる
...BUT HOW WILL I EVER PREPARE FOR A DATE THAT ISN'T FOR WORK?!
WHAT SORT OF OUTFIT SHOULD I WEAR?
I THOUGHT I BROUGHT MY "A" GAME TO MY LAST DATE, BUT IT WASN'T A BIG HIT...
MAYBE THE "PRIM AND PROPER" LOOK DOESN'T SUIT ME?!

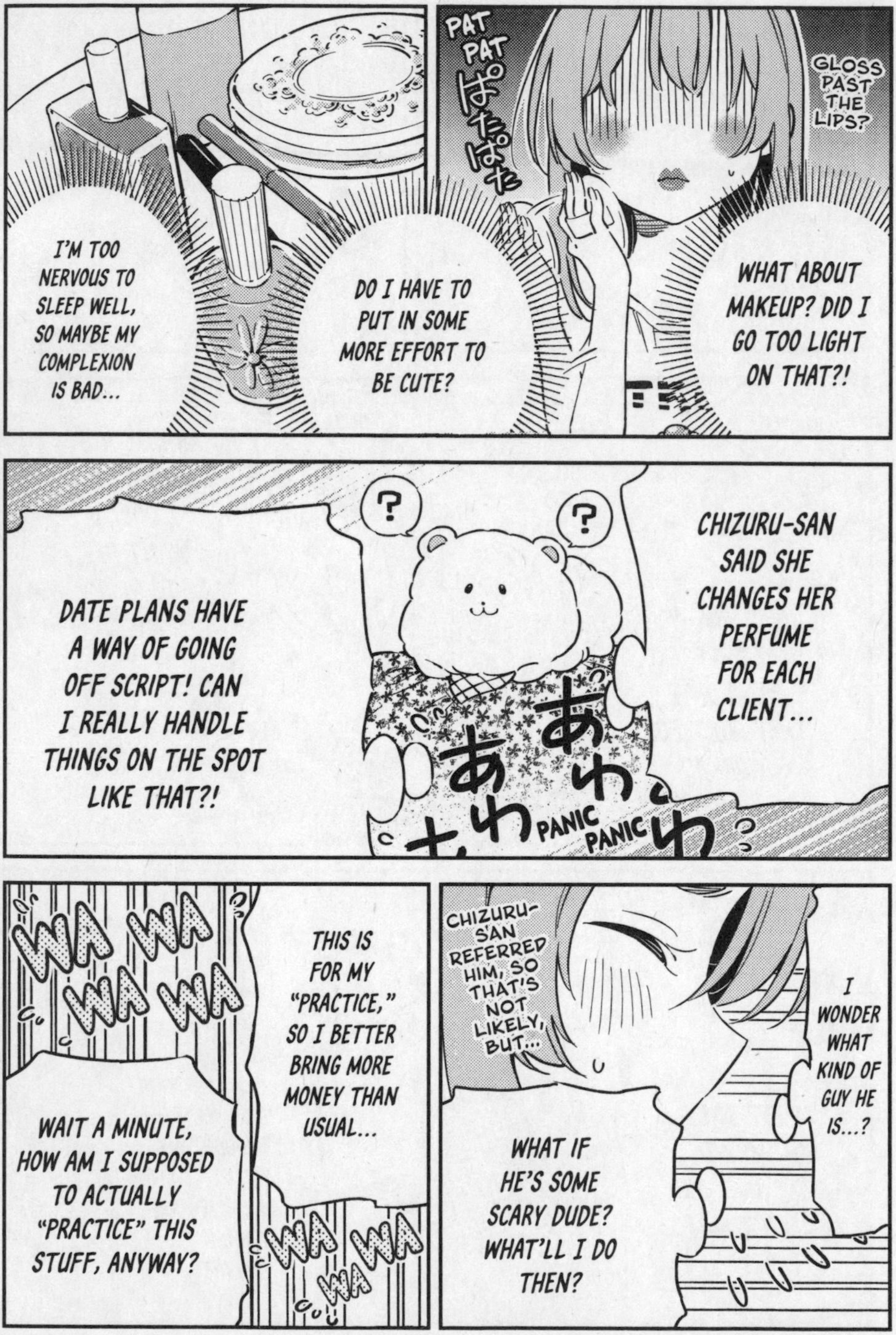
PAT PAT ぱたぱた
GLOSS PAST THE LIPS?
WHAT ABOUT MAKEUP? DID I GO TOO LIGHT ON THAT?!
DO I HAVE TO PUT IN SOME MORE EFFORT TO BE CUTE?
I'M TOO NERVOUS TO SLEEP WELL, SO MAYBE MY COMPLEXION IS BAD...
CHIZURU-SAN SAID SHE CHANGES HER PERFUME FOR EACH CLIENT...
DATE PLANS HAVE A WAY OF GOING OFF SCRIPT! CAN I REALLY HANDLE THINGS ON THE SPOT LIKE THAT?!
あわあわ PANIC PANIC
I WONDER WHAT KIND OF GUY HE IS...?
CHIZURU-SAN REFERRED HIM, SO THAT'S NOT LIKELY, BUT...
WHAT IF HE'S SOME SCARY DUDE? WHAT'LL I DO THEN?
THIS IS FOR MY "PRACTICE," SO I BETTER BRING MORE MONEY THAN USUAL...
WA WA WA WA
WAIT A MINUTE, HOW AM I SUPPOSED TO ACTUALLY "PRACTICE" THIS STUFF, ANYWAY?
WA WA WA

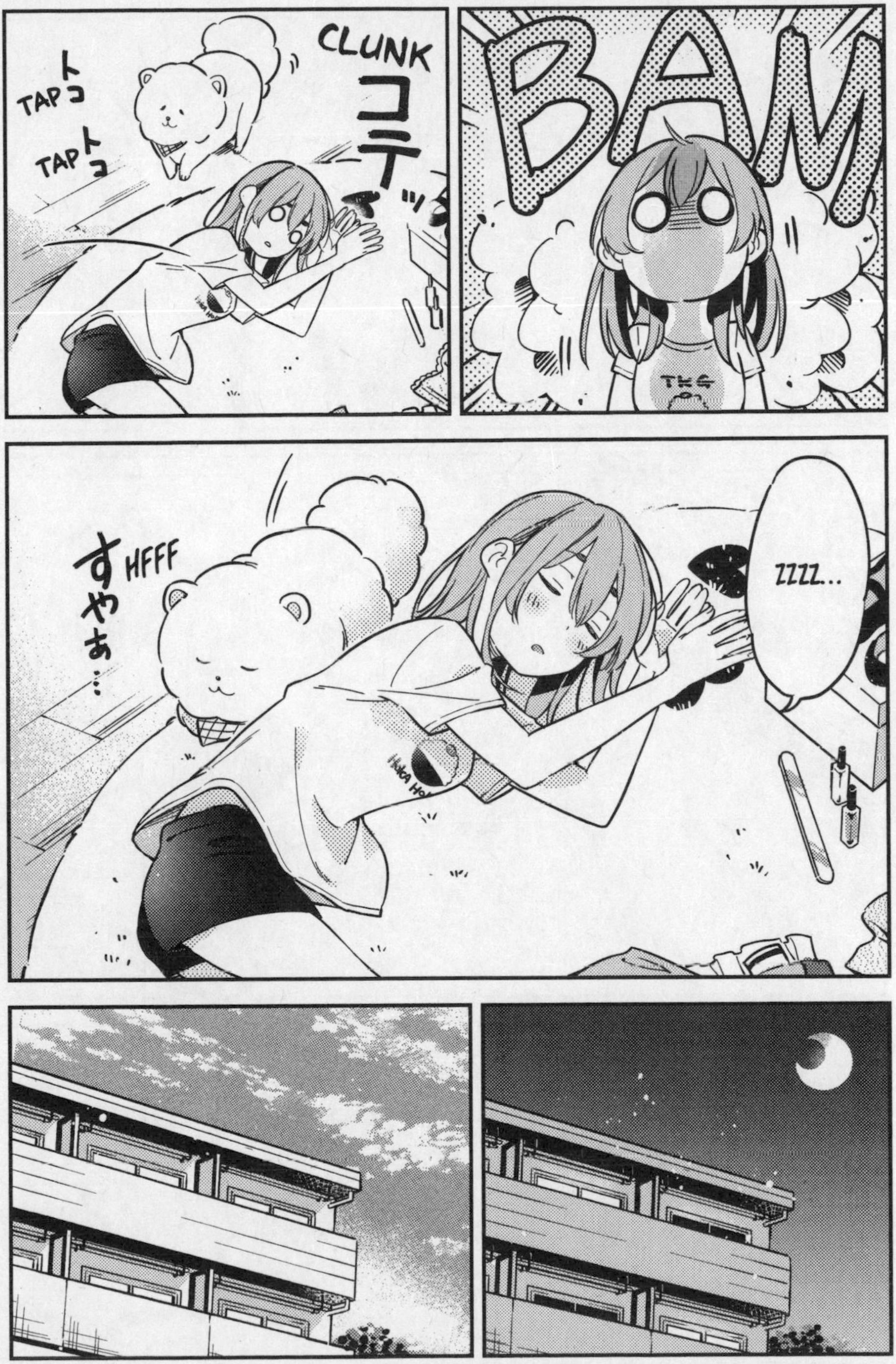
BAM
CLUNK
コテッ
TAP トコ
TAP トコ
ZZZZ...
すやぁ…
HFFF

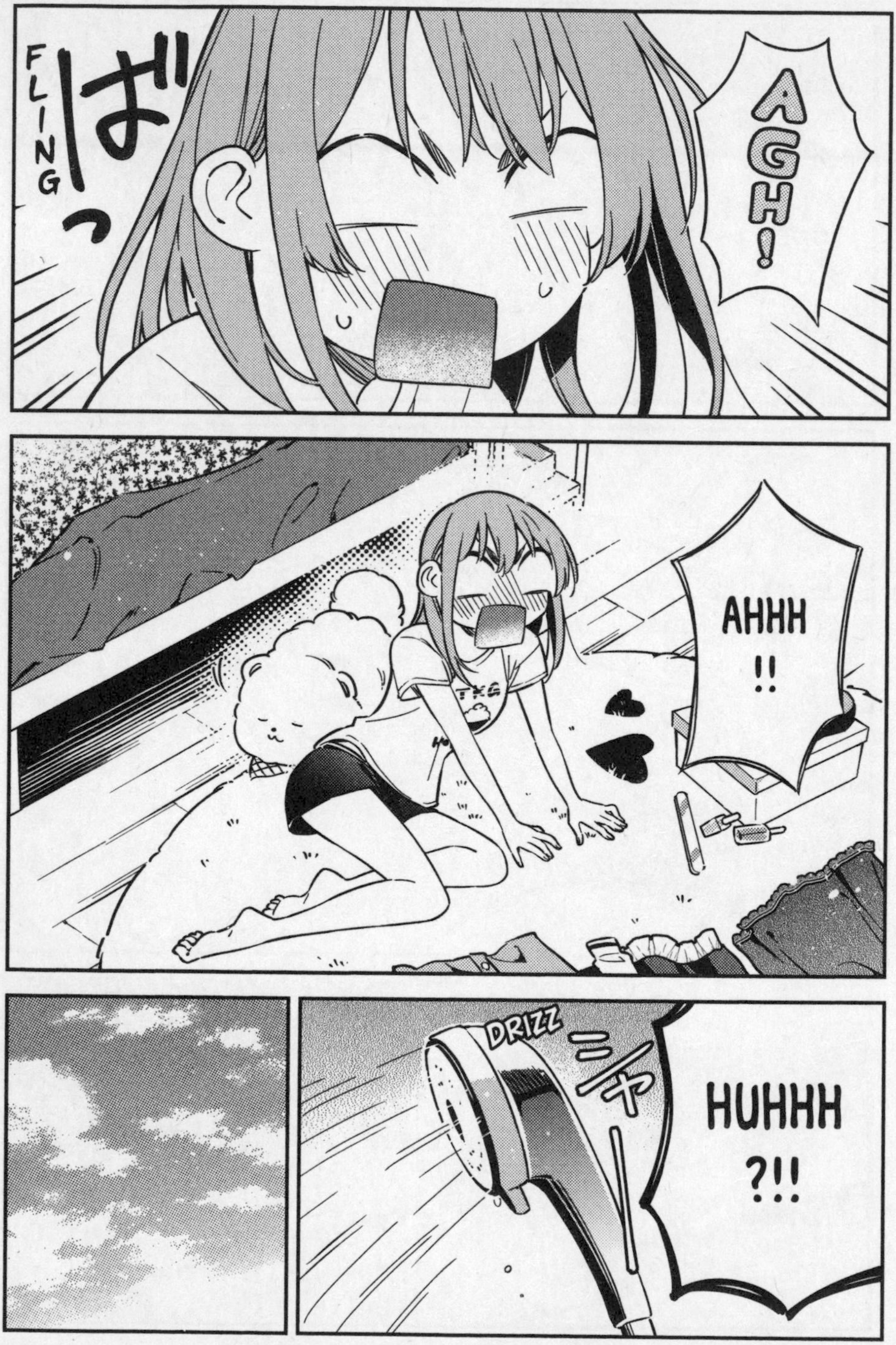
AGH!
FLING
ばっ
AHHH !!
DRIZZ
HUHHH ?!!

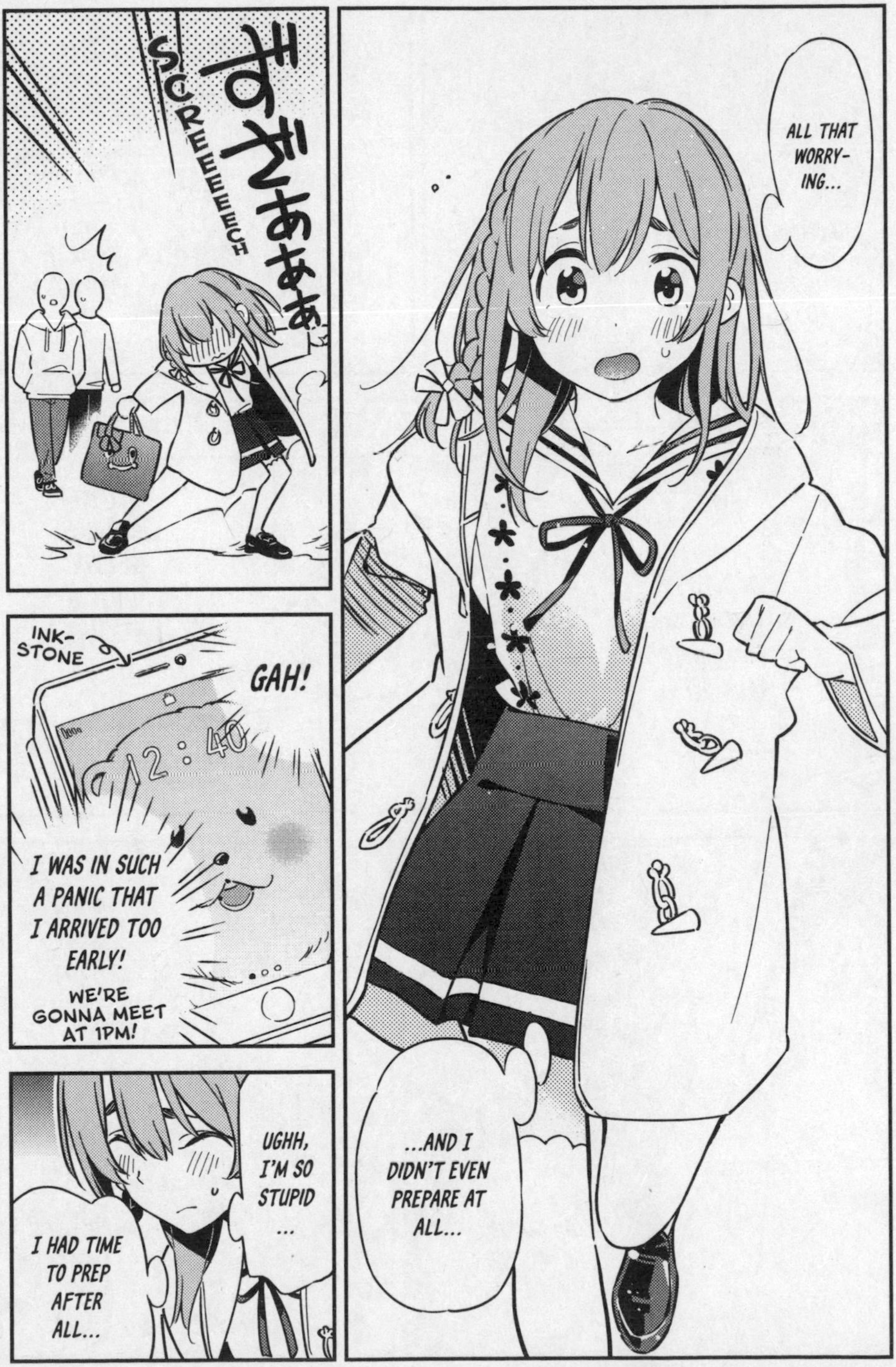
ALL THAT WORRY-ING...
...AND I DIDN'T EVEN PREPARE AT ALL...
ずざあああ
SCREEEEEECH
INK-STONE
GAH!
12:40
I WAS IN SUCH A PANIC THAT I ARRIVED TOO EARLY!
WE'RE GONNA MEET AT 1PM!
UGHH, I'M SO STUPID ...
I HAD TIME TO PREP AFTER ALL...

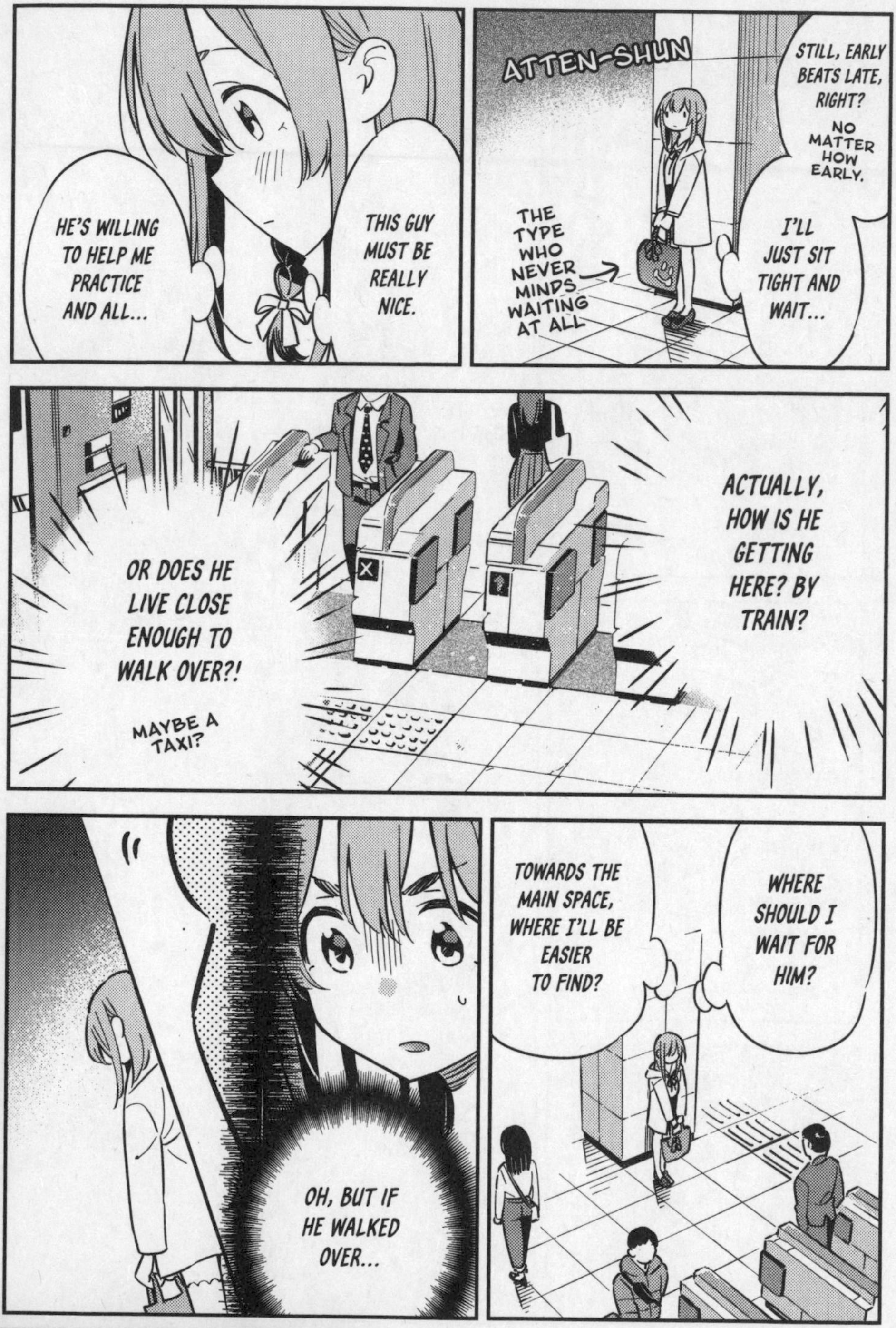
ATTEN-SHUN
STILL, EARLY BEATS LATE, RIGHT?
NO MATTER HOW EARLY.
I'LL JUST SIT TIGHT AND WAIT...
THE TYPE WHO NEVER MINDS WAITING AT ALL
THIS GUY MUST BE REALLY NICE.
HE'S WILLING TO HELP ME PRACTICE AND ALL...
ACTUALLY, HOW IS HE GETTING HERE? BY TRAIN?
OR DOES HE LIVE CLOSE ENOUGH TO WALK OVER?!
MAYBE A TAXI?
WHERE SHOULD I WAIT FOR HIM?
TOWARDS THE MAIN SPACE, WHERE I'LL BE EASIER TO FIND?
OH, BUT IF HE WALKED OVER...

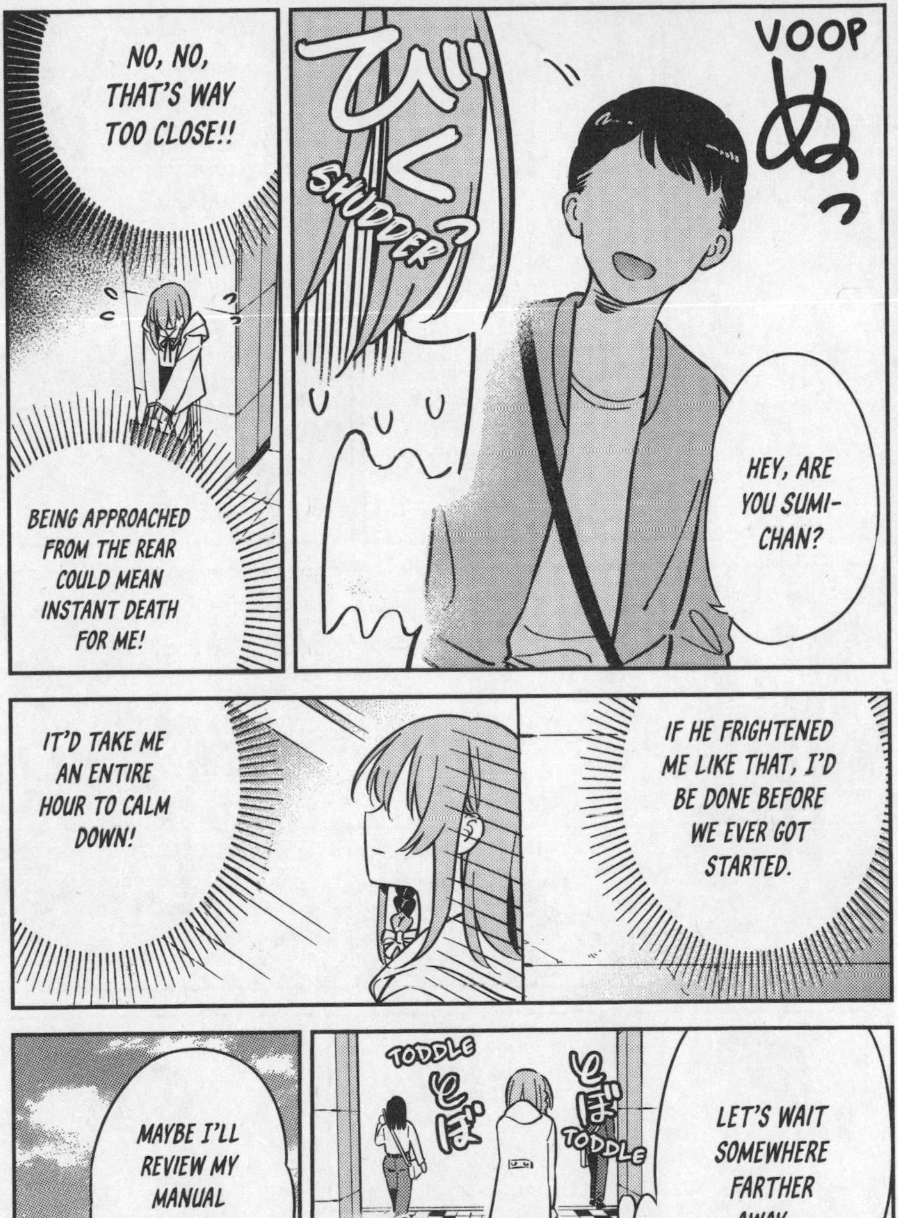

VOOP
ぬっ
HEY, ARE YOU SUMI-CHAN?
びくっ
SHUDDER
NO, NO, THAT'S WAY TOO CLOSE!!
BEING APPROACHED FROM THE REAR COULD MEAN INSTANT DEATH FOR ME!
IF HE FRIGHTENED ME LIKE THAT, I'D BE DONE BEFORE WE EVER GOT STARTED.
IT'D TAKE ME AN ENTIRE HOUR TO CALM DOWN!
LET'S WAIT SOMEWHERE FARTHER AWAY...
とぼ
TODDLE
とぼ
TODDLE
SOME-PLACE WHERE I CAN SEE THE WHOLE AREA...
MAYBE I'LL REVIEW MY MANUAL AGAIN...

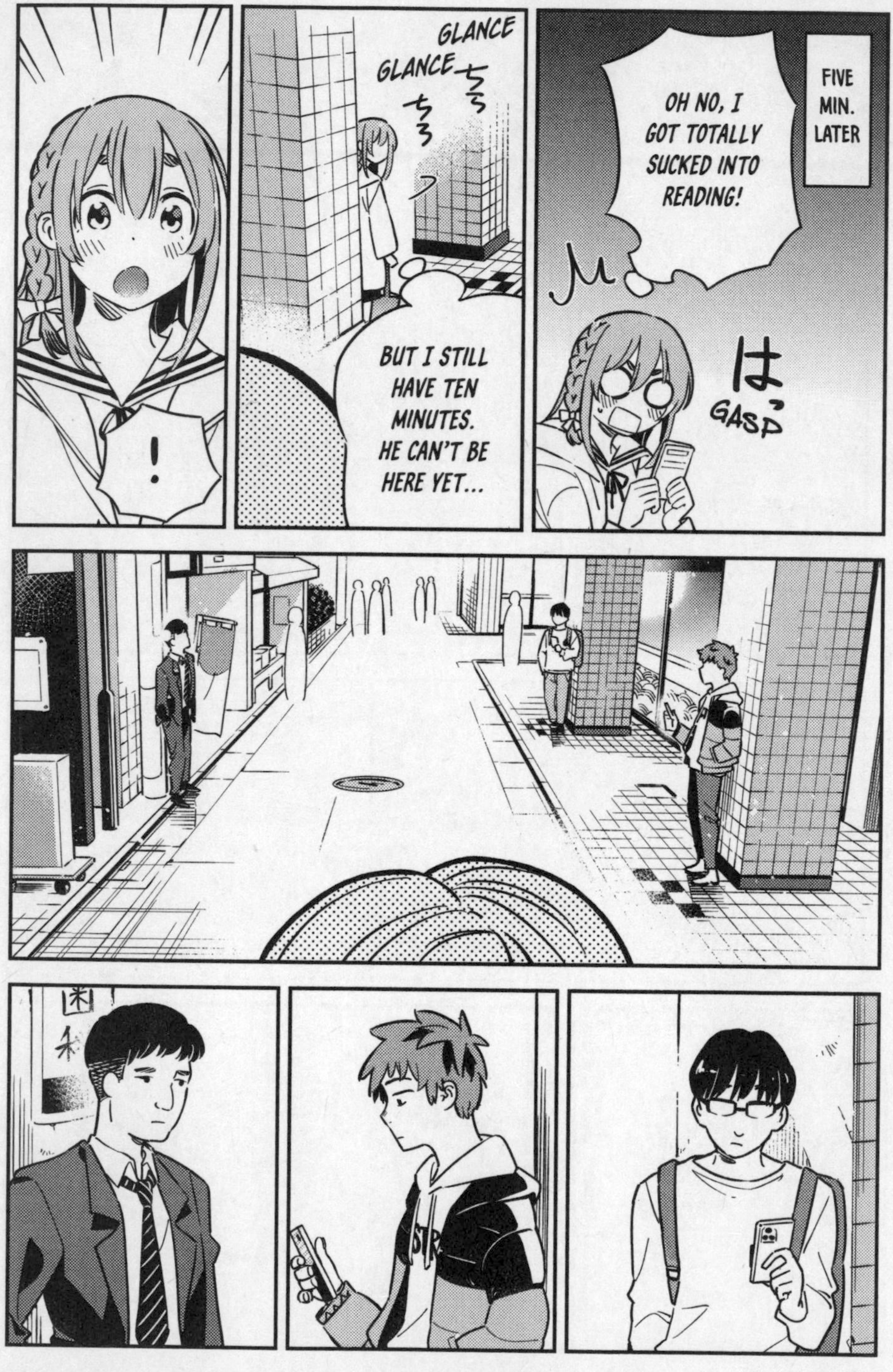
FIVE MIN. LATER
OH NO, I GOT TOTALLY SUCKED INTO READING!
は
GASP
GLANCE
ちら
GLANCE
ちら
BUT I STILL HAVE TEN MINUTES. HE CAN'T BE HERE YET...
!

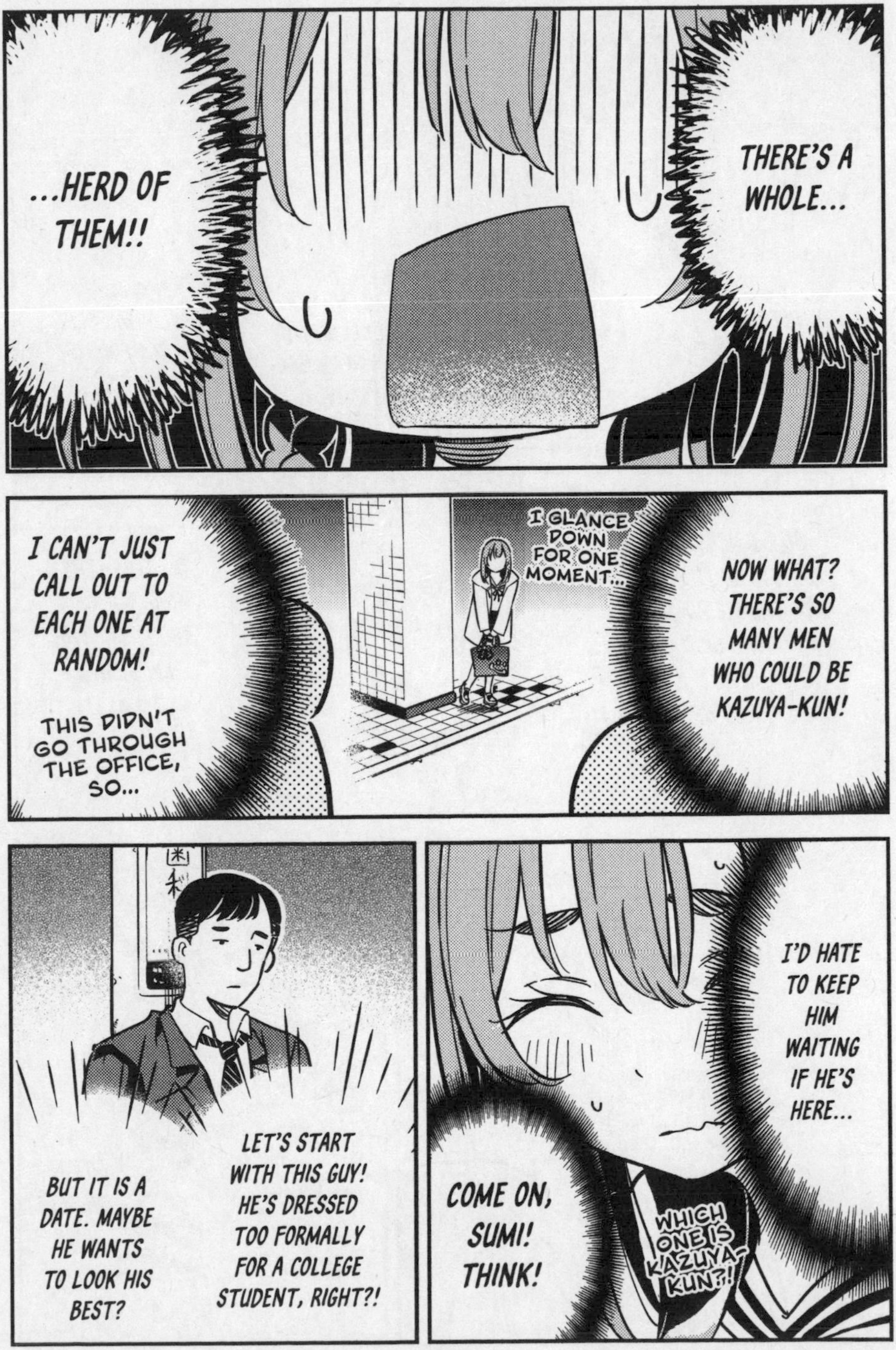
THERE'S A WHOLE...
...HERD OF THEM!!
NOW WHAT? THERE'S SO MANY MEN WHO COULD BE KAZUYA-KUN!
I GLANCE DOWN FOR ONE MOMENT...
I CAN'T JUST CALL OUT TO EACH ONE AT RANDOM!
THIS DIDN'T GO THROUGH THE OFFICE, SO...
I'D HATE TO KEEP HIM WAITING IF HE'S HERE...
WHICH ONE IS KAZUYA-KUN?!
COME ON, SUMI! THINK!
LET'S START WITH THIS GUY! HE'S DRESSED TOO FORMALLY FOR A COLLEGE STUDENT, RIGHT?!
BUT IT IS A DATE. MAYBE HE WANTS TO LOOK HIS BEST?

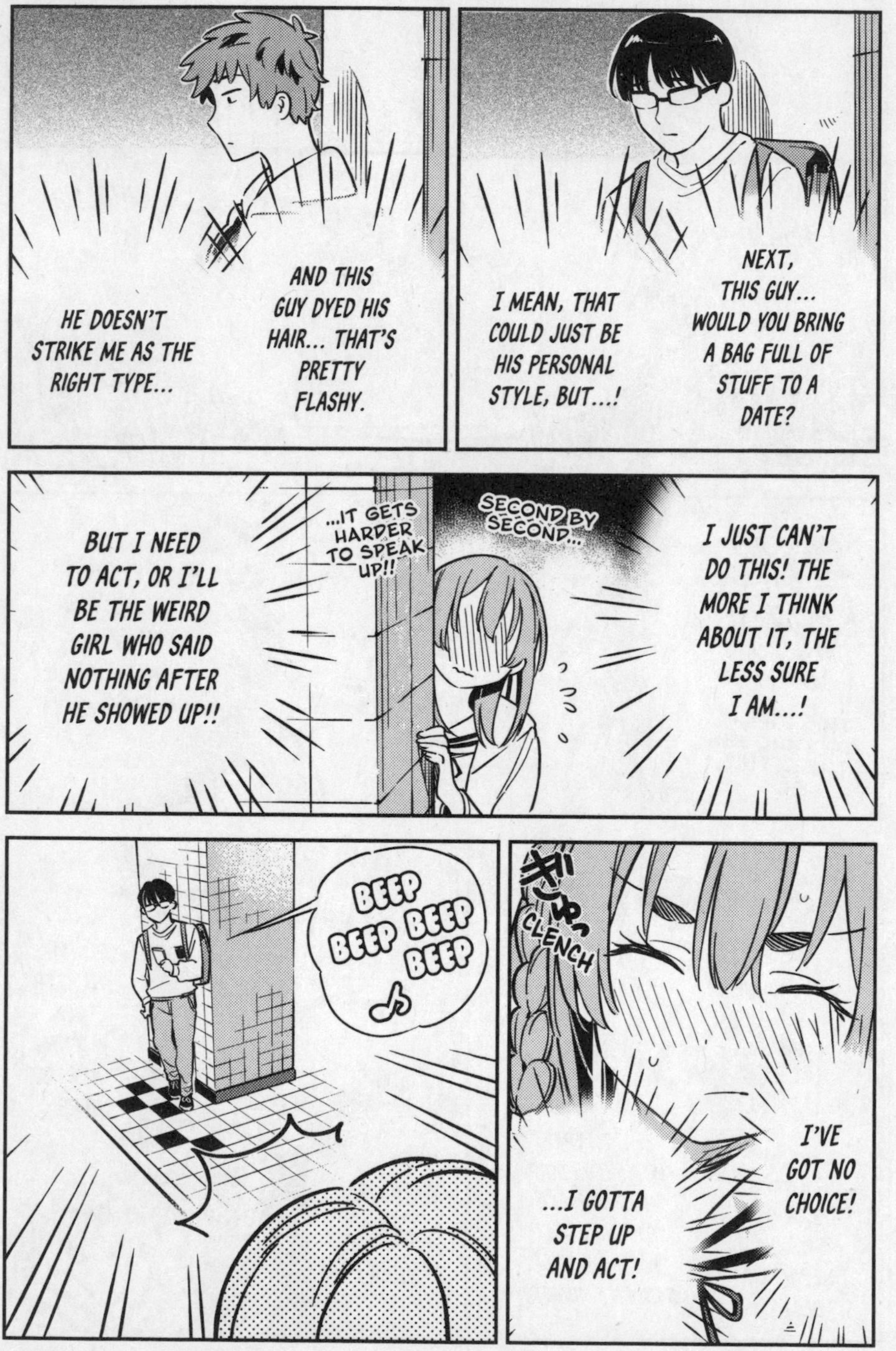
NEXT, THIS GUY... WOULD YOU BRING A BAG FULL OF STUFF TO A DATE?
I MEAN, THAT COULD JUST BE HIS PERSONAL STYLE, BUT...!
AND THIS GUY DYED HIS HAIR... THAT'S PRETTY FLASHY.
HE DOESN'T STRIKE ME AS THE RIGHT TYPE...
I JUST CAN'T DO THIS! THE MORE I THINK ABOUT IT, THE LESS SURE I AM...!
SECOND BY SECOND...
...IT GETS HARDER TO SPEAK UP!!
BUT I NEED TO ACT, OR I'LL BE THE WEIRD GIRL WHO SAID NOTHING AFTER HE SHOWED UP!!
ぎゅっ
CLENCH
I'VE GOT NO CHOICE!
...I GOTTA STEP UP AND ACT!
BEEP BEEP BEEP BEEP ♪

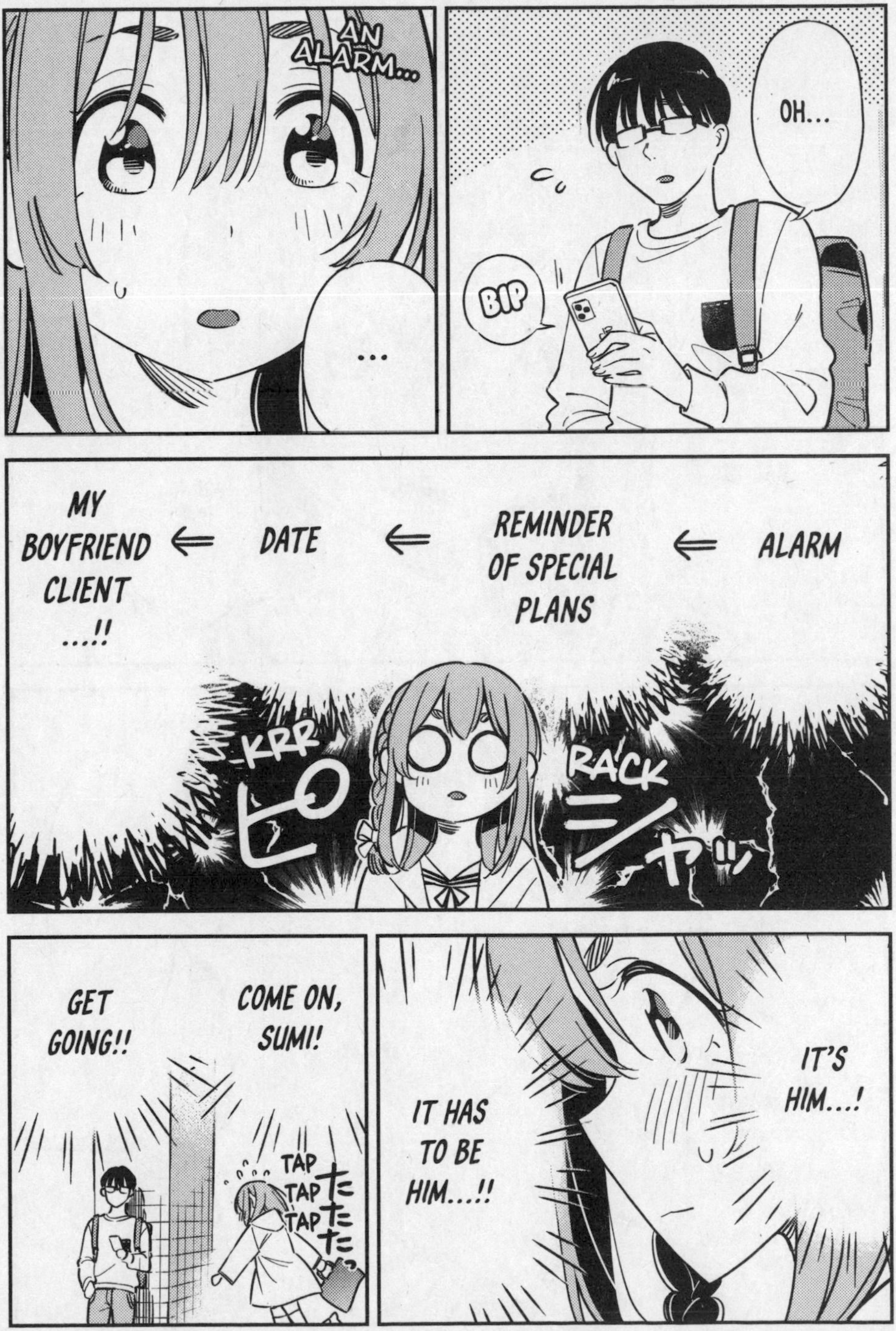
OH...
BIP
AN ALARM...
...
ALARM
⇐
REMINDER OF SPECIAL PLANS
⇐
DATE
⇐
MY BOYFRIEND CLIENT ...!!
RACK
シャッ
KRR
ピ
IT'S HIM...!
IT HAS TO BE HIM...!!
COME ON, SUMI!
GET GOING!!
TAP TAP TAP
たたた

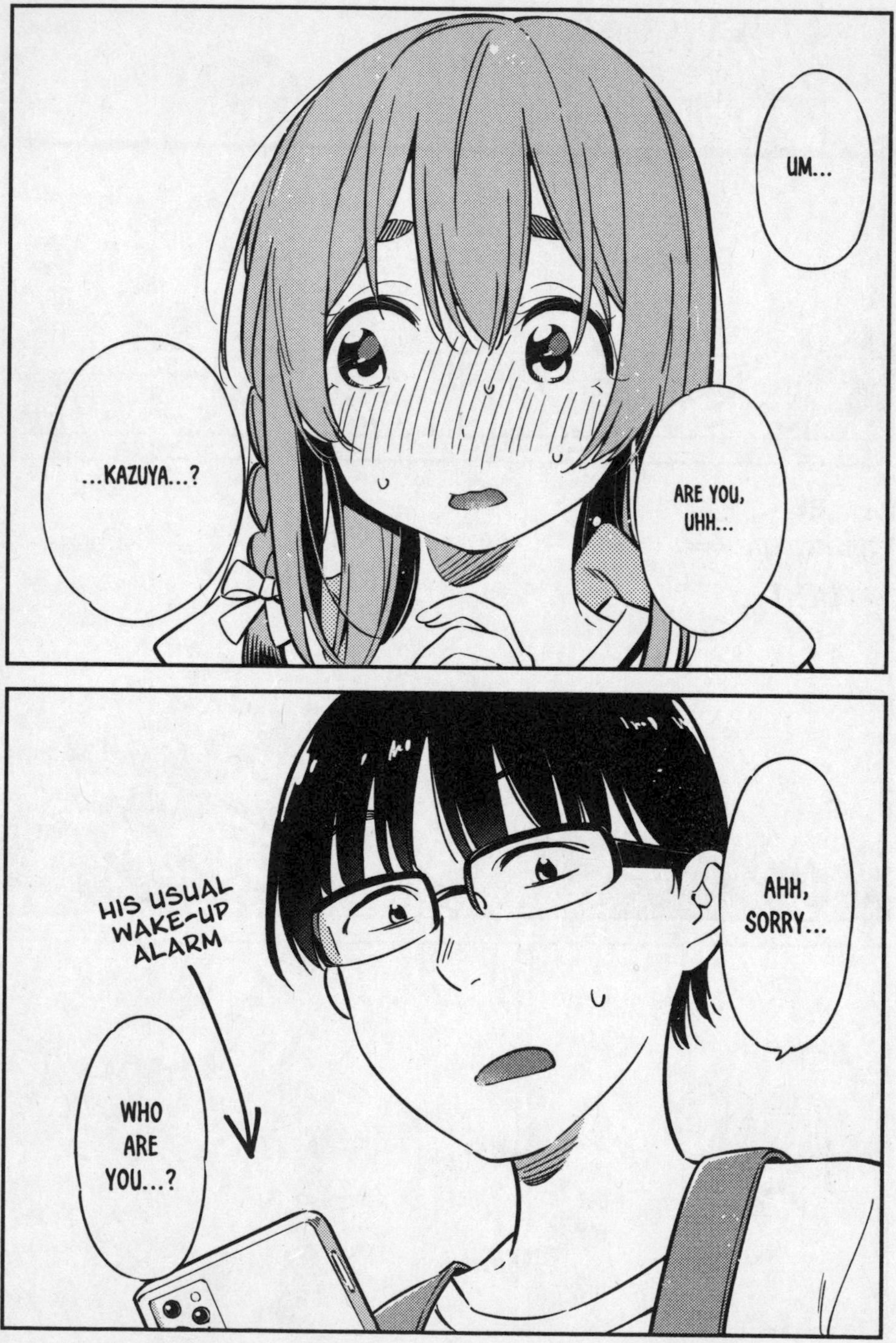
UM...
ARE YOU, UHH...
...KAZUYA...?
AHH, SORRY...
HIS USUAL WAKE-UP ALARM
WHO ARE YOU...?

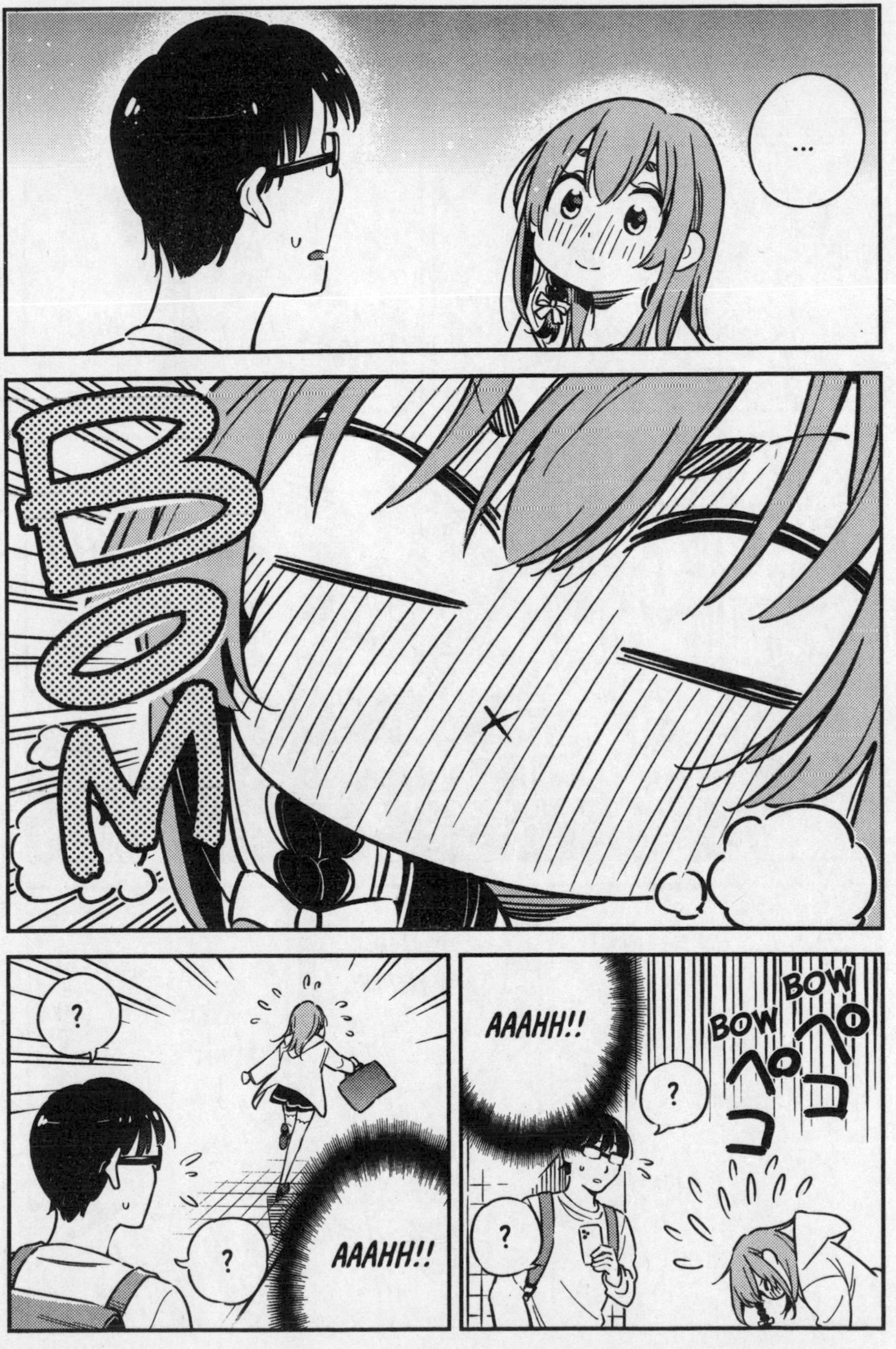
...
BOOM
AAAHH!!
BOW
BOW
ペコペコ
?
?
?
?
AAAHH!!

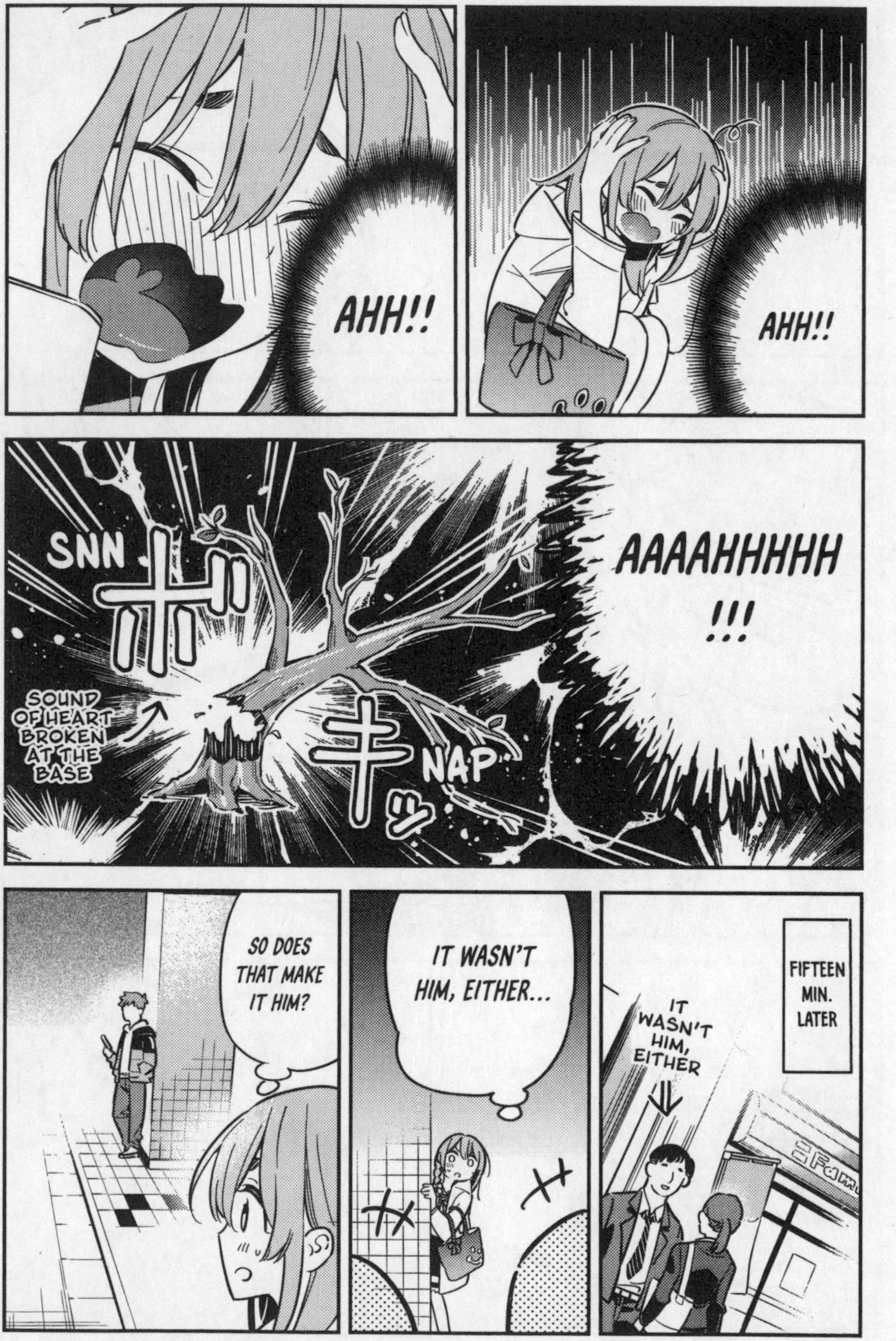
AHH!!
AHH!!
AAAAHHHH !!!
SNN
SOUND OF HEART BROKEN AT THE BASE
NAP
FIFTEEN MIN. LATER
IT WASN'T HIM, EITHER
IT WASN'T HIM, EITHER...
SO DOES THAT MAKE IT HIM?

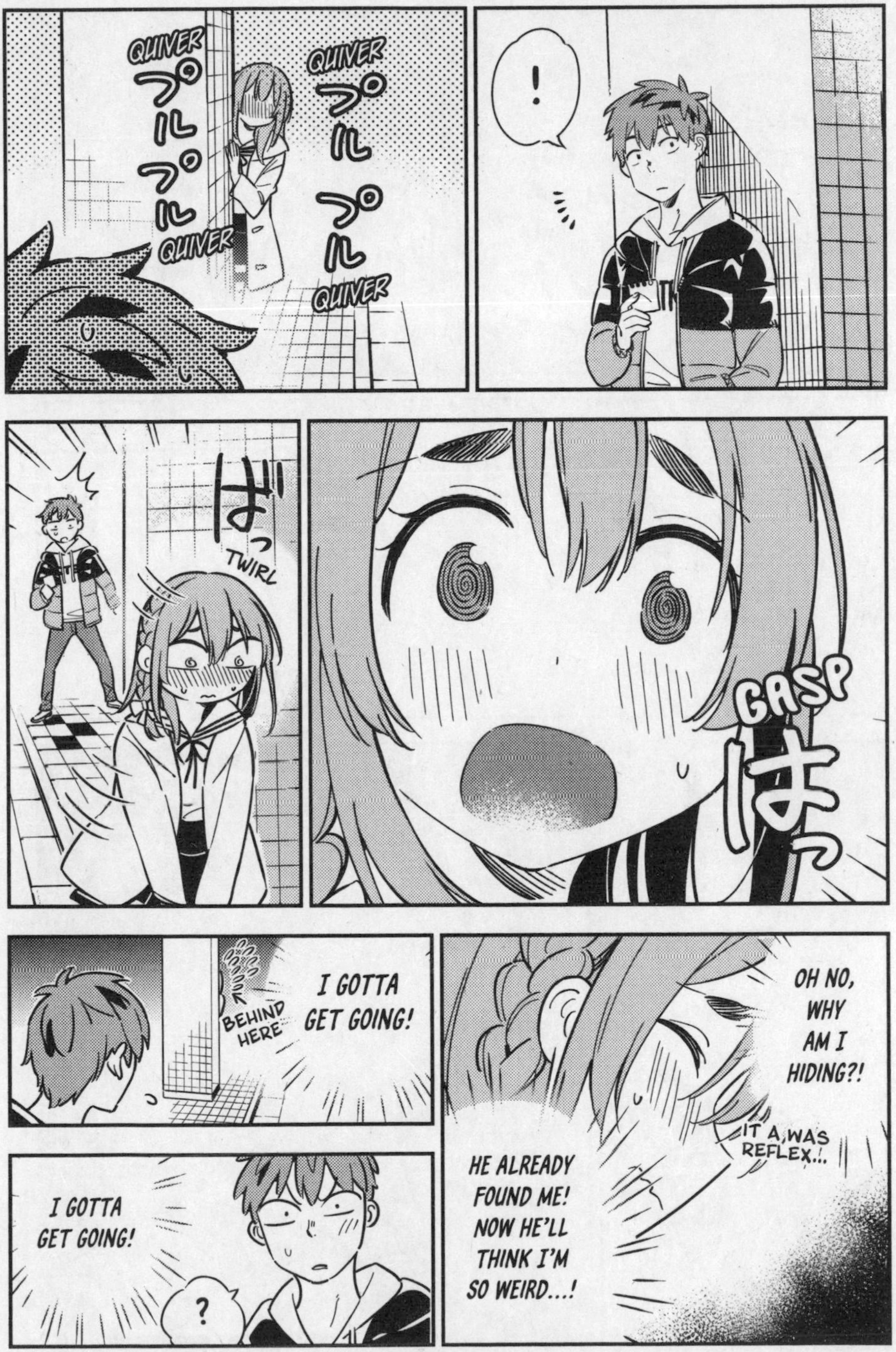
!
QUIVER
プルプル
QUIVER
QUIVER
プルプル
QUIVER
GASP
はっ
ばっ
TWIRL
OH NO, WHY AM I HIDING?!
IT A WAS REFLEX...!
HE ALREADY FOUND ME! NOW HE'LL THINK I'M SO WEIRD...!
I GOTTA GET GOING!
BEHIND HERE
I GOTTA GET GOING!
?

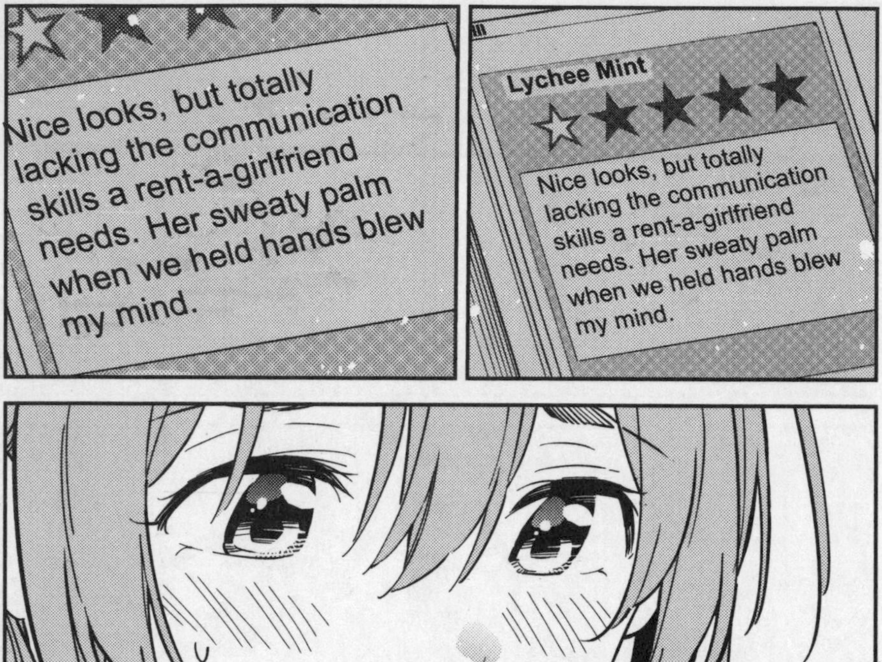
Lychee Mint
Nice looks, but totally lacking the communication skills a rent-a-girlfriend needs. Her sweaty palm when we held hands blew my mind.
Nice looks, but totally lacking the communication skills a rent-a-girlfriend needs. Her sweaty palm when we held hands blew my mind.
AW, WHAT A LOVELY DREAM THAT IS!
GULP

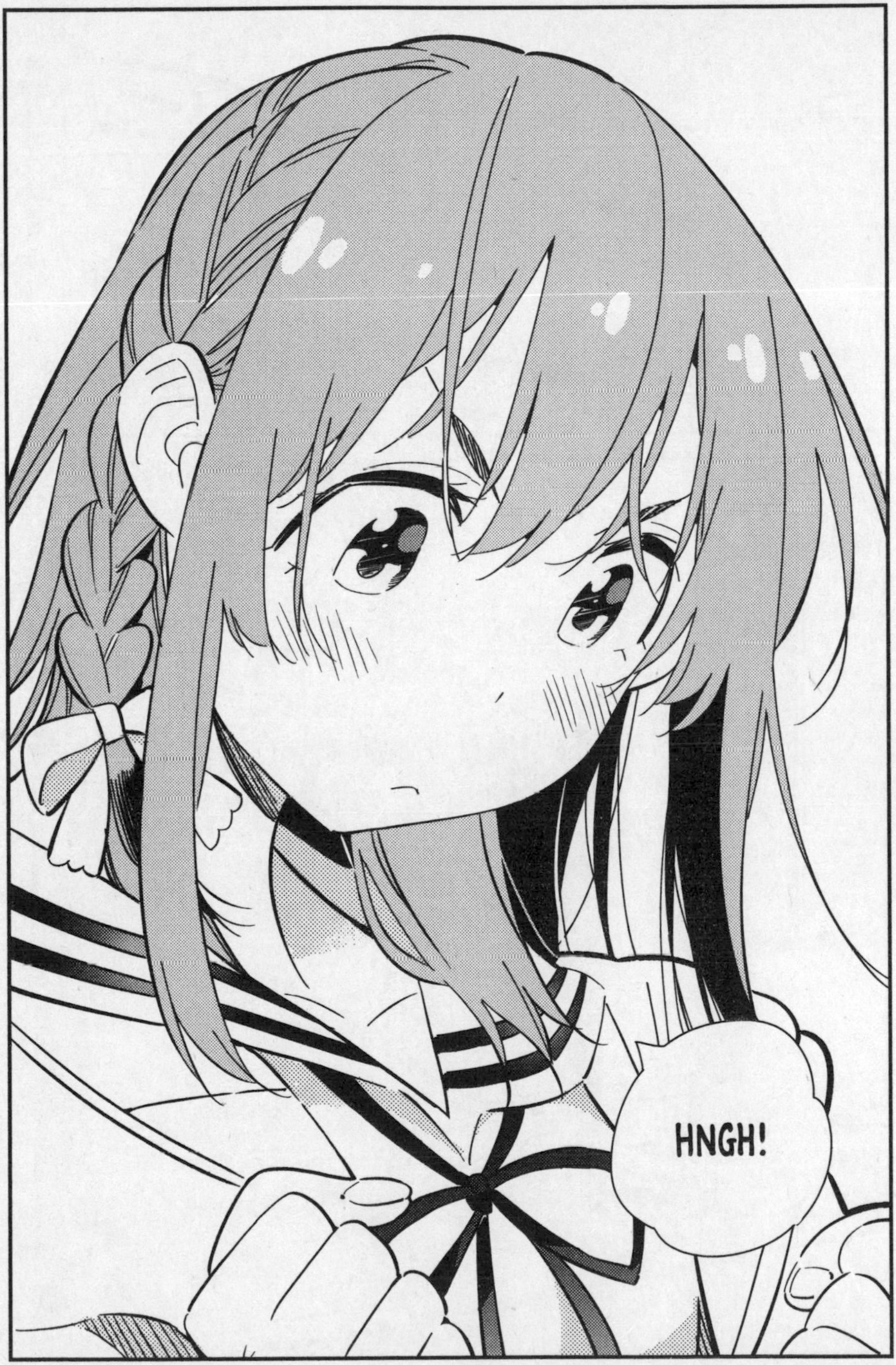
HNGH!

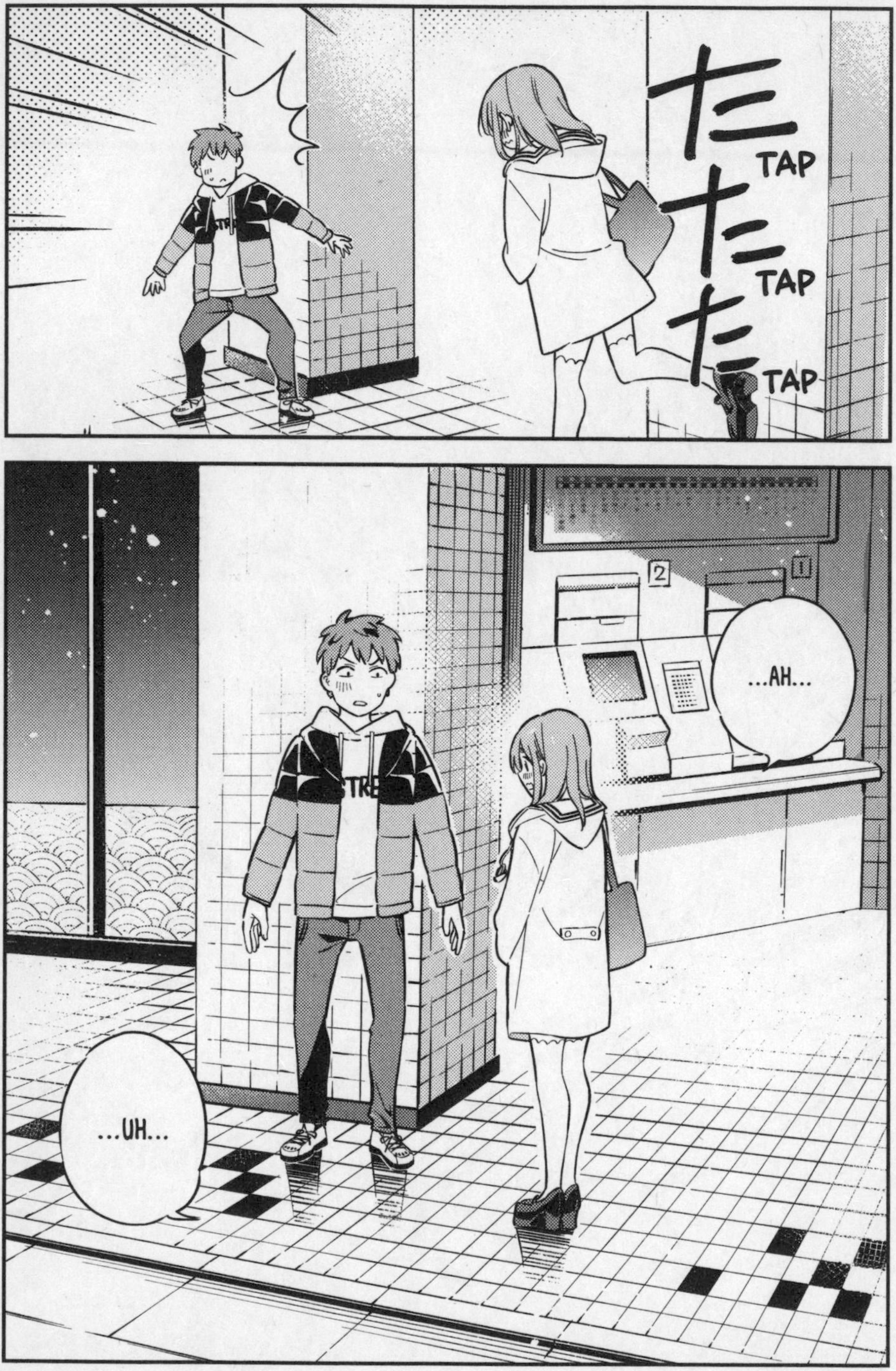
たたた
TAP
TAP
TAP
...AH...
...UH...

RATING 8 SUMI AND KAZUYA-KUN (2)

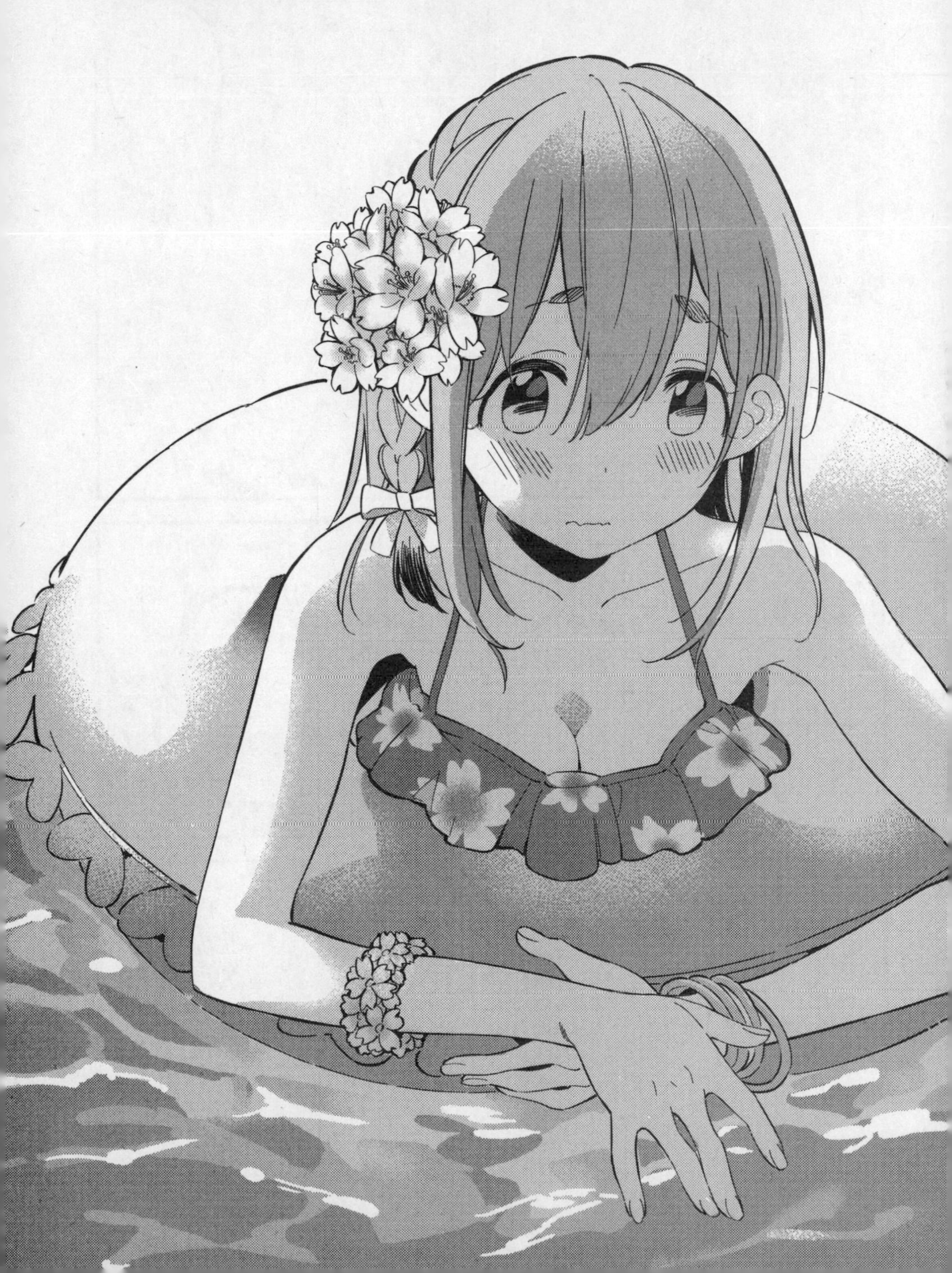

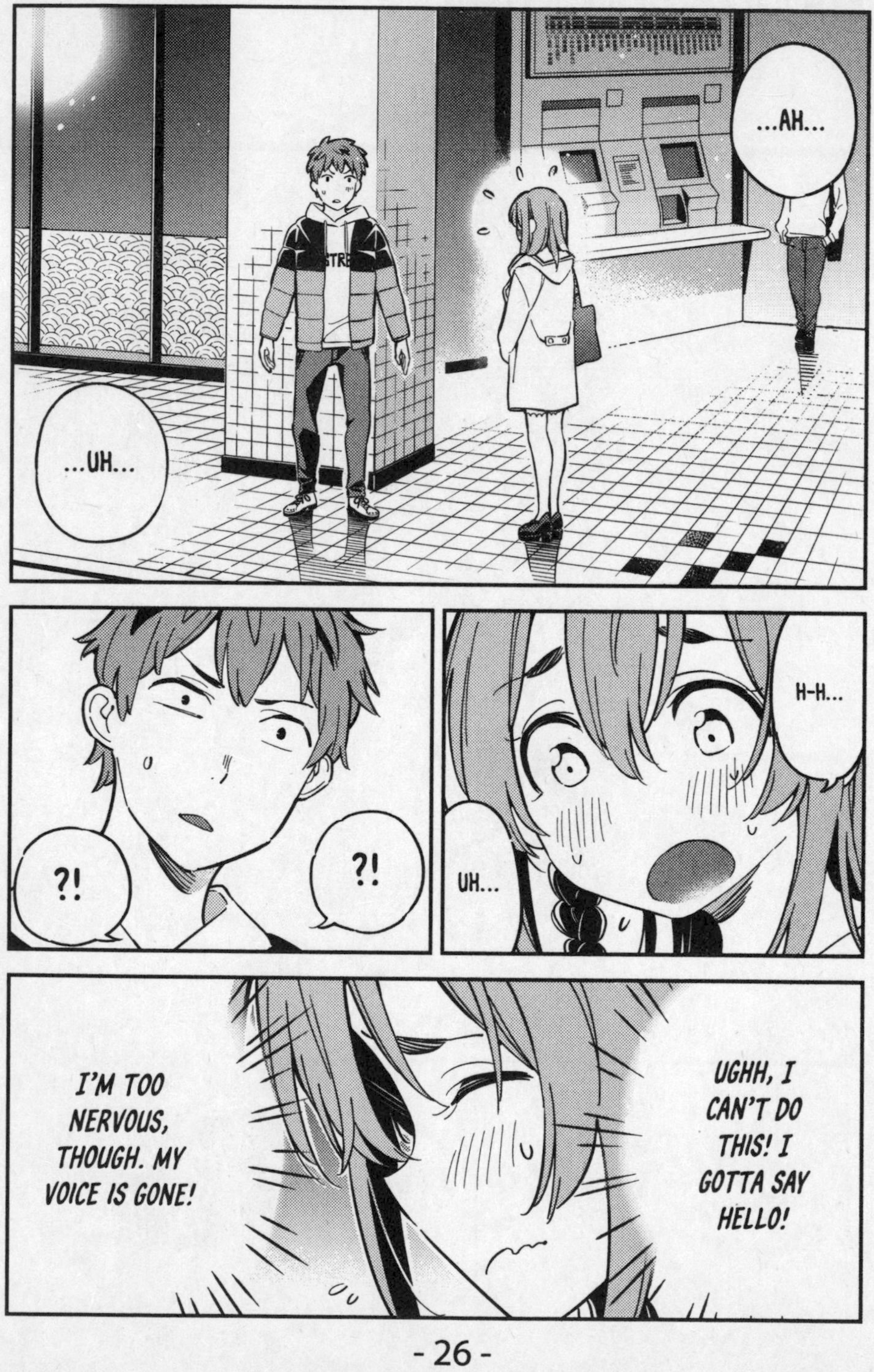
...AH...
...UH...
H-H...
UH...
?!
?!
UGHH, I CAN'T DO THIS! I GOTTA SAY HELLO!
I'M TOO NERVOUS, THOUGH. MY VOICE IS GONE!

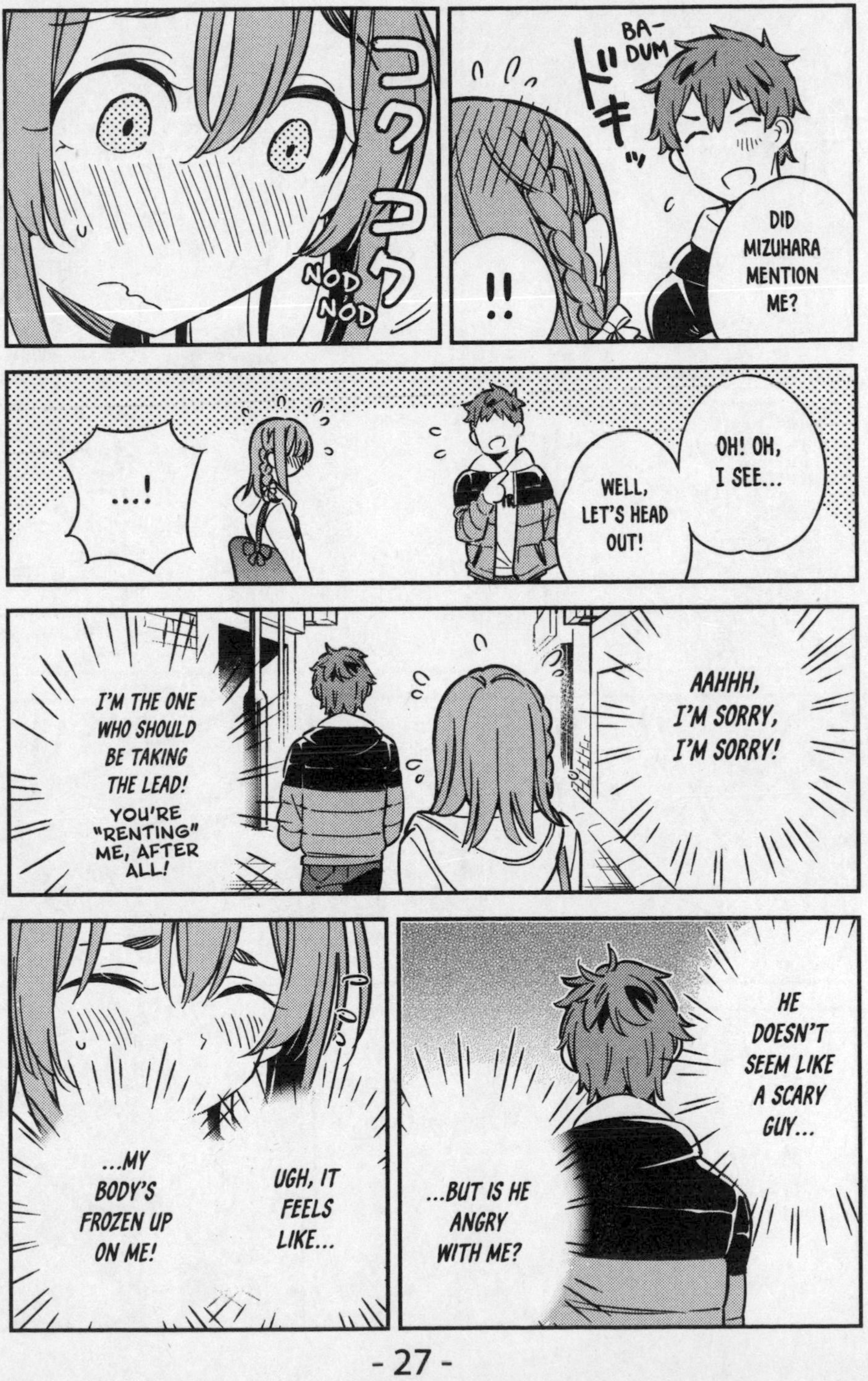
ドキッ
BA-DUM
DID MIZUHARA MENTION ME?
!!
コクコク
NOD NOD
OH! OH, I SEE...
WELL, LET'S HEAD OUT!
...!
AAHHH, I'M SORRY, I'M SORRY!
I'M THE ONE WHO SHOULD BE TAKING THE LEAD!
YOU'RE "RENTING" ME, AFTER ALL!
HE DOESN'T SEEM LIKE A SCARY GUY...
...BUT IS HE ANGRY WITH ME?
UGH, IT FEELS LIKE...
...MY BODY'S FROZEN UP ON ME!

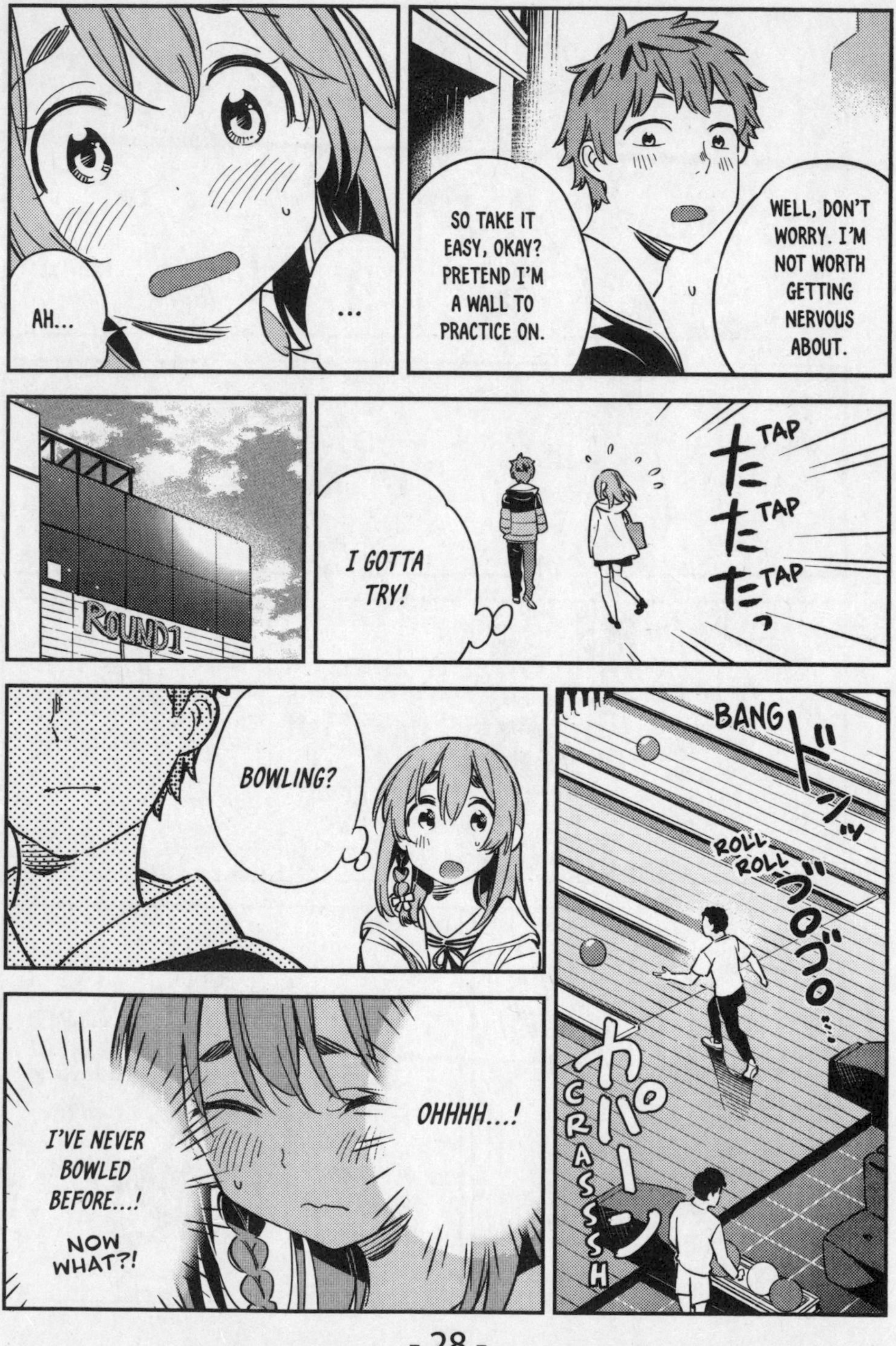
WELL, DON'T WORRY. I'M NOT WORTH GETTING NERVOUS ABOUT.
SO TAKE IT EASY, OKAY? PRETEND I'M A WALL TO PRACTICE ON.
...
AH...
たたたっ
TAP TAP TAP
I GOTTA TRY!
ROUND1
BANG
ROLL ROLL
CRASSSH
BOWLING?
OHHHH...!
I'VE NEVER BOWLED BEFORE...!
NOW WHAT?!

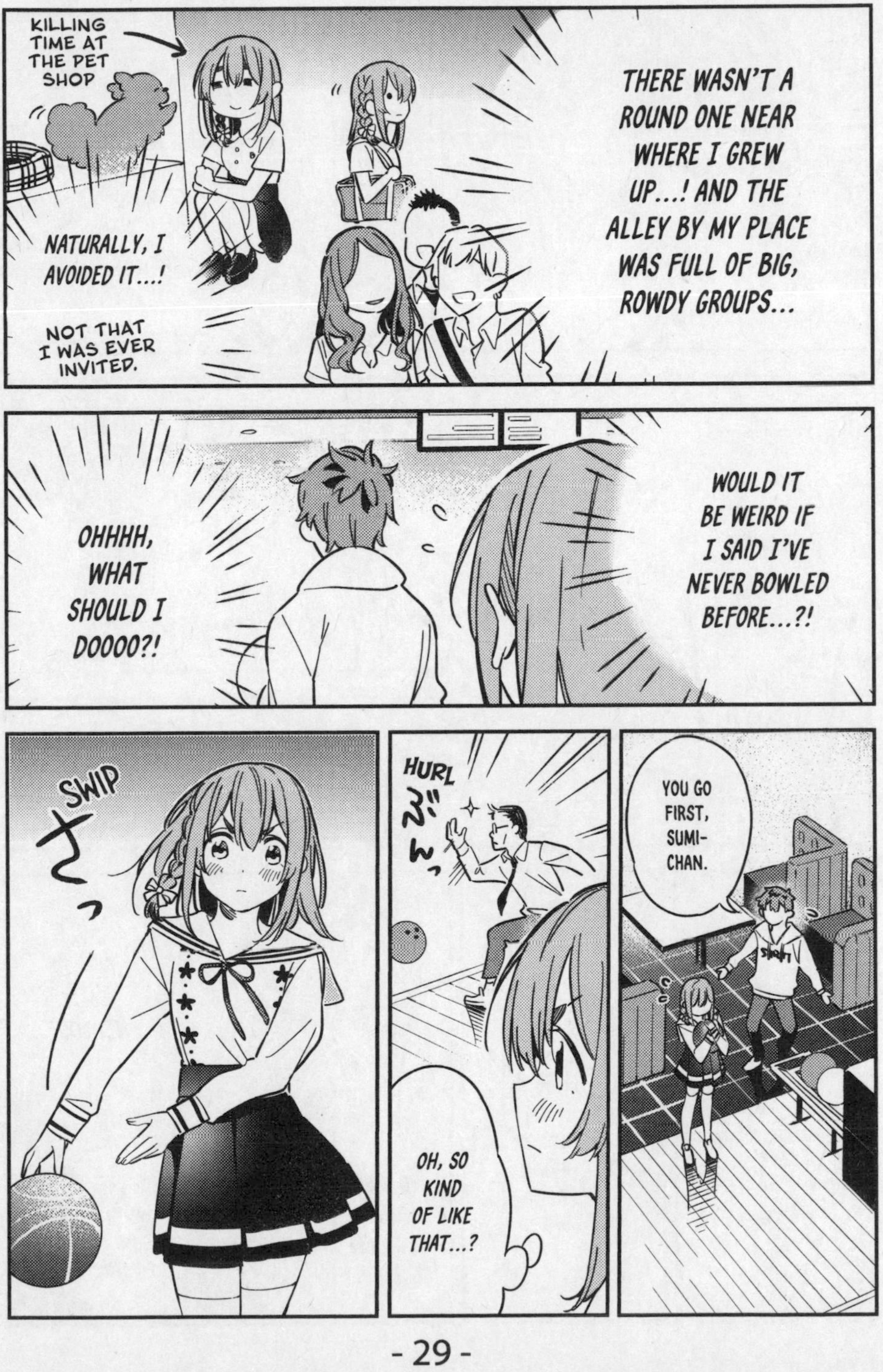
THERE WASN'T A ROUND ONE NEAR WHERE I GREW UP...! AND THE ALLEY BY MY PLACE WAS FULL OF BIG, ROWDY GROUPS...
KILLING TIME AT THE PET SHOP
NATURALLY, I AVOIDED IT...!
NOT THAT I WAS EVER INVITED.
WOULD IT BE WEIRD IF I SAID I'VE NEVER BOWLED BEFORE...?!
OHHHH, WHAT SHOULD I DOOOO?!
YOU GO FIRST, SUMI-CHAN.
HURL
ぶんっ
OH, SO KIND OF LIKE THAT...?
SWIP
さっ

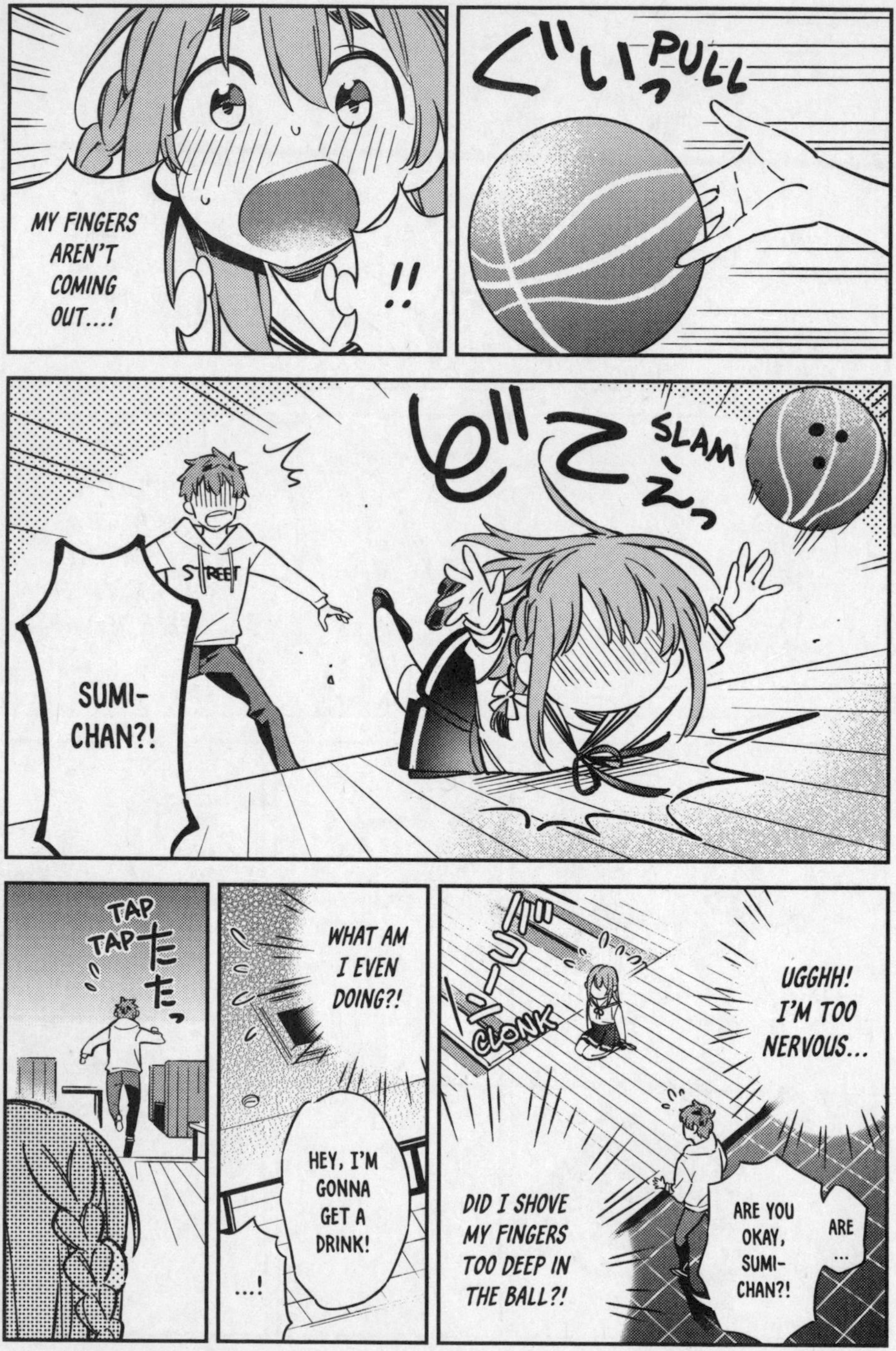
ぐいっ
PULL
MY FINGERS AREN'T COMING OUT...!
!!
どてぇっ
SLAM
SUMI-CHAN?!
UGGHH! I'M TOO NERVOUS...
ゴーン
CLONK
ARE ...
ARE YOU OKAY, SUMI-CHAN?!
DID I SHOVE MY FINGERS TOO DEEP IN THE BALL?!
WHAT AM I EVEN DOING?!
HEY, I'M GONNA GET A DRINK!
...!
たたっ
TAP TAP

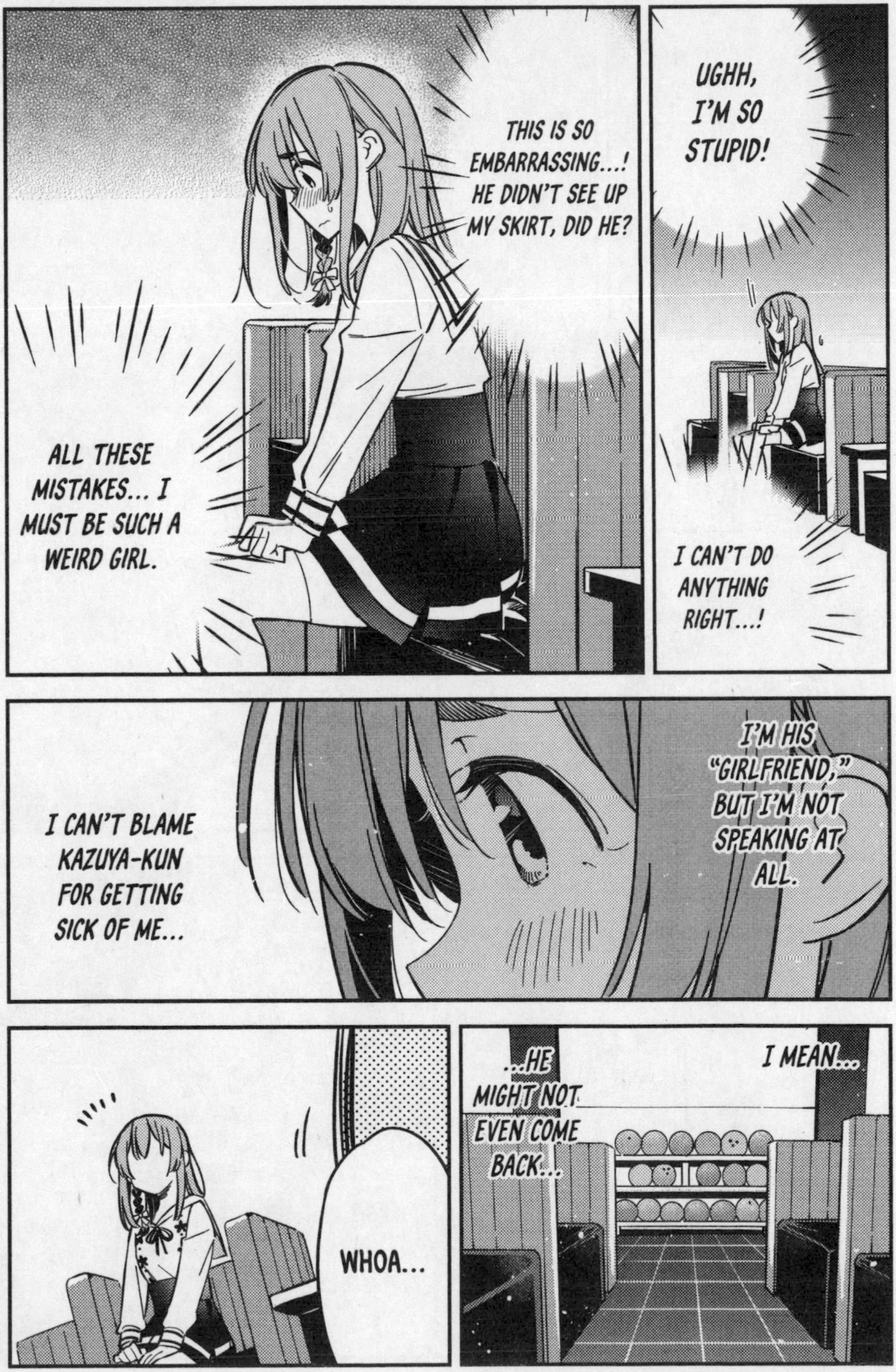
UGHH, I'M SO STUPID!
I CAN'T DO ANYTHING RIGHT...!
THIS IS SO EMBARRASSING...! HE DIDN'T SEE UP MY SKIRT, DID HE?
ALL THESE MISTAKES... I MUST BE SUCH A WEIRD GIRL.
I'M HIS "GIRLFRIEND," BUT I'M NOT SPEAKING AT ALL.
I CAN'T BLAME KAZUYA-KUN FOR GETTING SICK OF ME...
I MEAN...
...HE MIGHT NOT EVEN COME BACK...
WHOA...

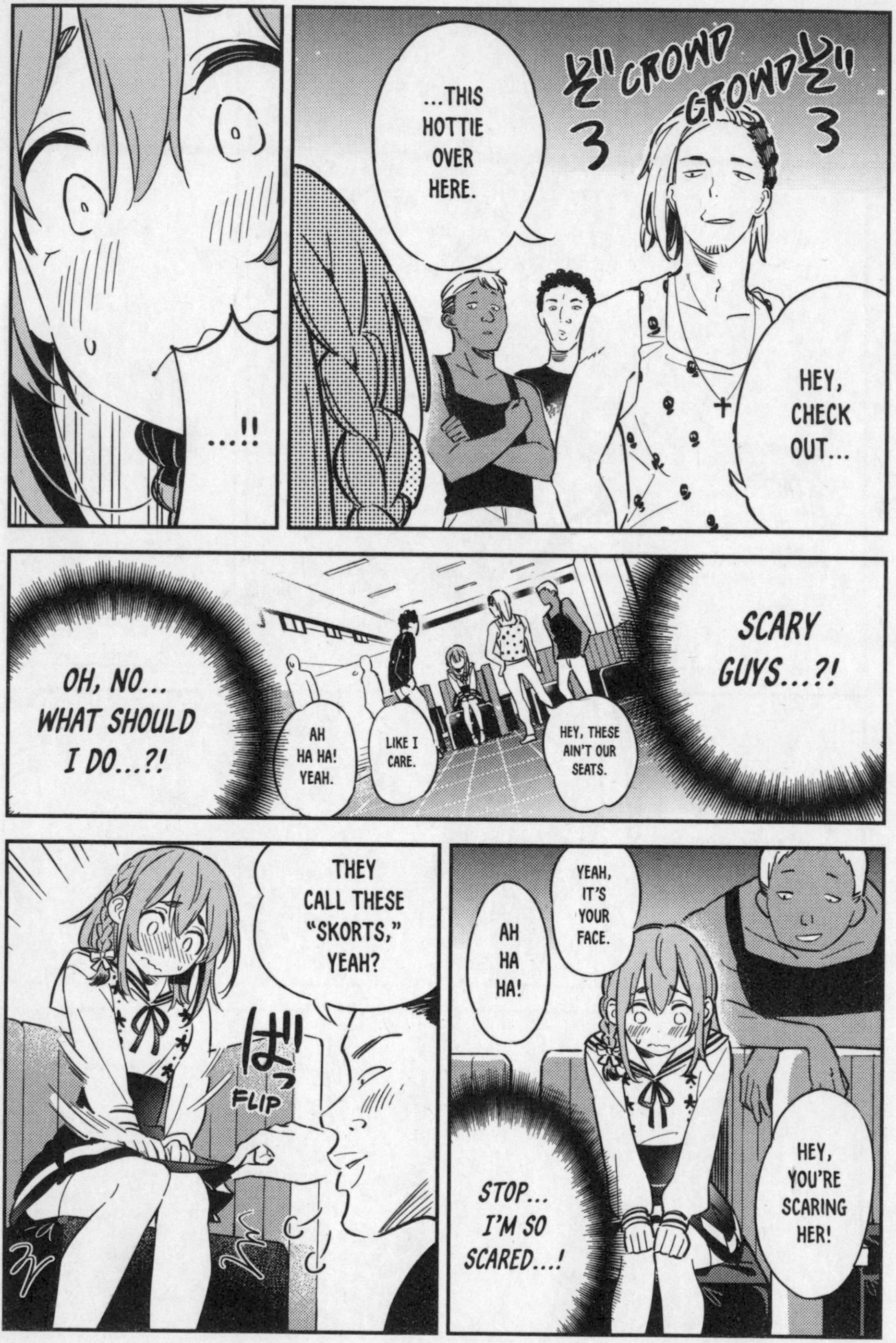
CROWD
CROWD
HEY, CHECK OUT...
...THIS HOTTIE OVER HERE.
...!!
SCARY GUYS...?!
HEY, THESE AIN'T OUR SEATS.
LIKE I CARE.
AH HA HA! YEAH.
OH, NO... WHAT SHOULD I DO...?!
YEAH, IT'S YOUR FACE.
AH HA HA!
HEY, YOU'RE SCARING HER!
STOP... I'M SO SCARED...!
THEY CALL THESE "SKORTS," YEAH?
ぱっ
FLIP

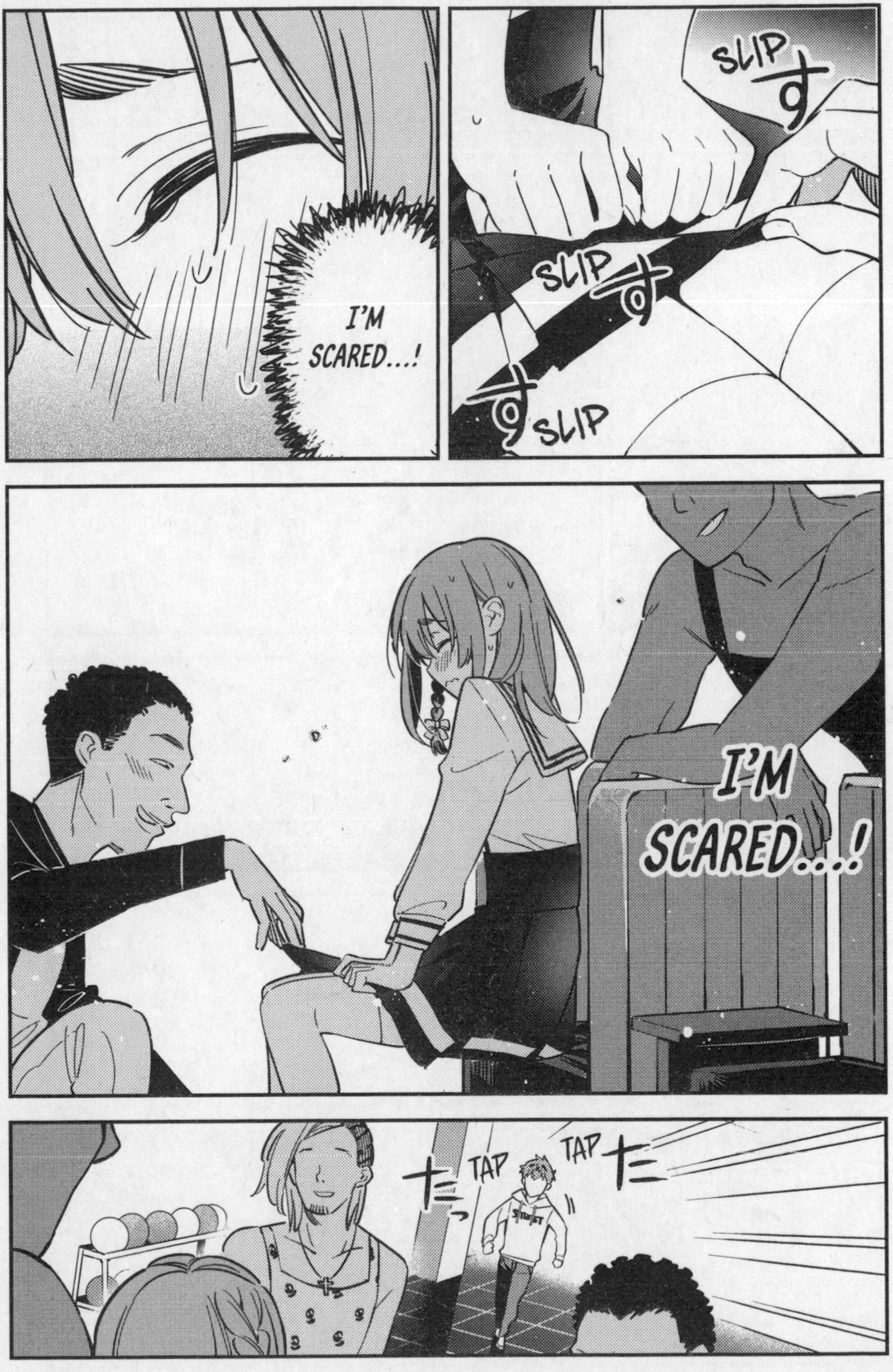
SLIP す
SLIP す
す SLIP
I'M SCARED...!
I'M SCARED...!
TAP た
たっ TAP

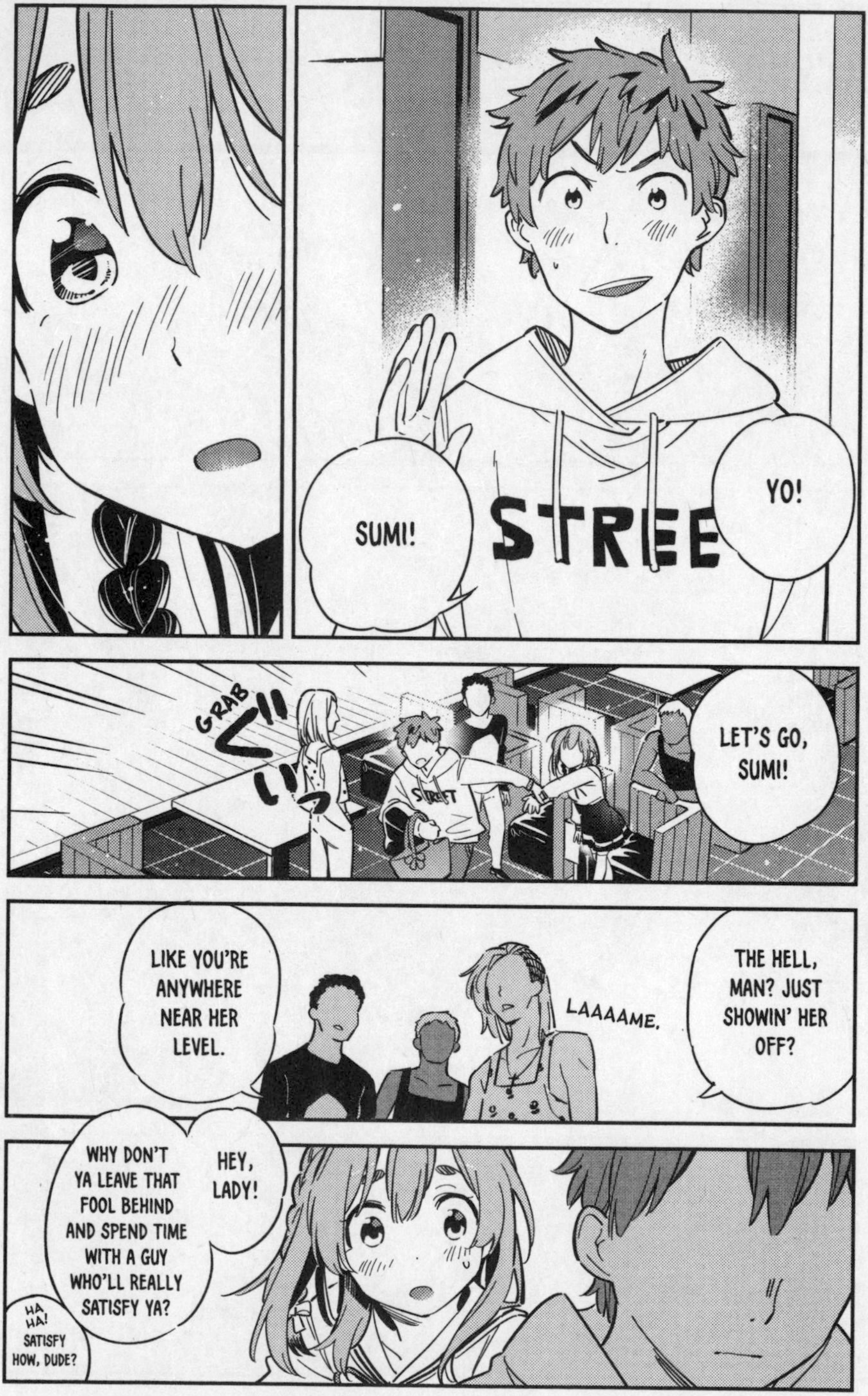
YO!
SUMI!
LET'S GO, SUMI!
GRAB
THE HELL, MAN? JUST SHOWIN' HER OFF?
LAAAAME.
LIKE YOU'RE ANYWHERE NEAR HER LEVEL.
HEY, LADY!
WHY DON'T YA LEAVE THAT FOOL BEHIND AND SPEND TIME WITH A GUY WHO'LL REALLY SATISFY YA?
HA HA! SATISFY HOW, DUDE?

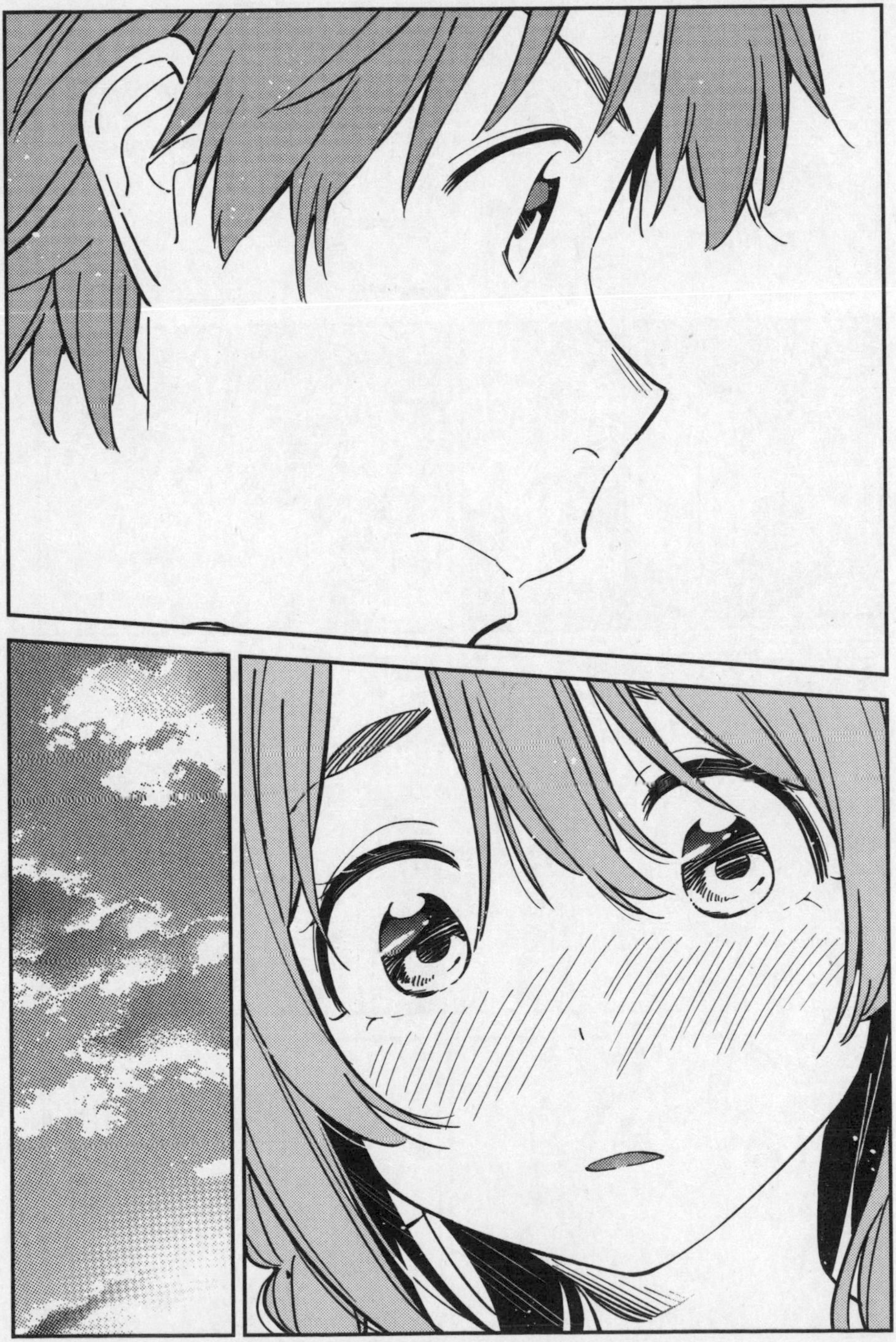

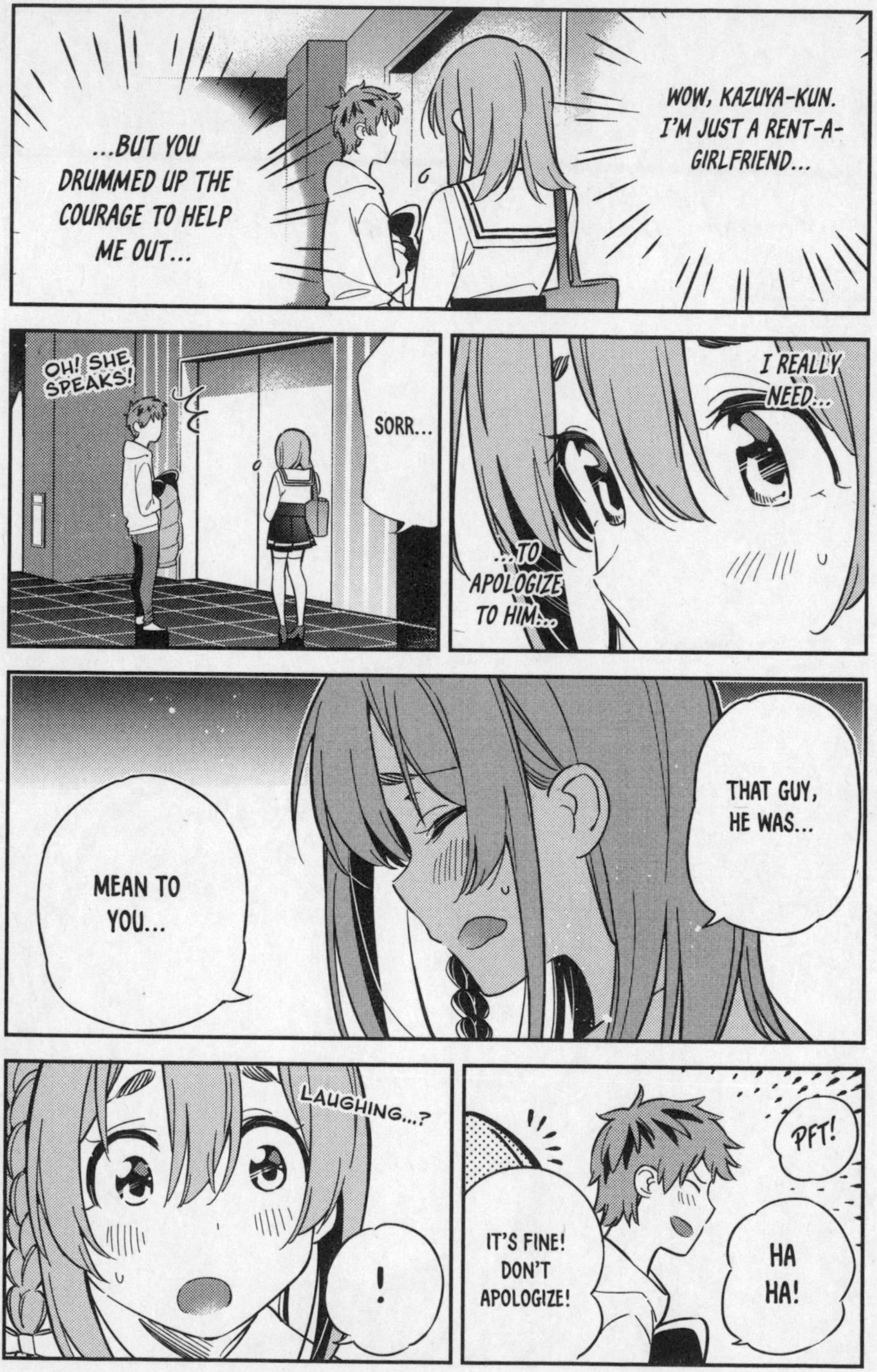
WOW, KAZUYA-KUN. I'M JUST A RENT-A-GIRLFRIEND...
...BUT YOU DRUMMED UP THE COURAGE TO HELP ME OUT...
I REALLY NEED...
...TO APOLOGIZE TO HIM...
SORR...
OH! SHE SPEAKS!
THAT GUY, HE WAS...
MEAN TO YOU...
PFT!
HA HA!
IT'S FINE! DON'T APOLOGIZE!
LAUGHING...?
!

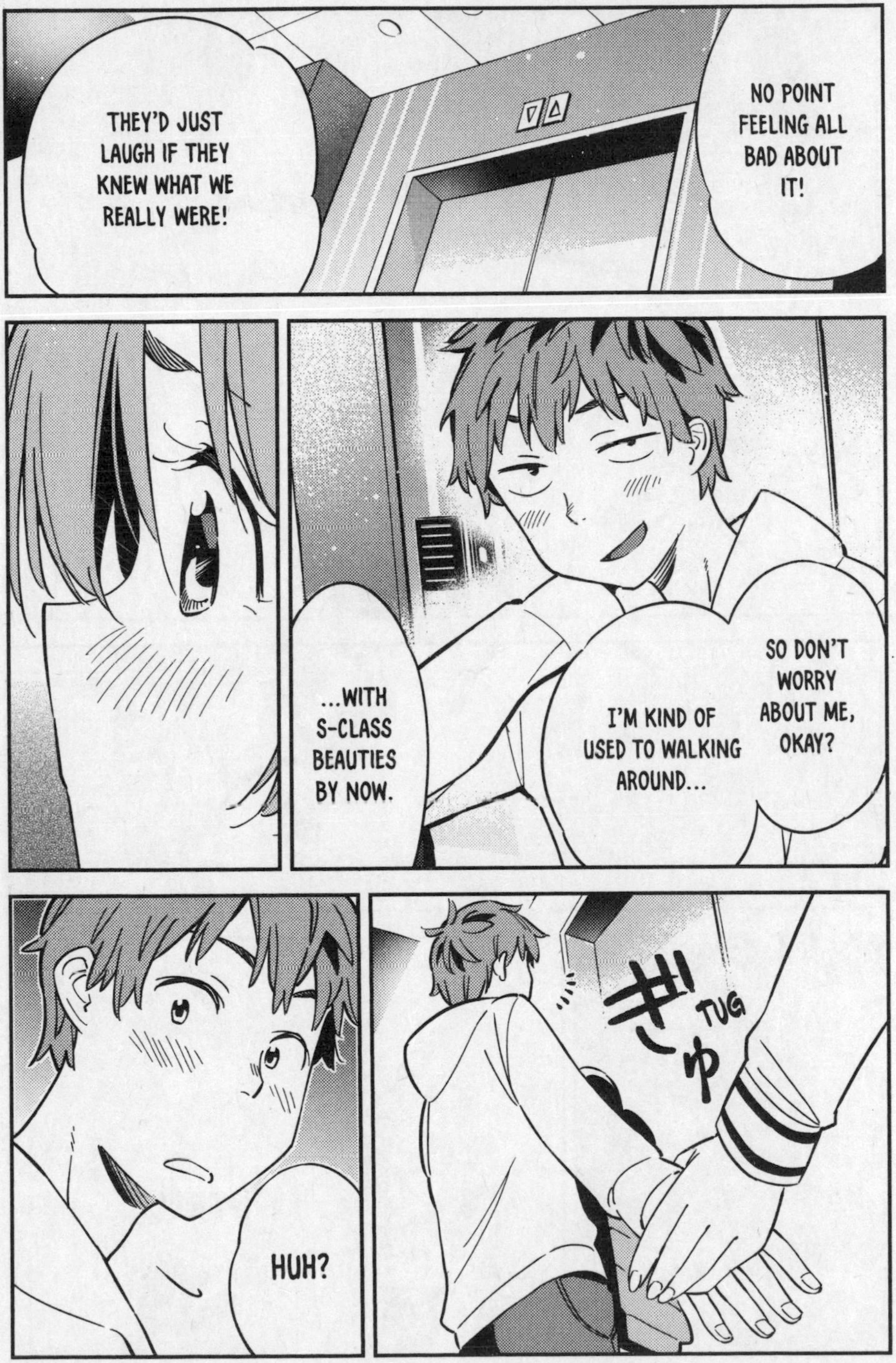
NO POINT FEELING ALL BAD ABOUT IT!
THEY'D JUST LAUGH IF THEY KNEW WHAT WE REALLY WERE!
SO DON'T WORRY ABOUT ME, OKAY?
I'M KIND OF USED TO WALKING AROUND...
...WITH S-CLASS BEAUTIES BY NOW.
ぎゅ
TUG
HUH?

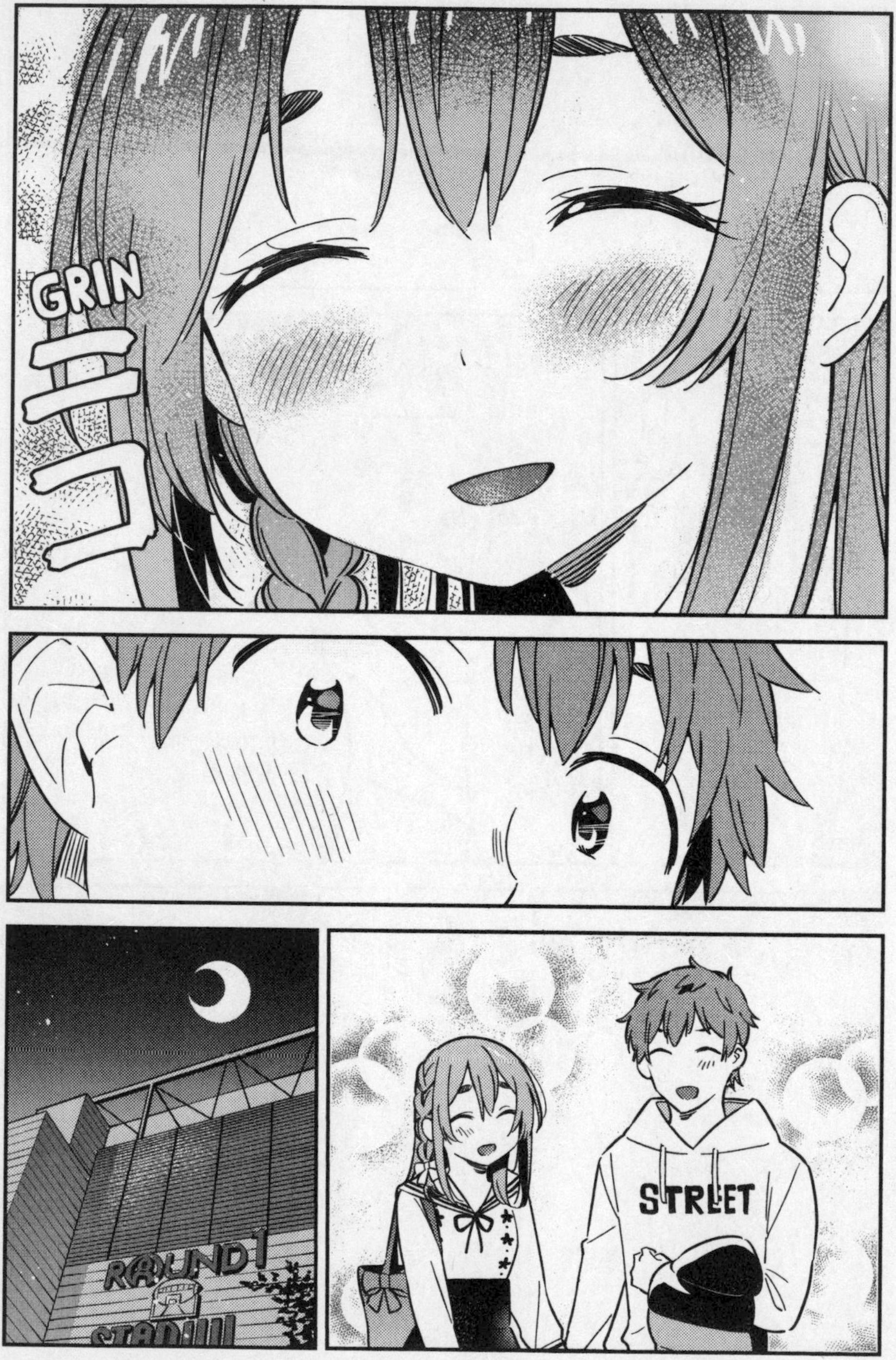
GRIN
ニコ
STREET
ROUND1

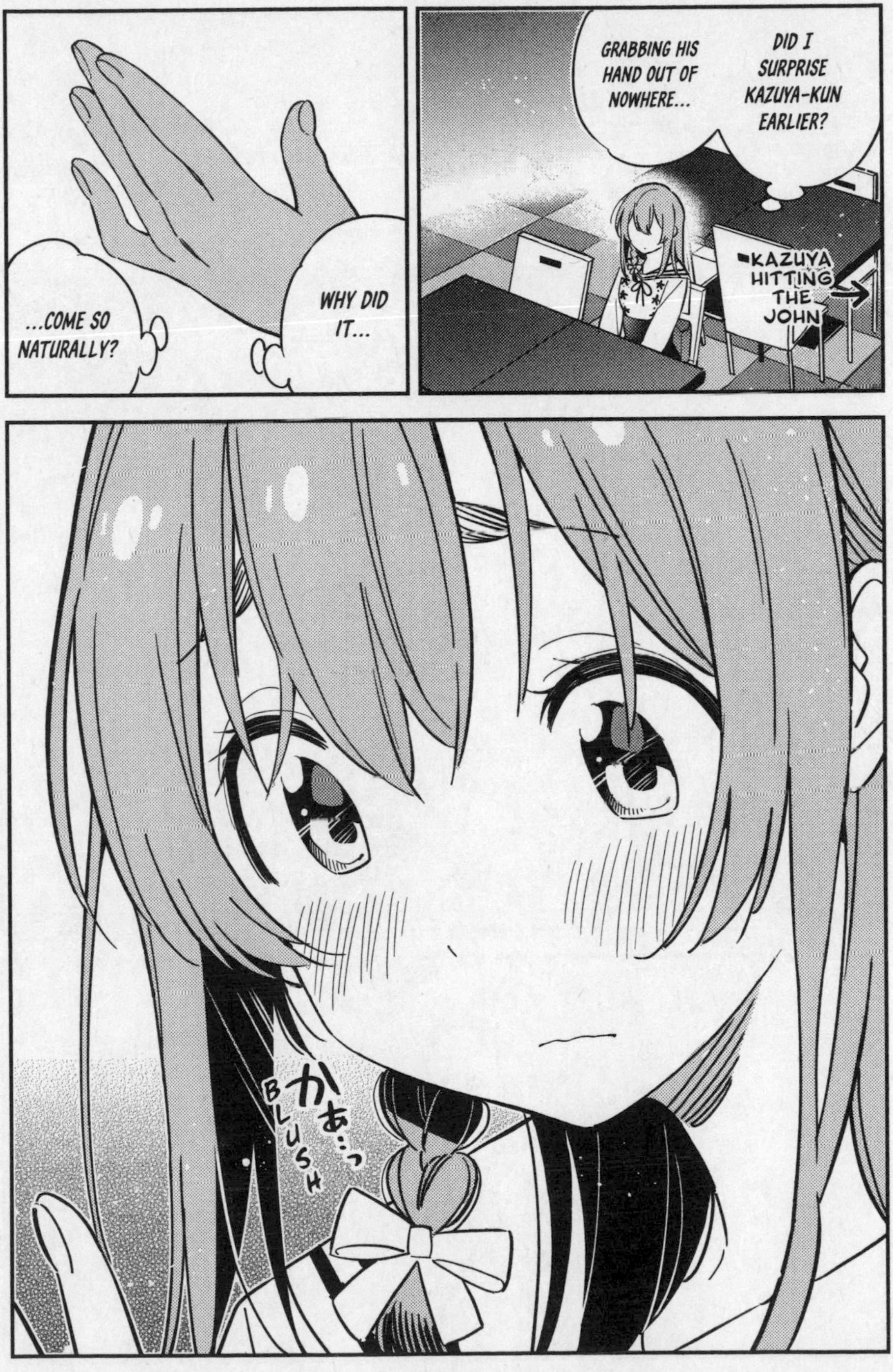
DID I SURPRISE KAZUYA-KUN EARLIER?
GRABBING HIS HAND OUT OF NOWHERE...
KAZUYA HITTING THE JOHN
WHY DID IT...
...COME SO NATURALLY?
かあ…っ
BLUSH

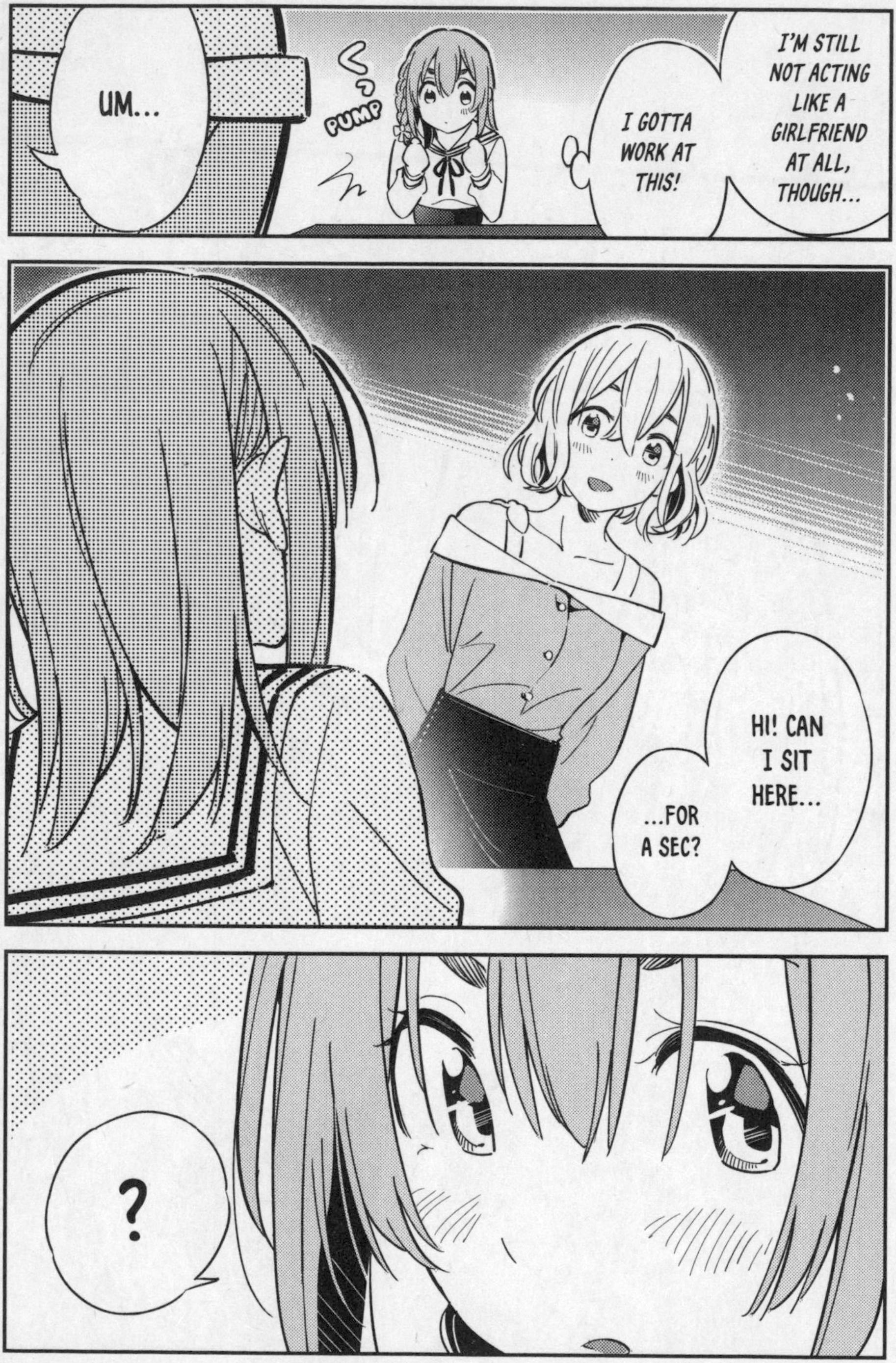
I'M STILL NOT ACTING LIKE A GIRLFRIEND AT ALL, THOUGH...
I GOTTA WORK AT THIS!
PUMP
UM...
HI! CAN I SIT HERE...
...FOR A SEC?
?

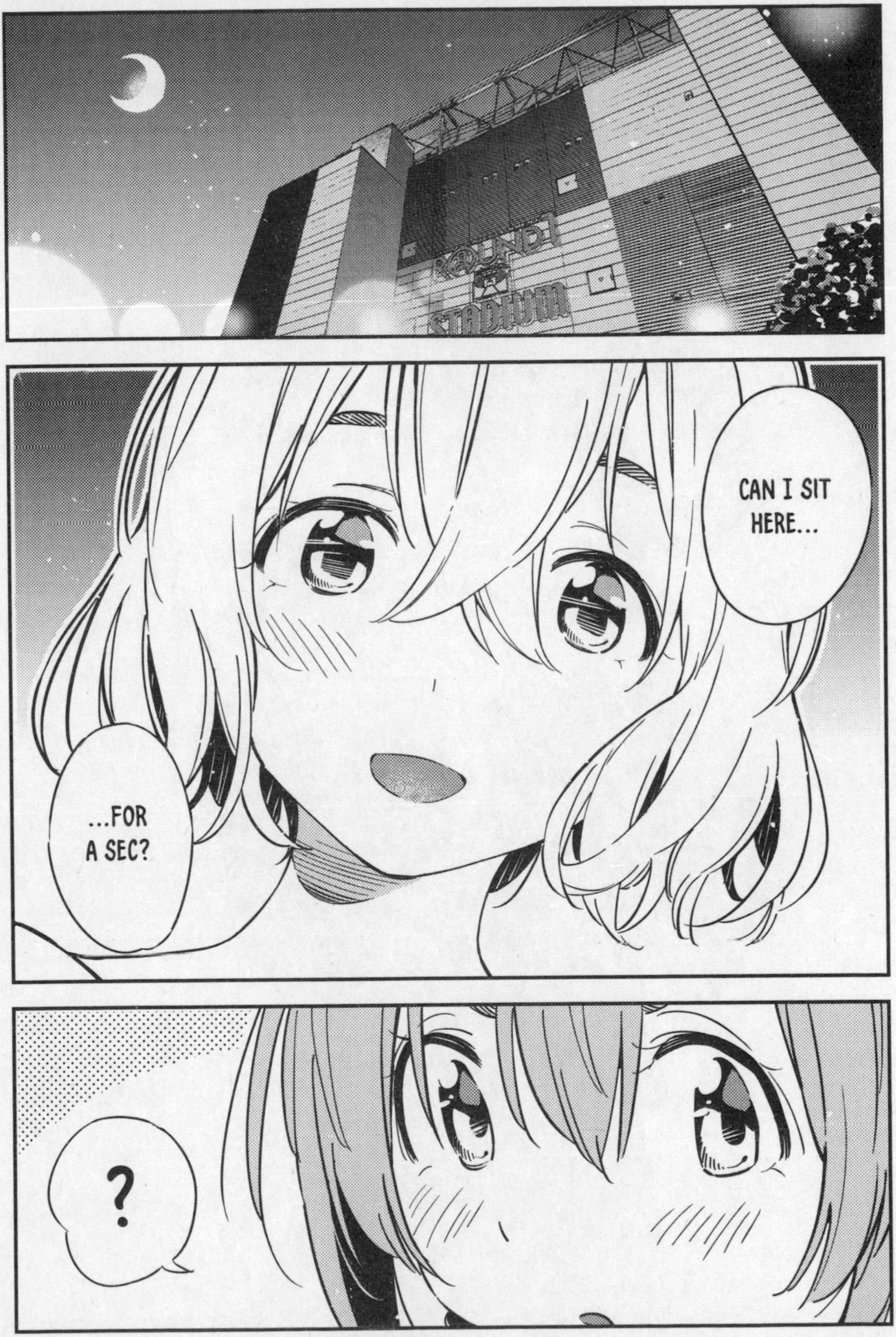
ROUND1
STADIUM
CAN I SIT HERE...
...FOR A SEC?
?

RATING 9 ★ SUMI AND KAZUYA-KUN'S FRIEND

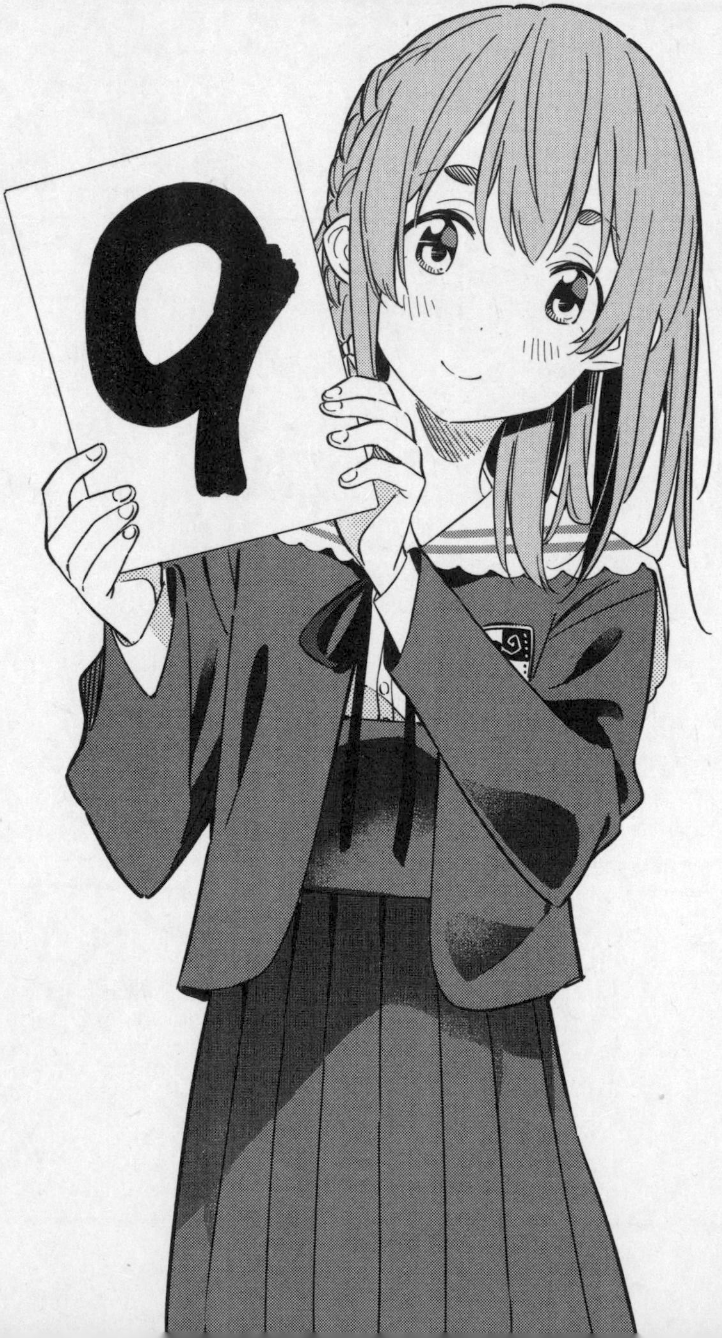
9

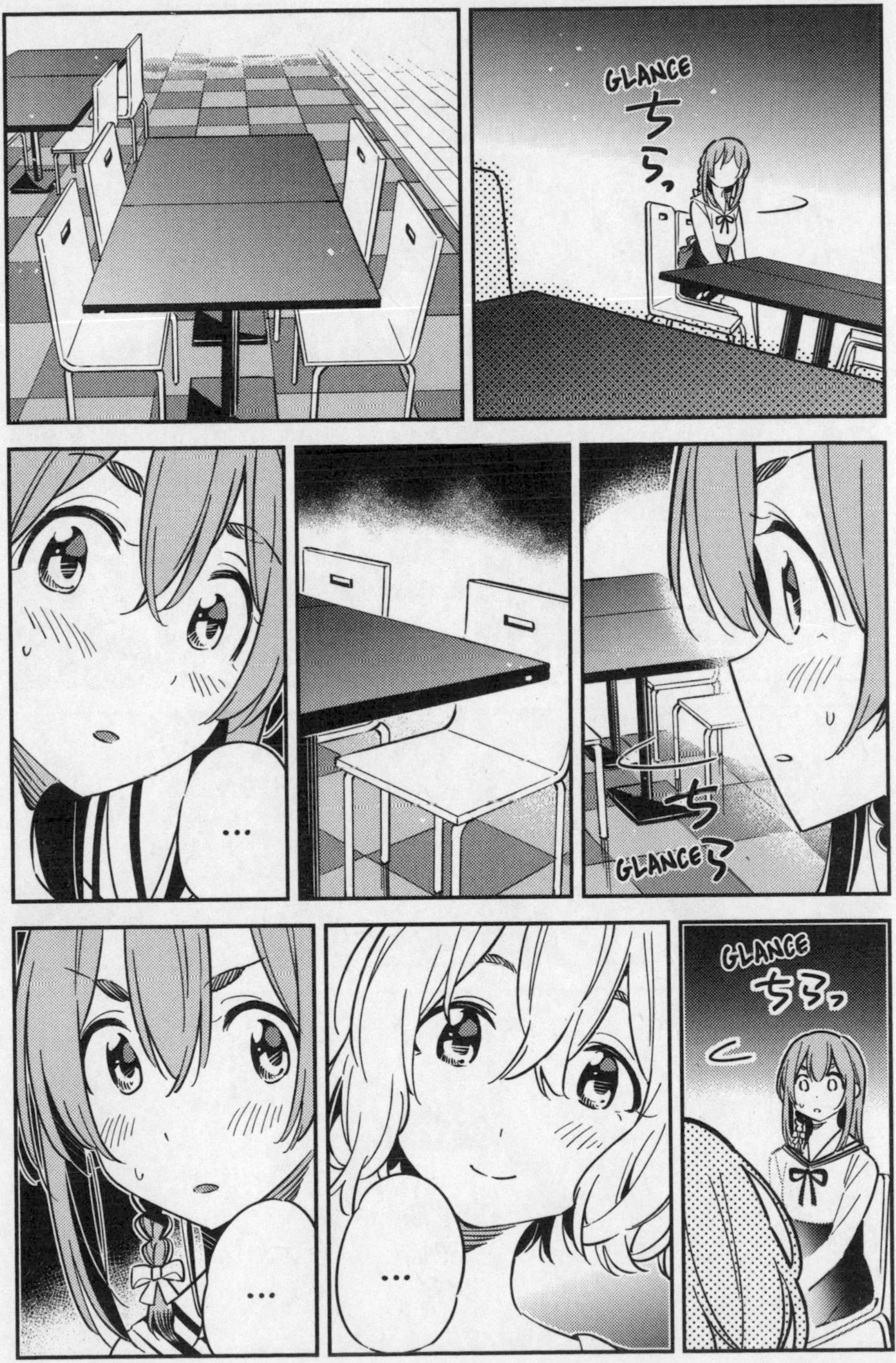
GLANCE
ちらっ
ち
GLANCE
ろ
...
GLANCE
ちろっ
...
...

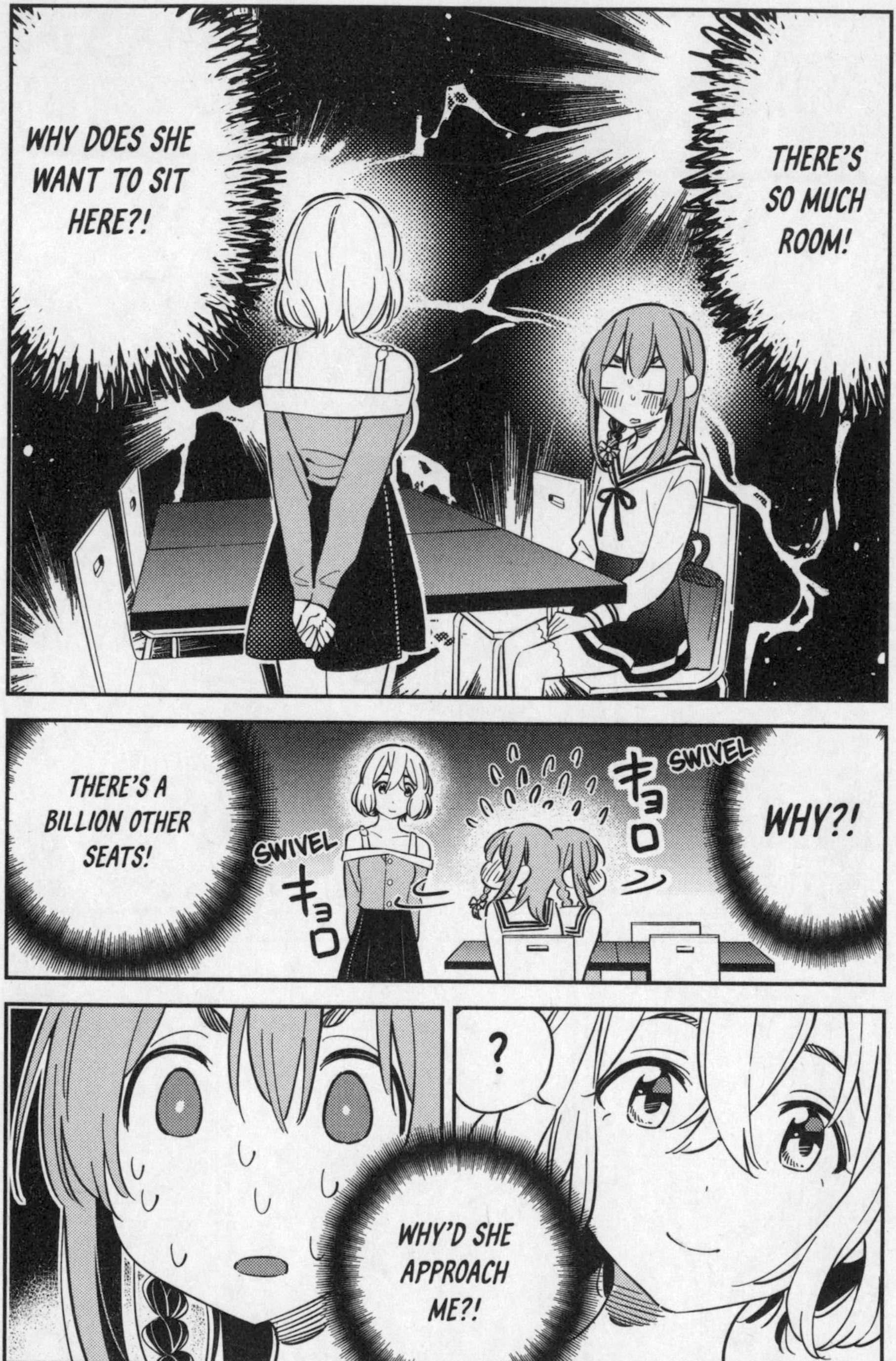
THERE'S SO MUCH ROOM!
WHY DOES SHE WANT TO SIT HERE?!
WHY?!
SWIVEL
キョロ
SWIVEL
キョロ
THERE'S A BILLION OTHER SEATS!
?
WHY'D SHE APPROACH ME?!

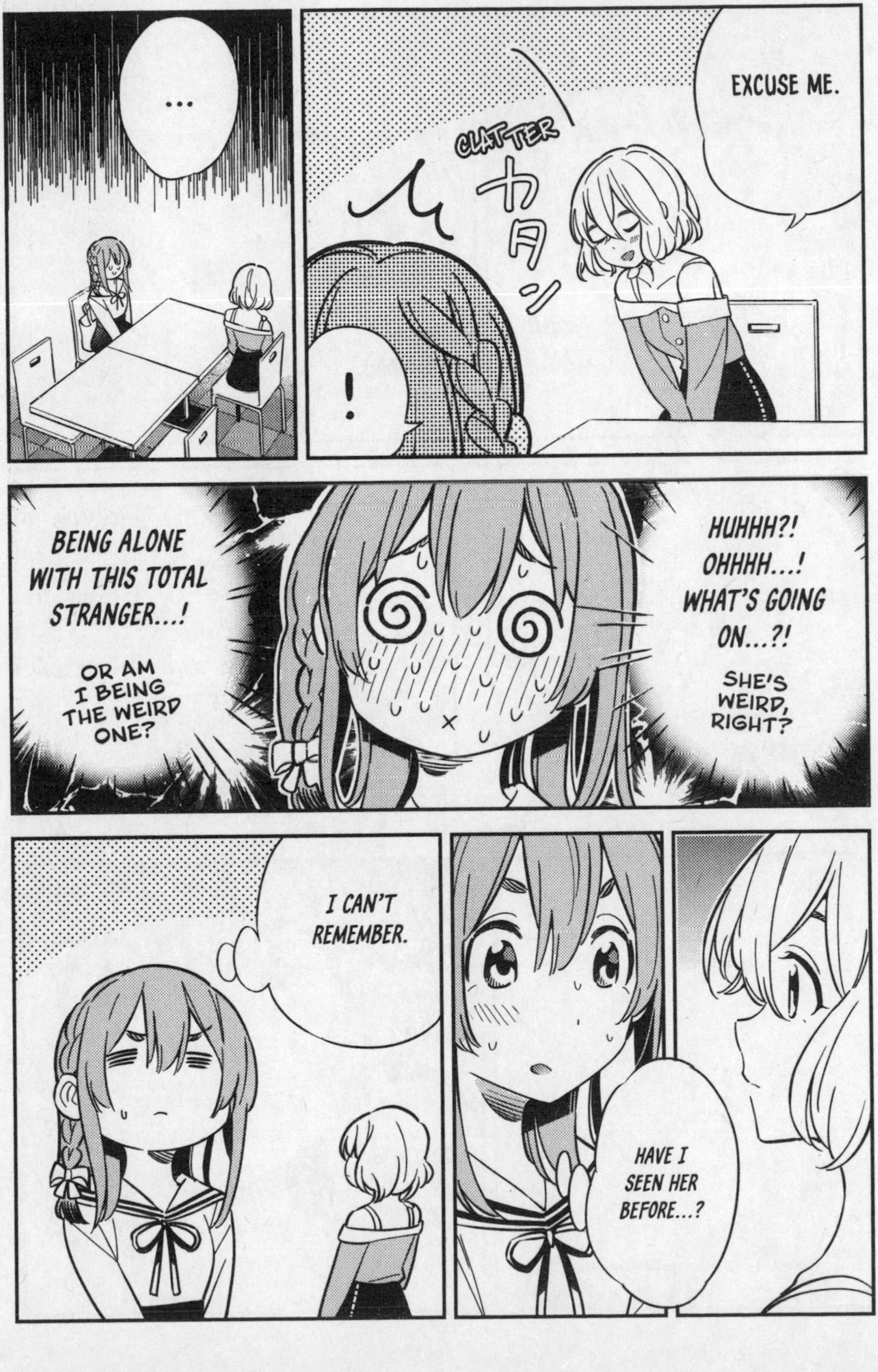
EXCUSE ME.
CLATTER
カタン
!
...
HUHHH?! OHHHH...! WHAT'S GOING ON...?!
BEING ALONE WITH THIS TOTAL STRANGER...!
SHE'S WEIRD, RIGHT?
OR AM I BEING THE WEIRD ONE?
HAVE I SEEN HER BEFORE...?
I CAN'T REMEMBER.

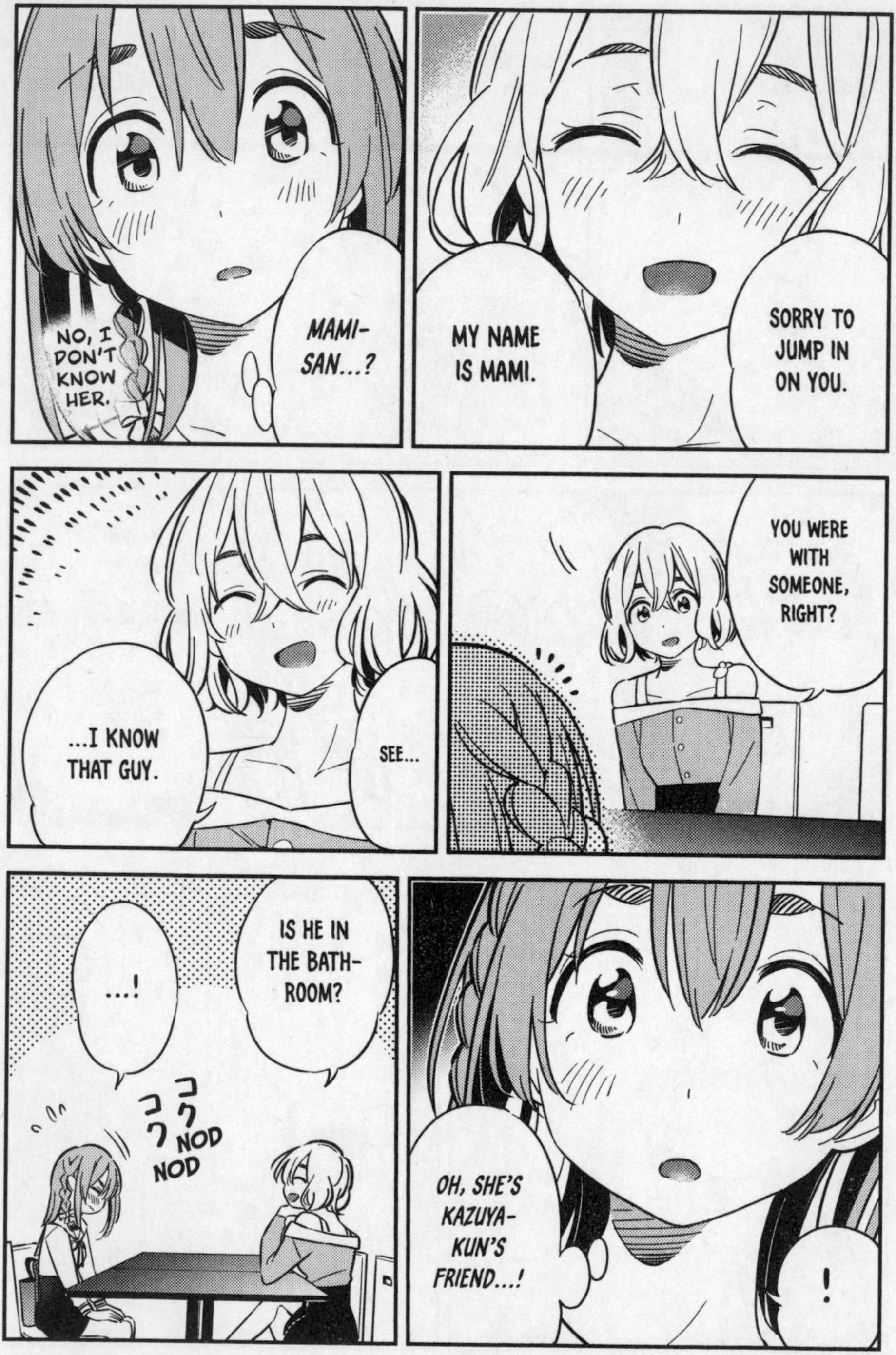
SORRY TO JUMP IN ON YOU.
MY NAME IS MAMI.
MAMI-SAN...?
NO, I DON'T KNOW HER.
YOU WERE WITH SOMEONE, RIGHT?
SEE...
...I KNOW THAT GUY.
!
OH, SHE'S KAZUYA-KUN'S FRIEND...!
IS HE IN THE BATH-ROOM?
...!
コクコク
NOD NOD

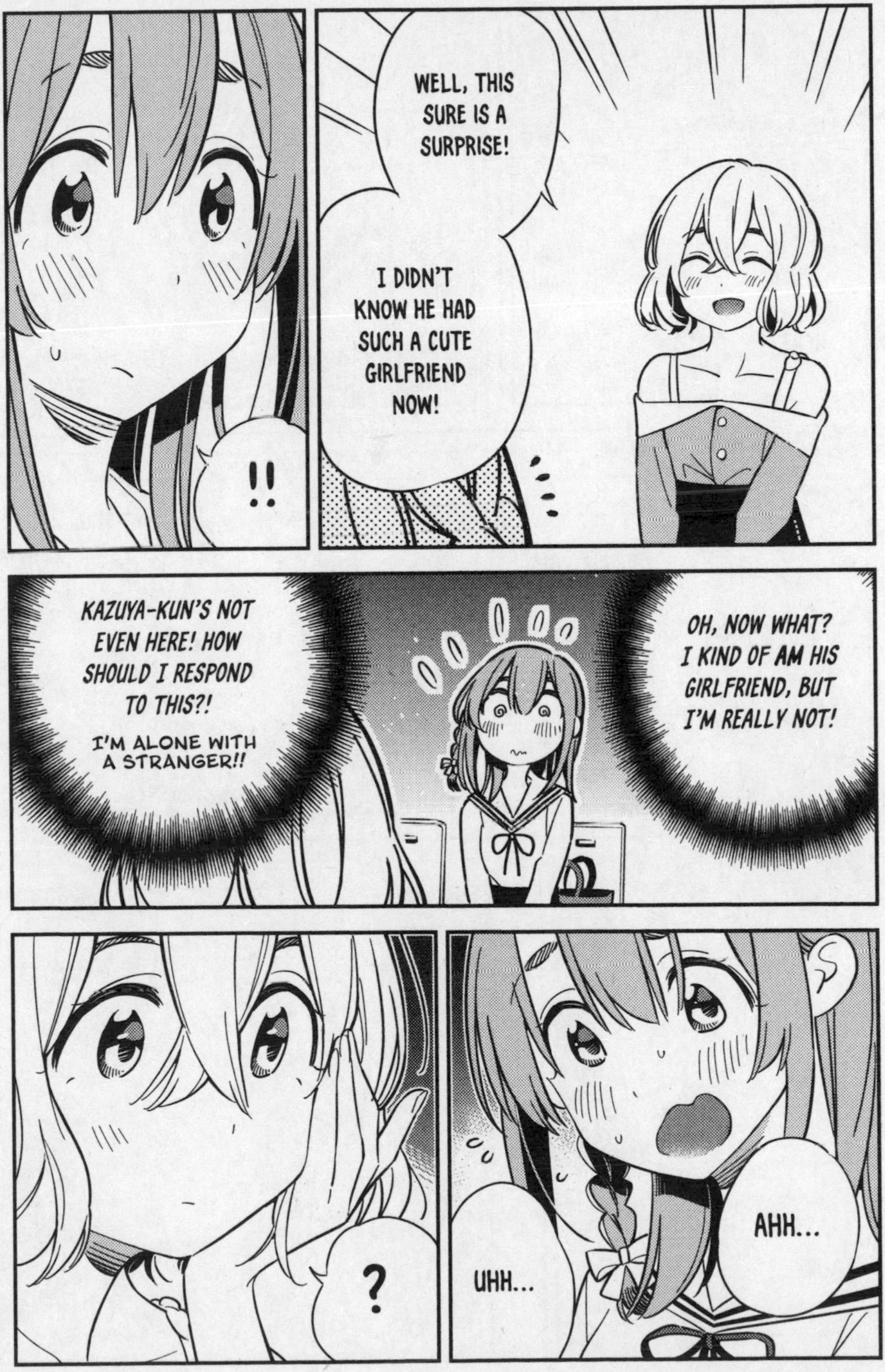
WELL, THIS SURE IS A SURPRISE!
I DIDN'T KNOW HE HAD SUCH A CUTE GIRLFRIEND NOW!
!!
OH, NOW WHAT? I KIND OF AM HIS GIRLFRIEND, BUT I'M REALLY NOT!
KAZUYA-KUN'S NOT EVEN HERE! HOW SHOULD I RESPOND TO THIS?!
I'M ALONE WITH A STRANGER!!
AHH...
UHH...
?

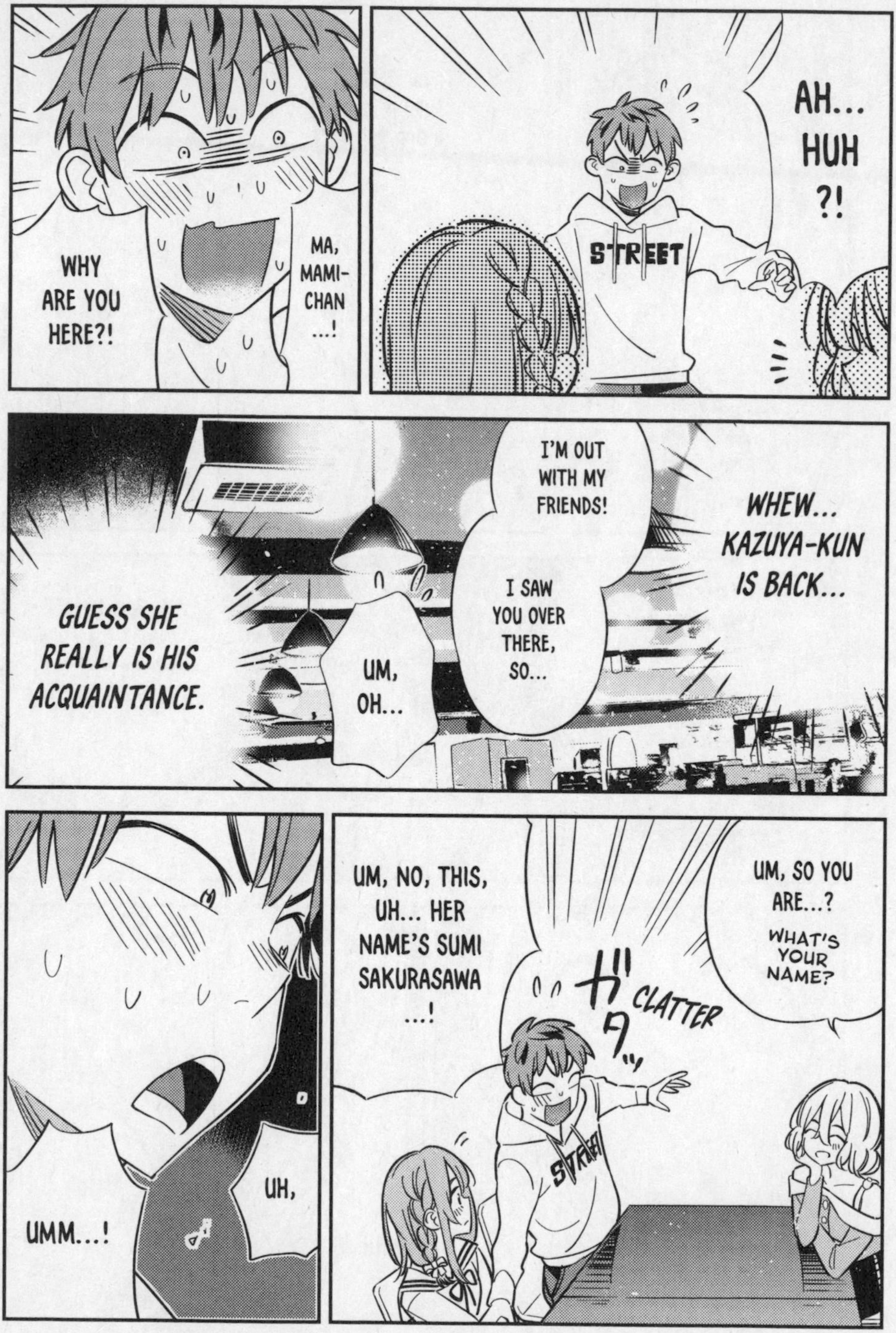
AH... HUH ?!
MA, MAMI-CHAN ...!
WHY ARE YOU HERE?!
WHEW... KAZUYA-KUN IS BACK...
I'M OUT WITH MY FRIENDS!
I SAW YOU OVER THERE, SO...
UM, OH...
GUESS SHE REALLY IS HIS ACQUAINTANCE.
UM, SO YOU ARE...?
WHAT'S YOUR NAME?
ガタッ
CLATTER
UM, NO, THIS, UH... HER NAME'S SUMI SAKURASAWA ...!
UH,
UMM...!

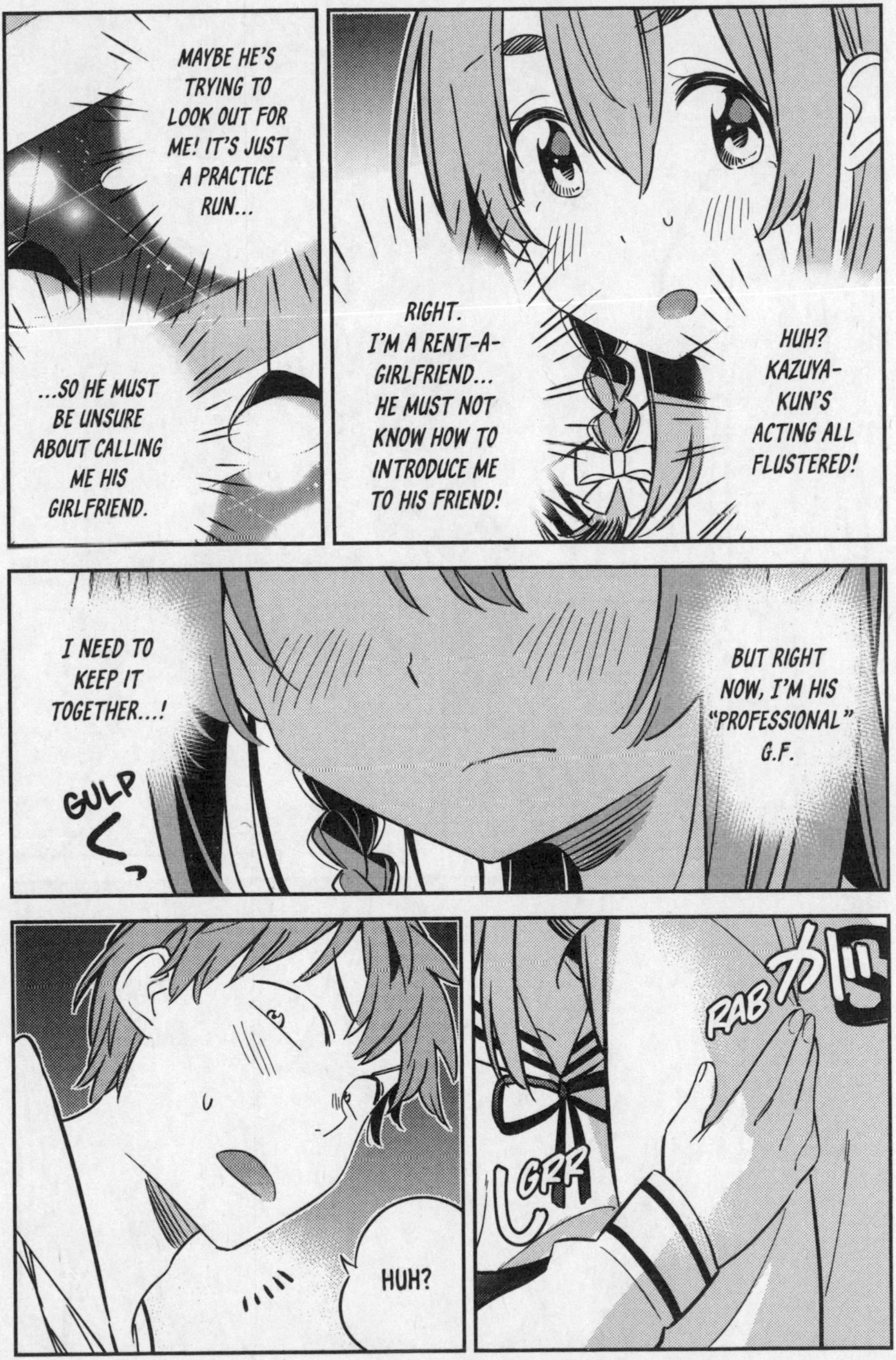
HUH? KAZUYA-KUN'S ACTING ALL FLUSTERED!
RIGHT. I'M A RENT-A-GIRLFRIEND... HE MUST NOT KNOW HOW TO INTRODUCE ME TO HIS FRIEND!
MAYBE HE'S TRYING TO LOOK OUT FOR ME! IT'S JUST A PRACTICE RUN...
...SO HE MUST BE UNSURE ABOUT CALLING ME HIS GIRLFRIEND.
BUT RIGHT NOW, I'M HIS "PROFESSIONAL" G.F.
I NEED TO KEEP IT TOGETHER...!
GULP
RAB
GRR
HUH?

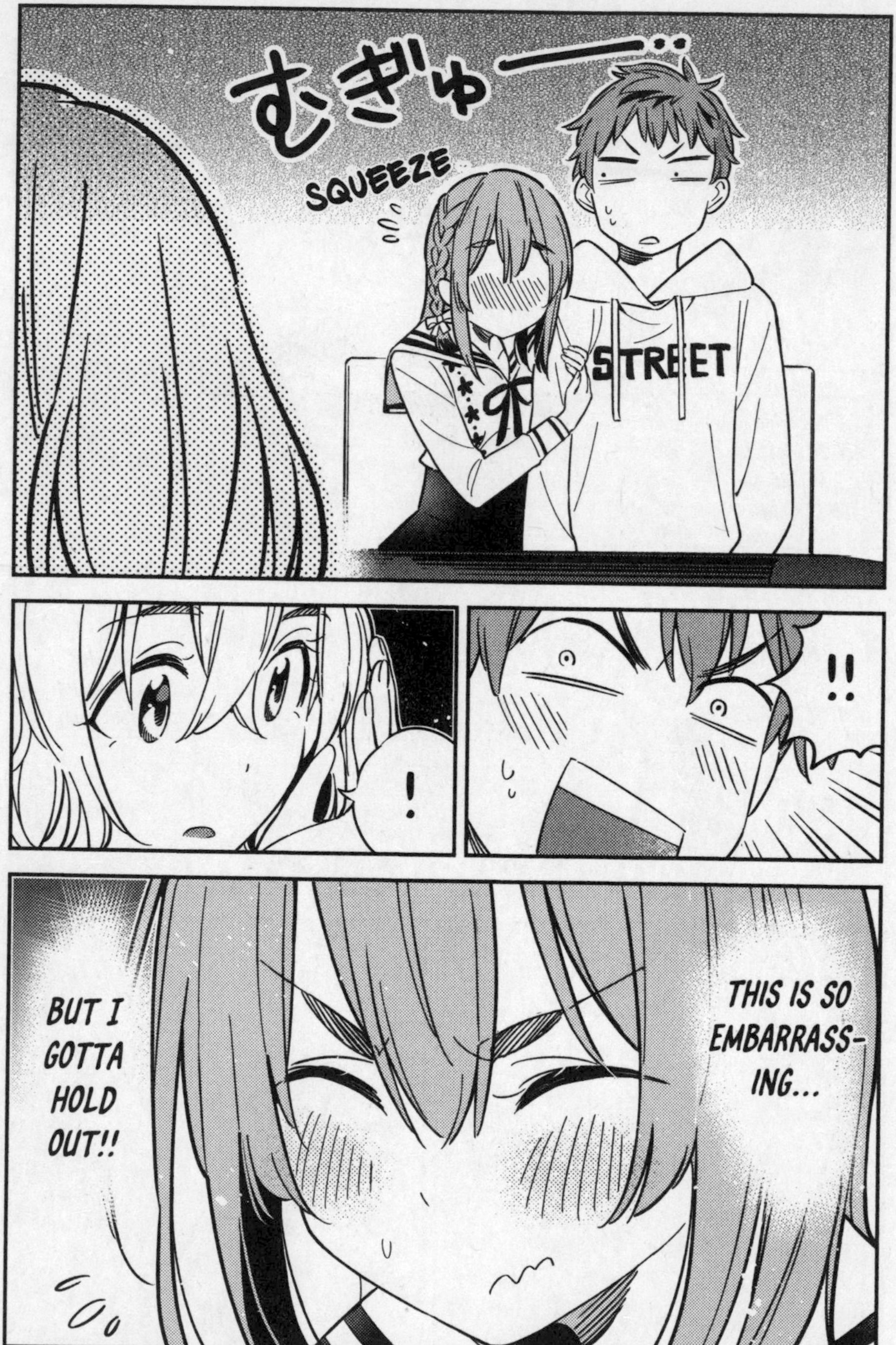
むぎゅー
SQUEEZE
STREET
!!
!
THIS IS SO EMBARRASS-ING...
BUT I GOTTA HOLD OUT!!

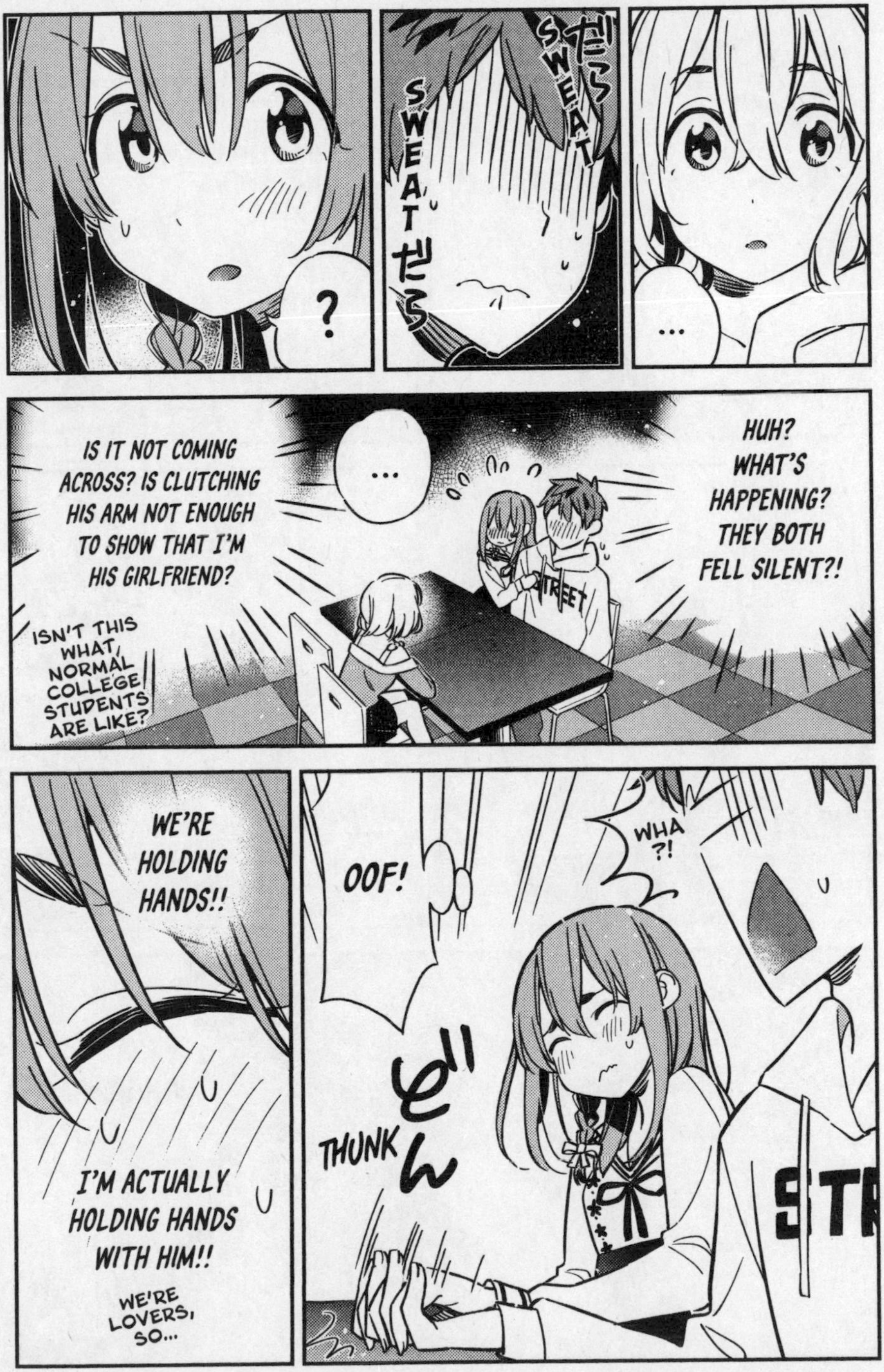
...
SWEAT だら
SWEAT だら
?
HUH? WHAT'S HAPPENING? THEY BOTH FELL SILENT?!
...
IS IT NOT COMING ACROSS? IS CLUTCHING HIS ARM NOT ENOUGH TO SHOW THAT I'M HIS GIRLFRIEND?
ISN'T THIS WHAT, NORMAL COLLEGE STUDENTS ARE LIKE?
WHA ?!
OOF!
どん
THUNK
WE'RE HOLDING HANDS!!
I'M ACTUALLY HOLDING HANDS WITH HIM!!
WE'RE LOVERS, SO...

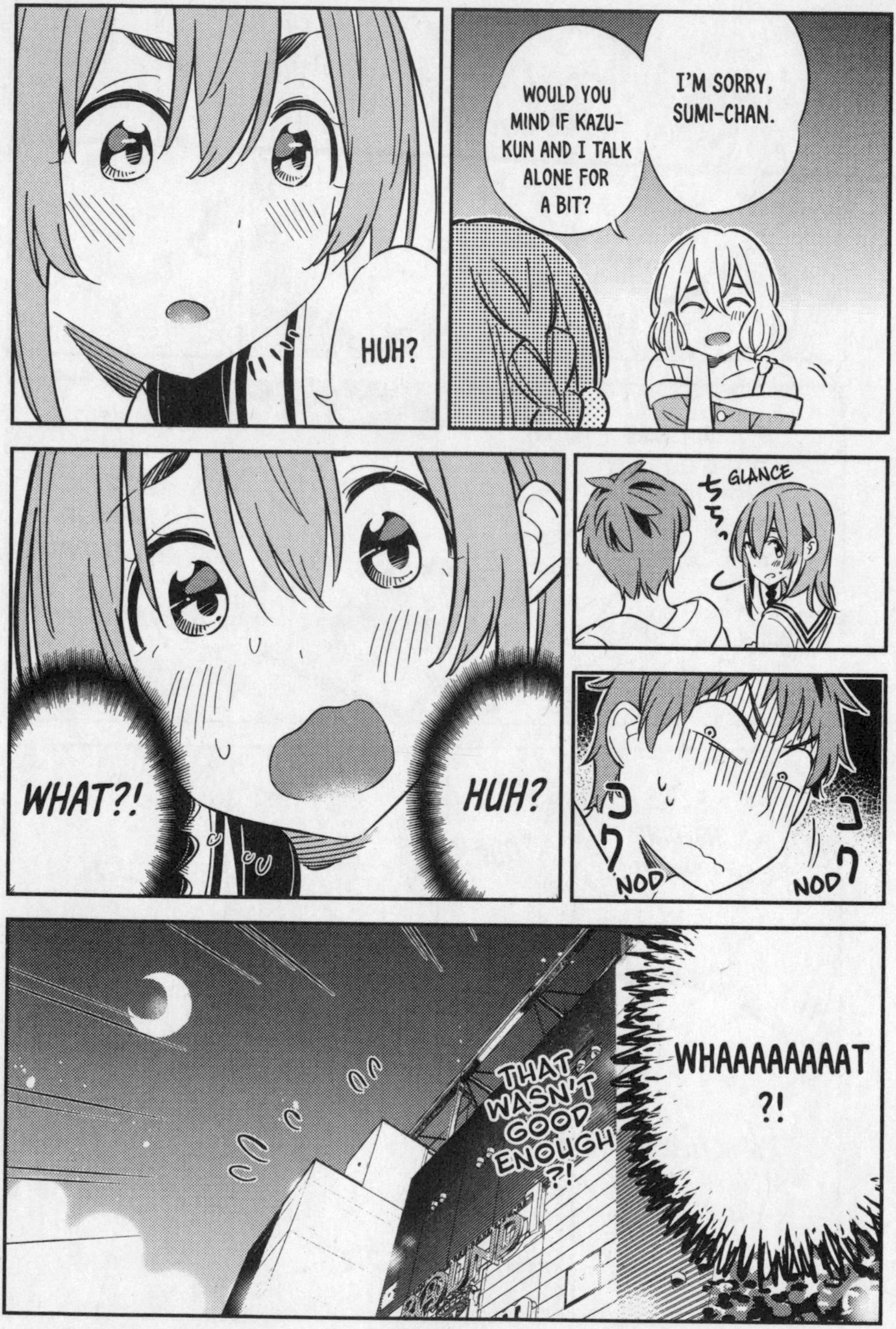
I'M SORRY, SUMI-CHAN.
WOULD YOU MIND IF KAZU-KUN AND I TALK ALONE FOR A BIT?
HUH?
ちらっ
GLANCE
コク
NOD
コク
NOD
HUH?
WHAT?!
WHAAAAAAAAT ?!
THAT WASN'T GOOD ENOUGH ?!

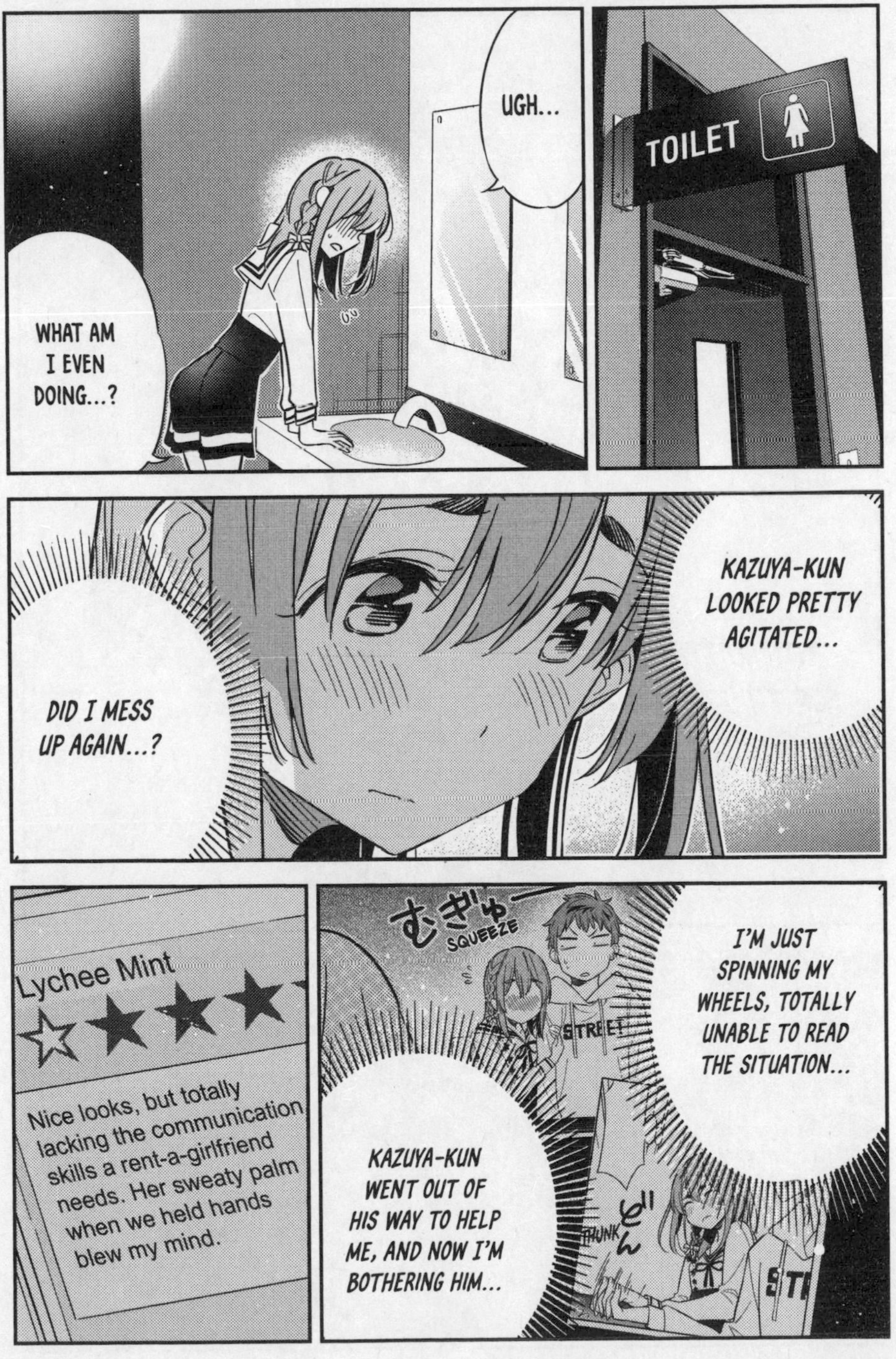
TOILET
UGH...
WHAT AM I EVEN DOING...?
KAZUYA-KUN LOOKED PRETTY AGITATED...
DID I MESS UP AGAIN...?
むぎゅー
SQUEEZE
STREET
I'M JUST SPINNING MY WHEELS, TOTALLY UNABLE TO READ THE SITUATION...
KAZUYA-KUN WENT OUT OF HIS WAY TO HELP ME, AND NOW I'M BOTHERING HIM...
どん
THUNK
Lychee Mint
Nice looks, but totally lacking the communication skills a rent-a-girlfriend needs. Her sweaty palm when we held hands blew my mind.

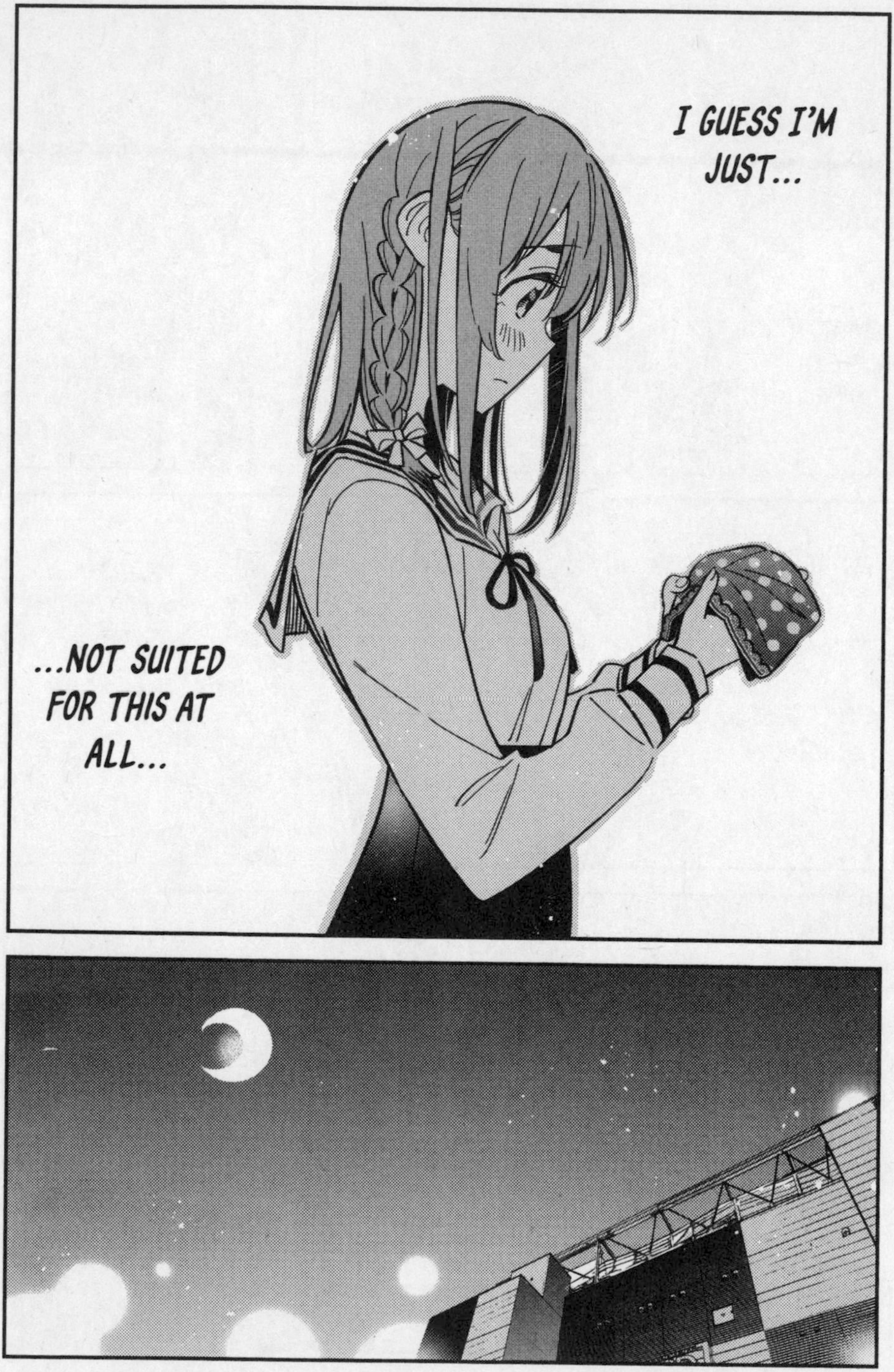
I GUESS I'M JUST...
...NOT SUITED FOR THIS AT ALL...

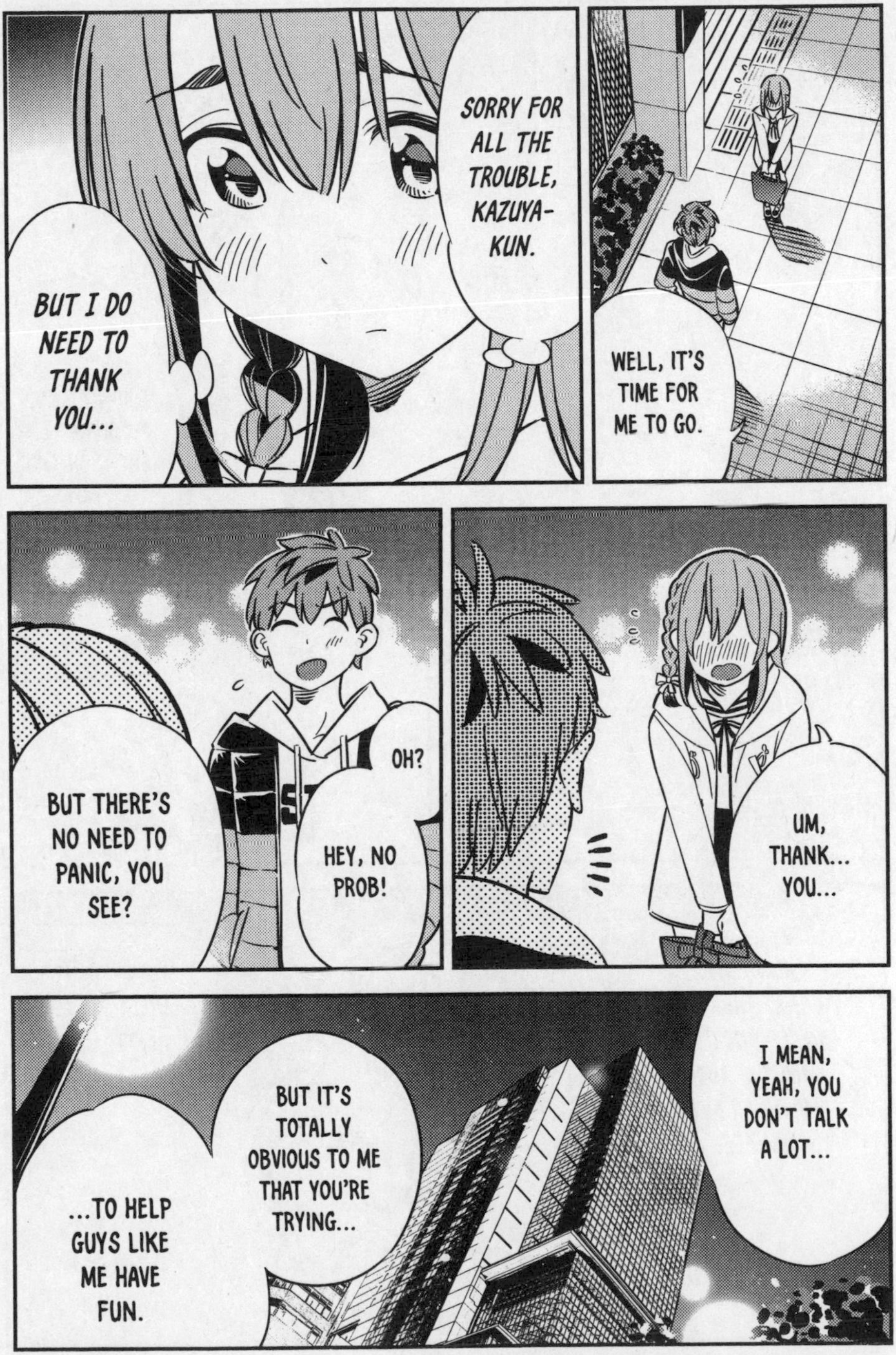
WELL, IT'S TIME FOR ME TO GO.
SORRY FOR ALL THE TROUBLE, KAZUYA-KUN.
BUT I DO NEED TO THANK YOU...
UM, THANK... YOU...
OH?
HEY, NO PROB!
BUT THERE'S NO NEED TO PANIC, YOU SEE?
I MEAN, YEAH, YOU DON'T TALK A LOT...
BUT IT'S TOTALLY OBVIOUS TO ME THAT YOU'RE TRYING...
...TO HELP GUYS LIKE ME HAVE FUN.

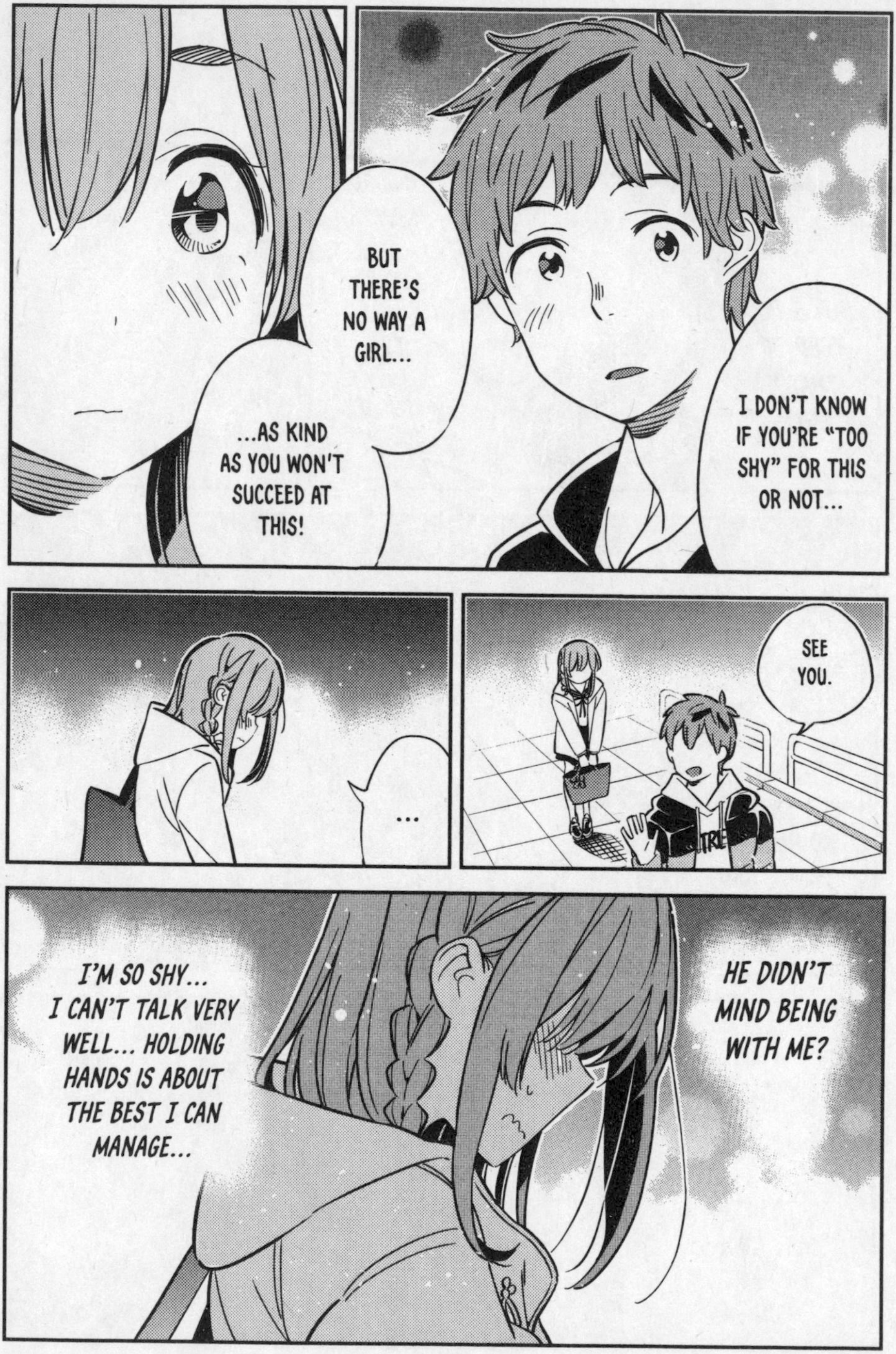
I DON'T KNOW IF YOU'RE "TOO SHY" FOR THIS OR NOT...
BUT THERE'S NO WAY A GIRL...
...AS KIND AS YOU WON'T SUCCEED AT THIS!
SEE YOU.
...
HE DIDN'T MIND BEING WITH ME?
I'M SO SHY... I CAN'T TALK VERY WELL... HOLDING HANDS IS ABOUT THE BEST I CAN MANAGE...

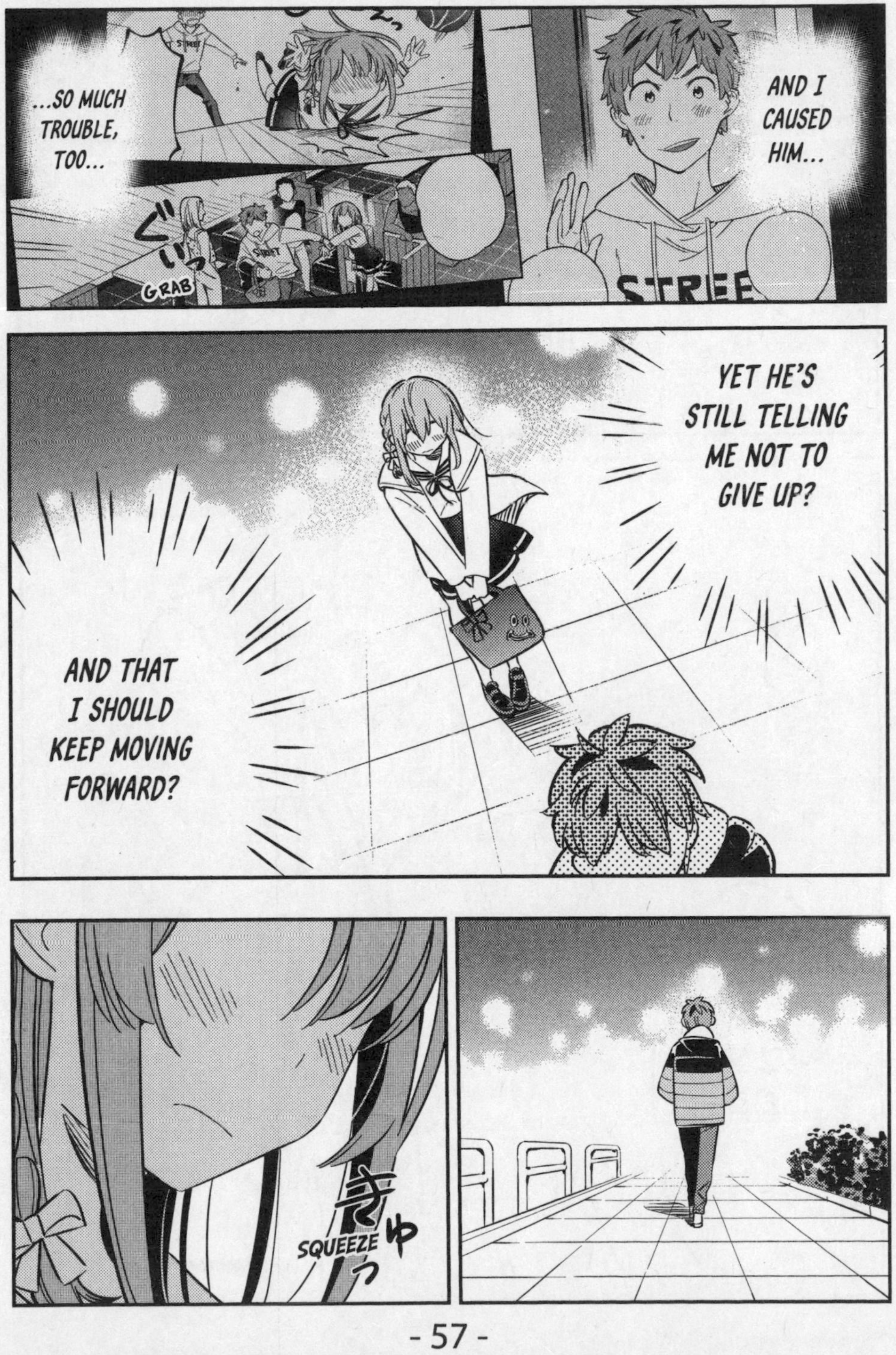
AND I CAUSED HIM...
...SO MUCH TROUBLE, TOO...
GRAB
YET HE'S STILL TELLING ME NOT TO GIVE UP?
AND THAT I SHOULD KEEP MOVING FORWARD?
SQUEEZE

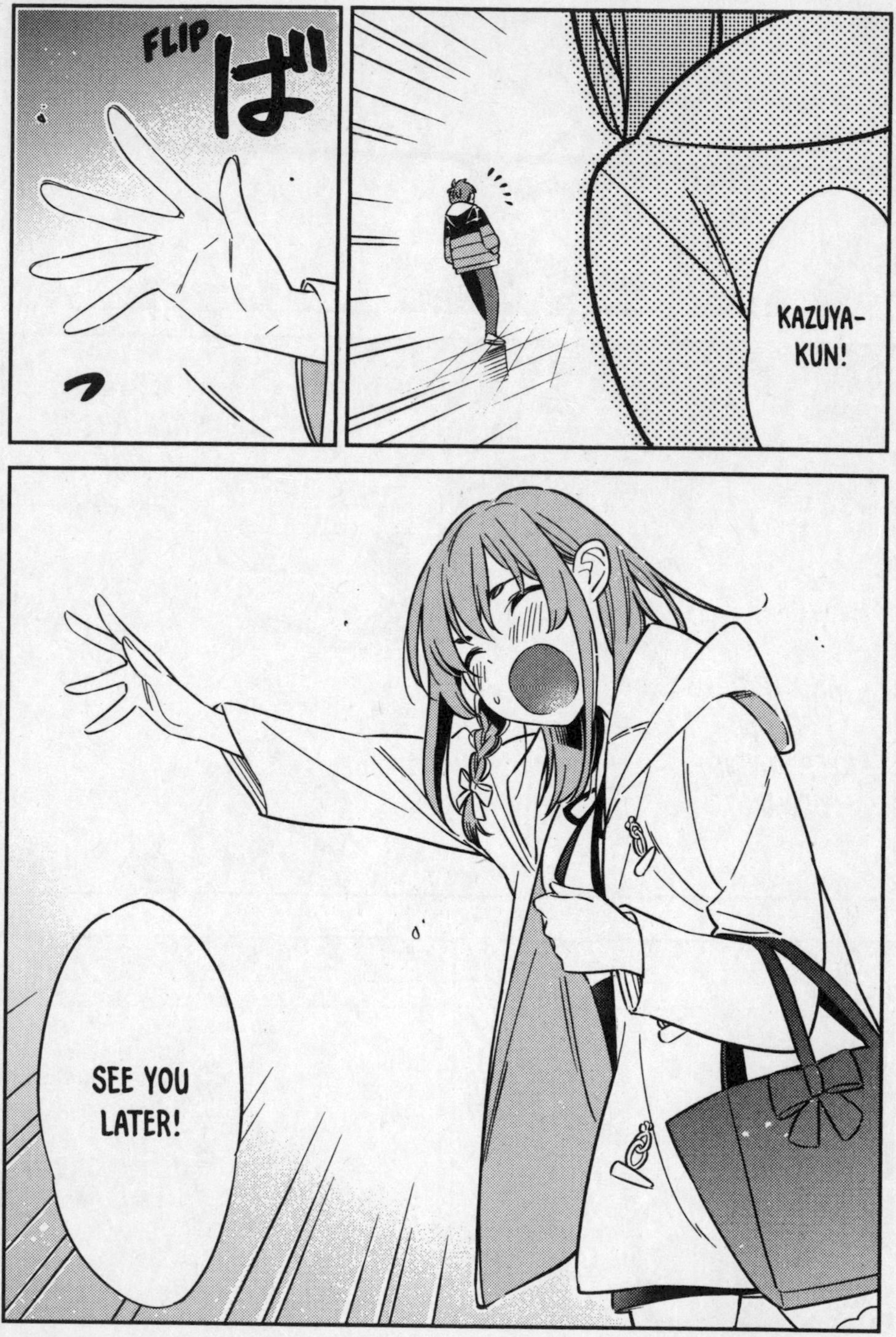
KAZUYA-KUN!
FLIP
ば
っ
SEE YOU LATER!

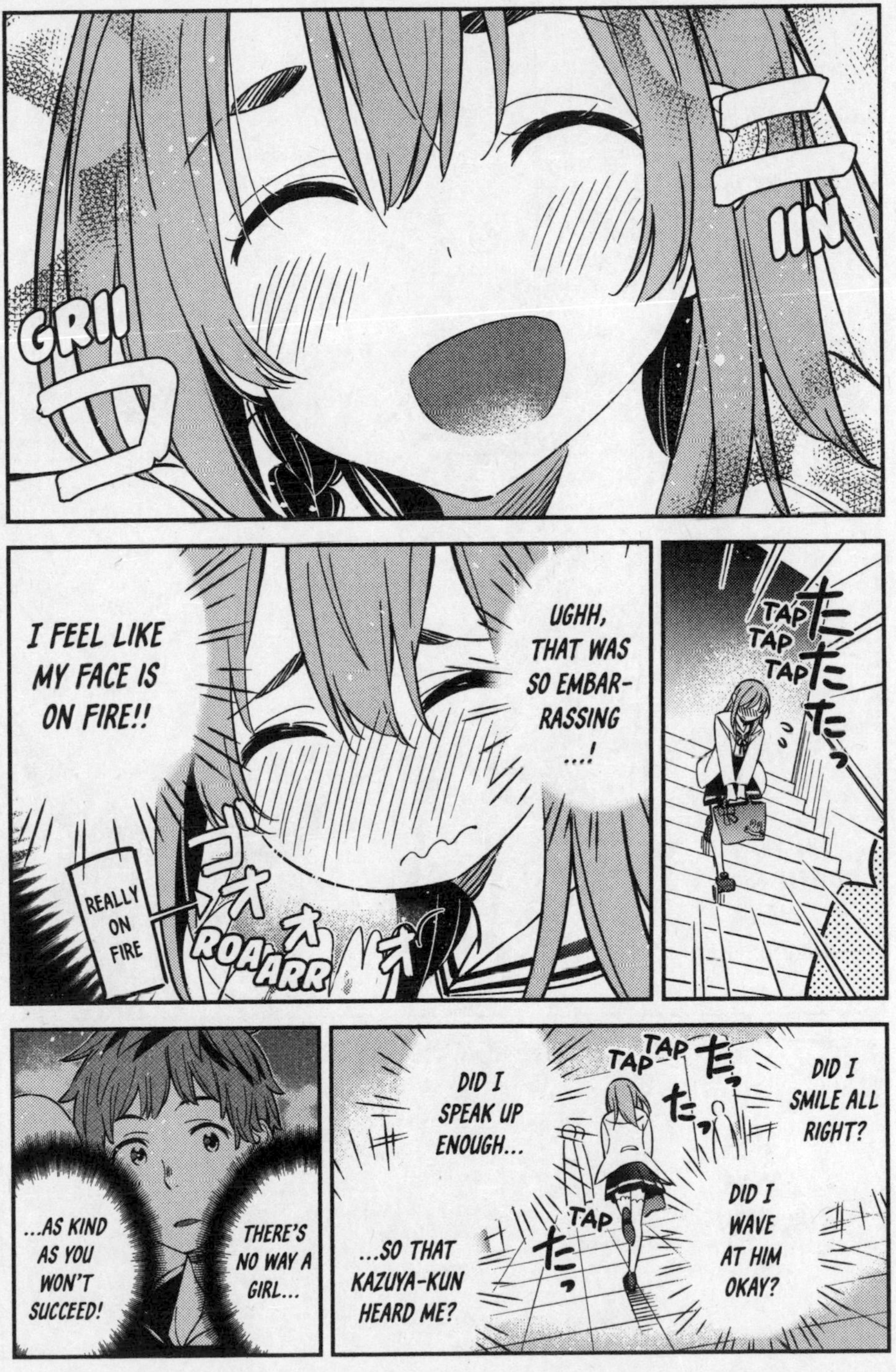
GRII
IIN
TAP TAP TAP
たたたっ
UGHH, THAT WAS SO EMBARRASSING ...!
I FEEL LIKE MY FACE IS ON FIRE!!
REALLY ON FIRE
ゴオオオ
ROAARR
DID I SMILE ALL RIGHT?
TAP TAP
たったっ
DID I SPEAK UP ENOUGH...
DID I WAVE AT HIM OKAY?
...SO THAT KAZUYA-KUN HEARD ME?
TAP
たっ
THERE'S NO WAY A GIRL...
...AS KIND AS YOU WON'T SUCCEED!

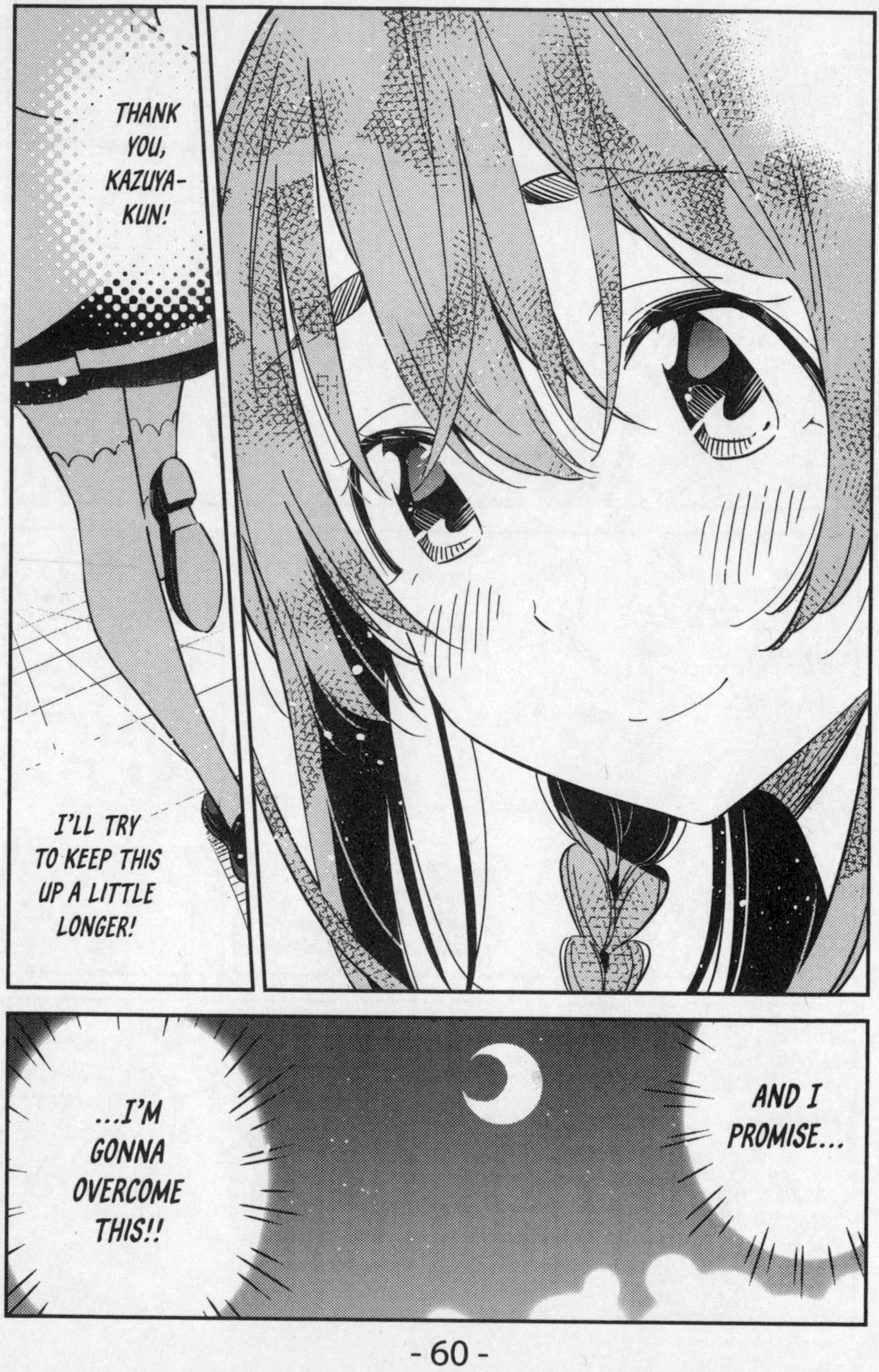
THANK YOU, KAZUYA-KUN!
I'LL TRY TO KEEP THIS UP A LITTLE LONGER!
AND I PROMISE...
...I'M GONNA OVERCOME THIS!!

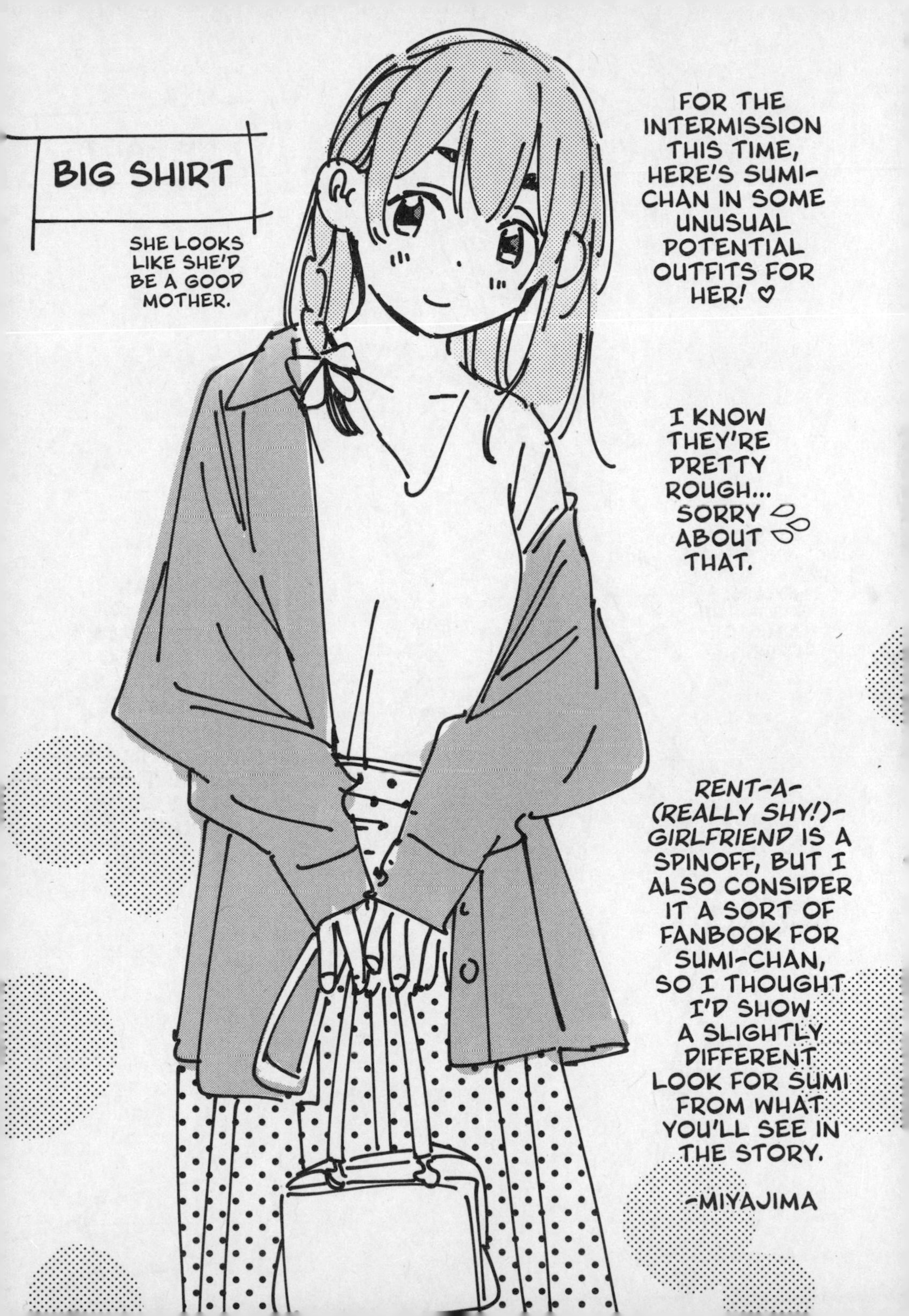
BIG SHIRT
SHE LOOKS LIKE SHE'D BE A GOOD MOTHER.
FOR THE INTERMISSION THIS TIME, HERE'S SUMI-CHAN IN SOME UNUSUAL POTENTIAL OUTFITS FOR HER! ♡
I KNOW THEY'RE PRETTY ROUGH... SORRY ABOUT THAT.
RENT-A-(REALLY SHY!)-GIRLFRIEND IS A SPINOFF, BUT I ALSO CONSIDER IT A SORT OF FANBOOK FOR SUMI-CHAN, SO I THOUGHT I'D SHOW A SLIGHTLY DIFFERENT LOOK FOR SUMI FROM WHAT YOU'LL SEE IN THE STORY.
-MIYAJIMA

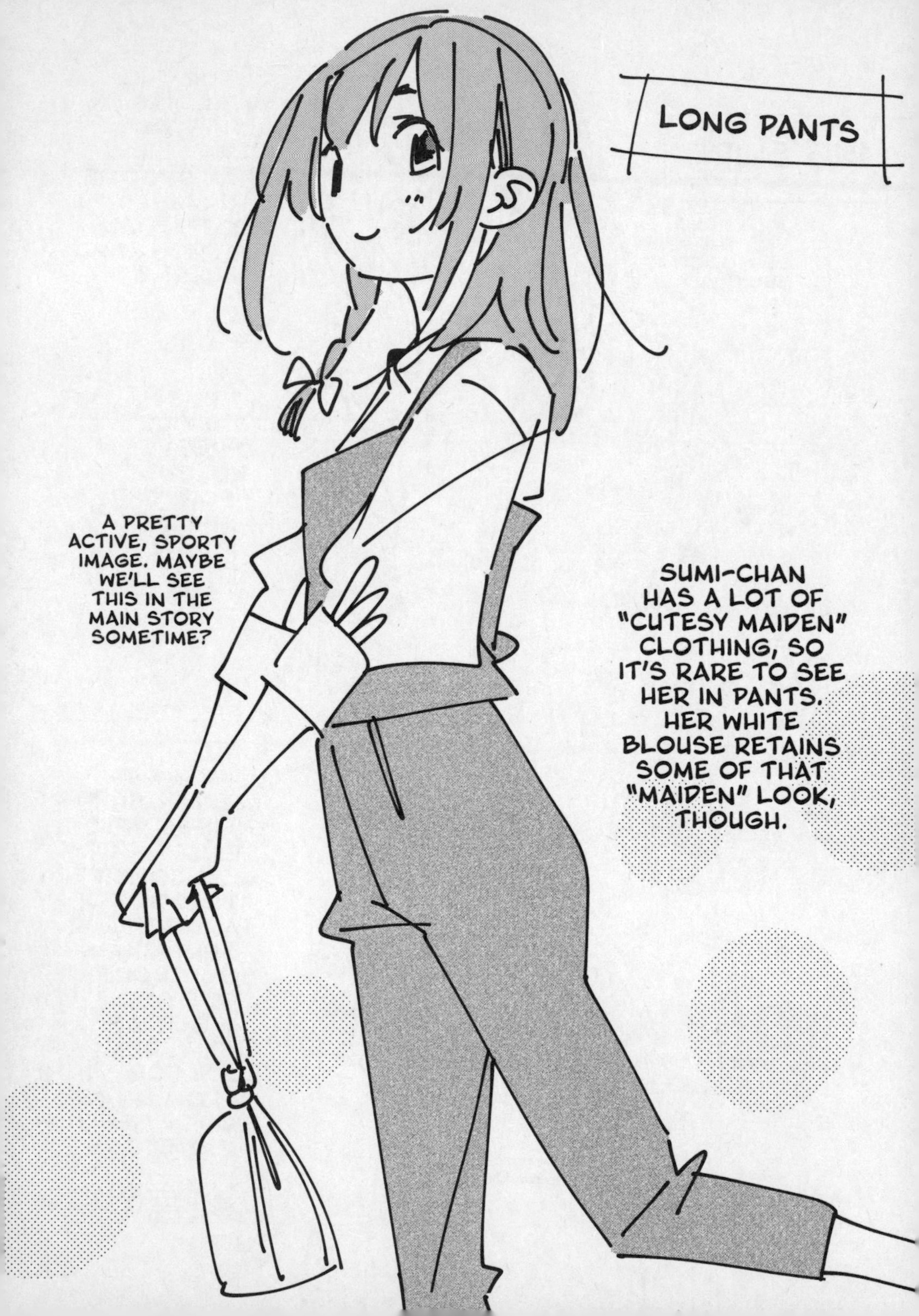
LONG PANTS
SUMI-CHAN HAS A LOT OF "CUTESY MAIDEN" CLOTHING, SO IT'S RARE TO SEE HER IN PANTS. HER WHITE BLOUSE RETAINS SOME OF THAT "MAIDEN" LOOK, THOUGH.
A PRETTY ACTIVE, SPORTY IMAGE. MAYBE WE'LL SEE THIS IN THE MAIN STORY SOMETIME?

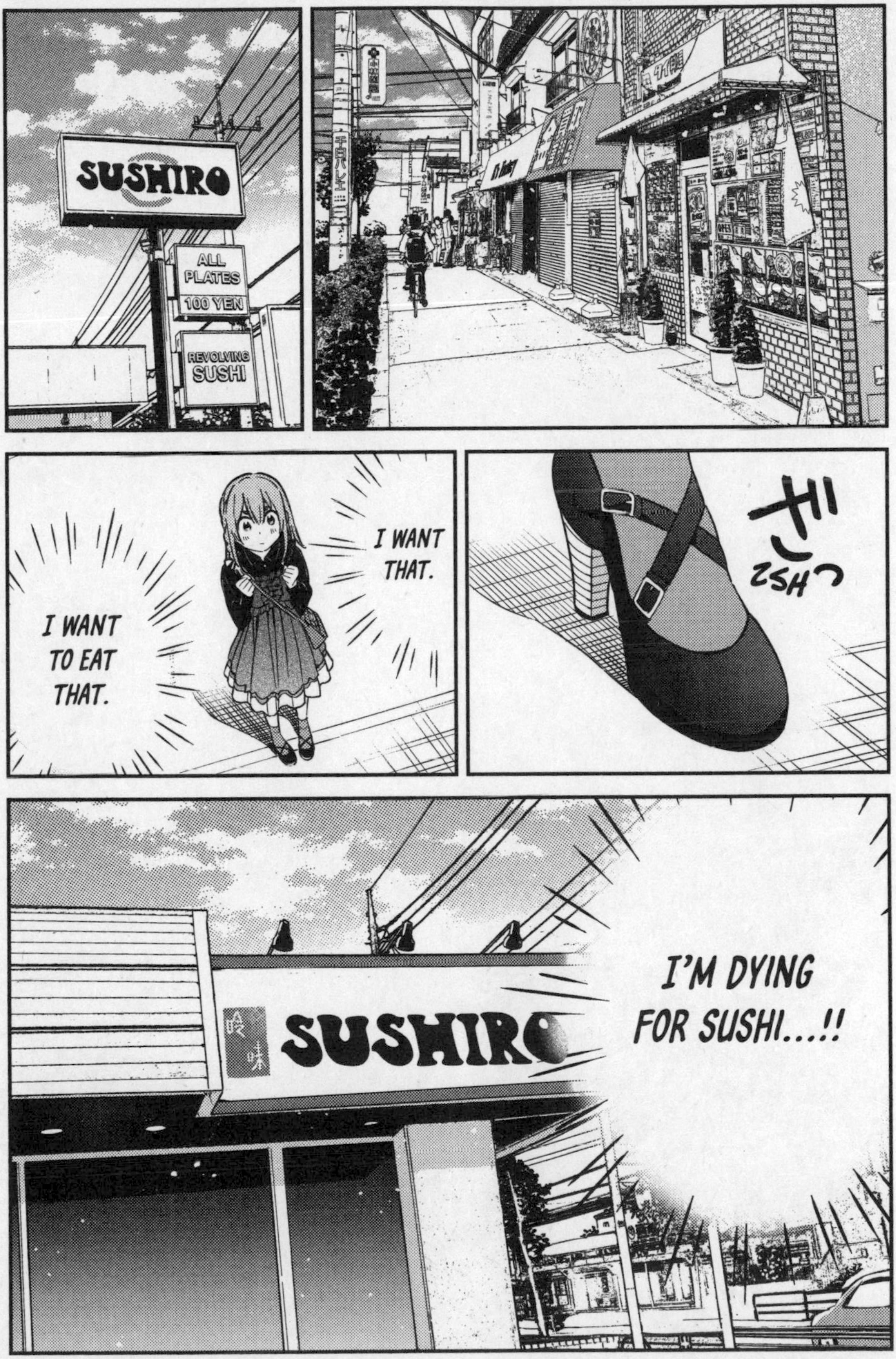
SUSHIRO
ALL PLATES
100 YEN
REVOLVING SUSHI
ZSH
I WANT THAT.
I WANT TO EAT THAT.
SUSHIRO
I'M DYING FOR SUSHI...!!

RATING 10 SUMI AND THE REVOLVING SUSHI BAR

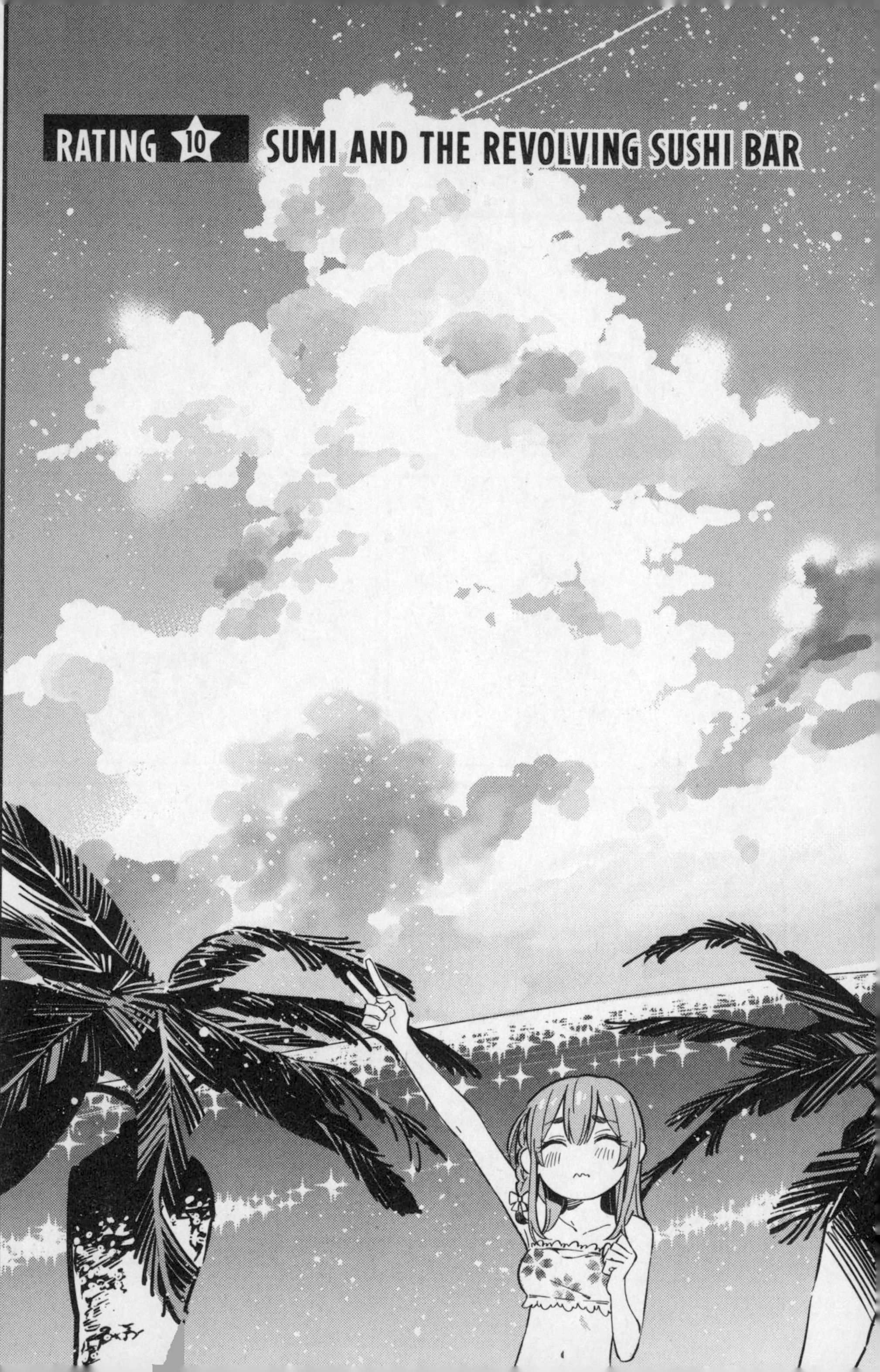

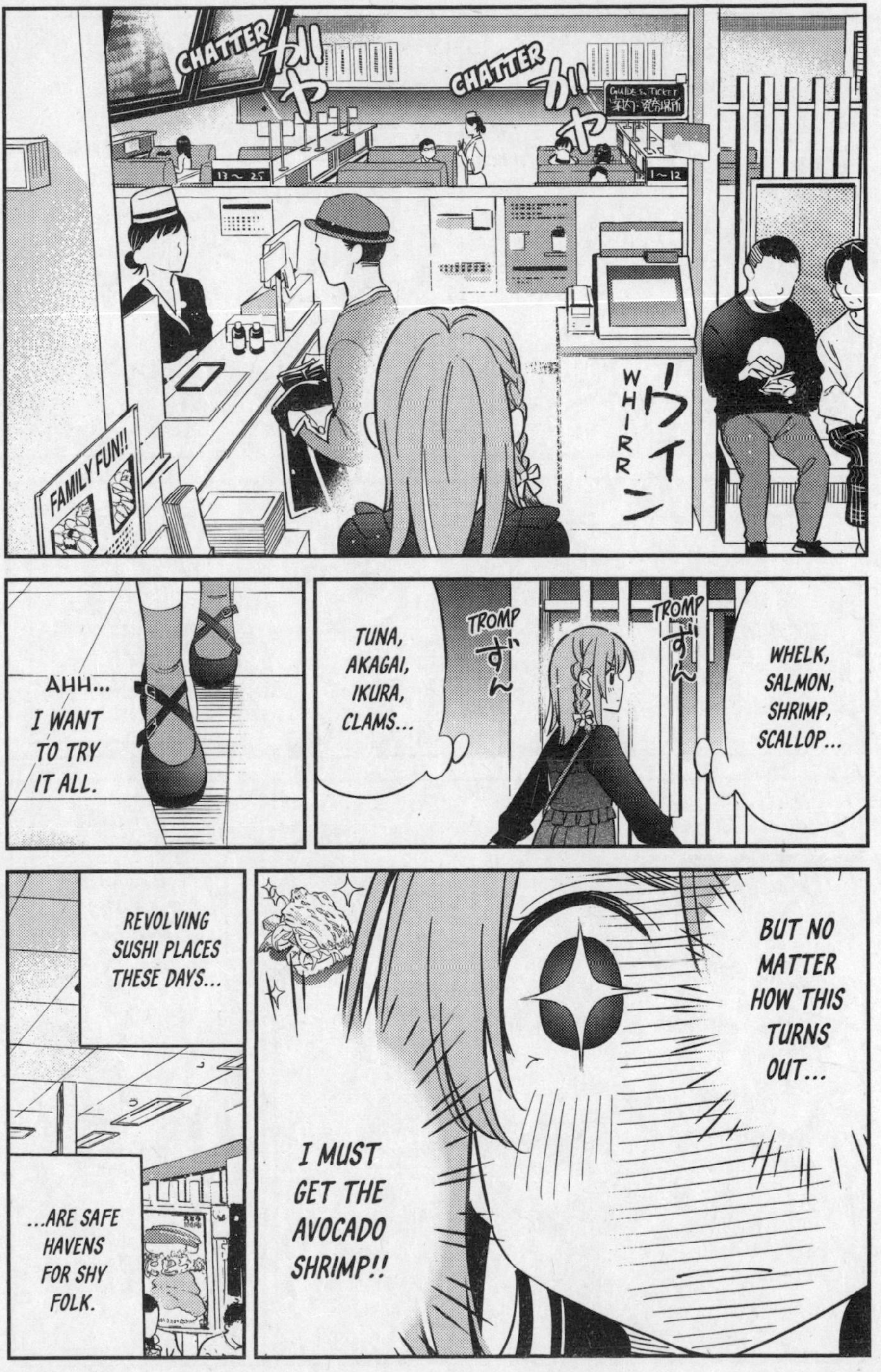
CHATTER がや
CHATTER がや
GUIDE & TICKET
案内・発券場所
13～25
1～12
WHIRR ウイーン
FAMILY FUN!!
WHELK, SALMON, SHRIMP, SCALLOP...
TROMP ずん
TROMP ずん
TUNA, AKAGAI, IKURA, CLAMS...
AHH... I WANT TO TRY IT ALL.
BUT NO MATTER HOW THIS TURNS OUT...
I MUST GET THE AVOCADO SHRIMP!!
REVOLVING SUSHI PLACES THESE DAYS...
...ARE SAFE HAVENS FOR SHY FOLK.

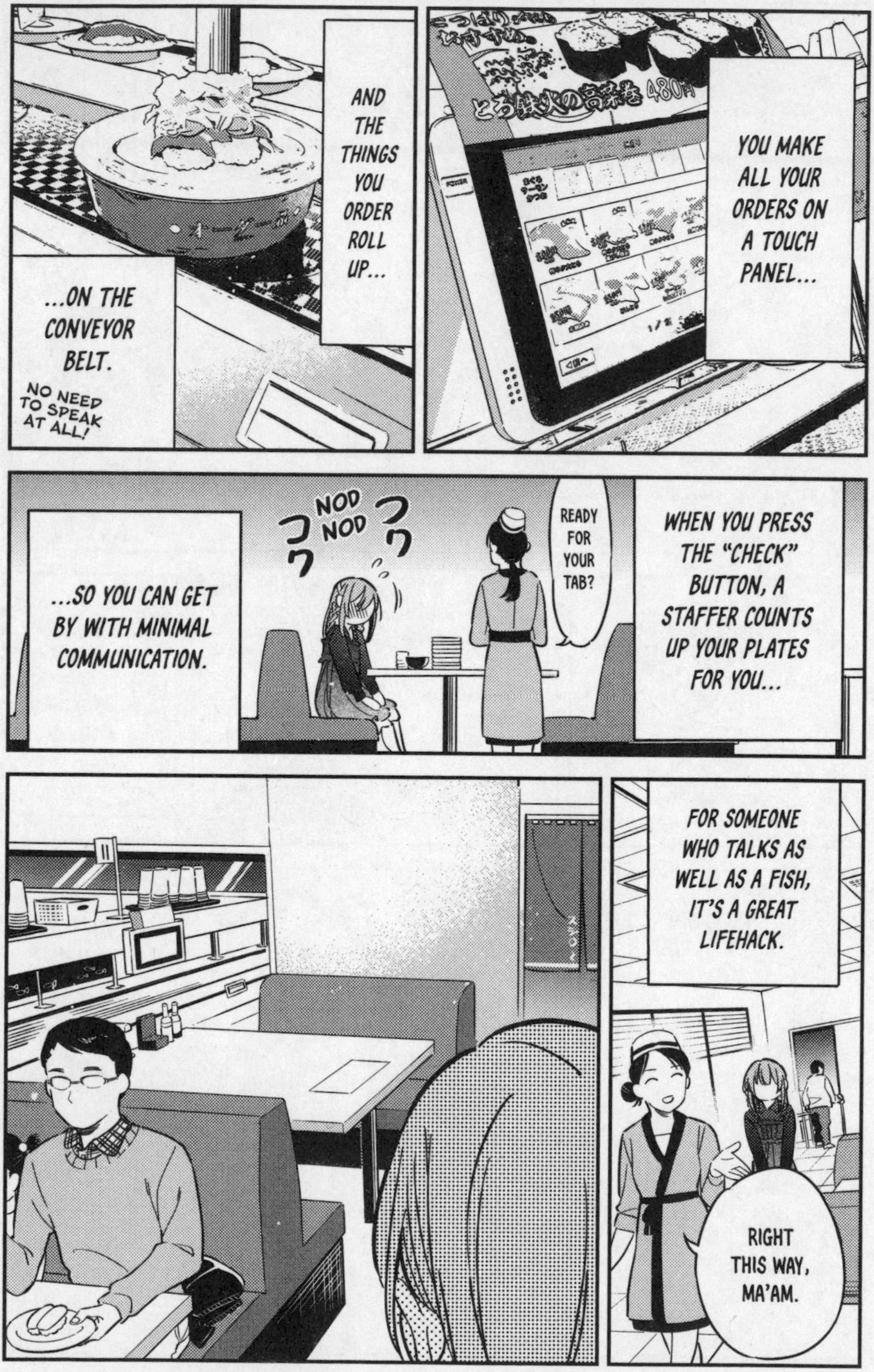
YOU MAKE ALL YOUR ORDERS ON A TOUCH PANEL...
AND THE THINGS YOU ORDER ROLL UP...
...ON THE CONVEYOR BELT.
NO NEED TO SPEAK AT ALL!
WHEN YOU PRESS THE "CHECK" BUTTON, A STAFFER COUNTS UP YOUR PLATES FOR YOU...
READY FOR YOUR TAB?
NOD NOD
...SO YOU CAN GET BY WITH MINIMAL COMMUNICATION.
FOR SOMEONE WHO TALKS AS WELL AS A FISH, IT'S A GREAT LIFEHACK.
RIGHT THIS WAY, MA'AM.

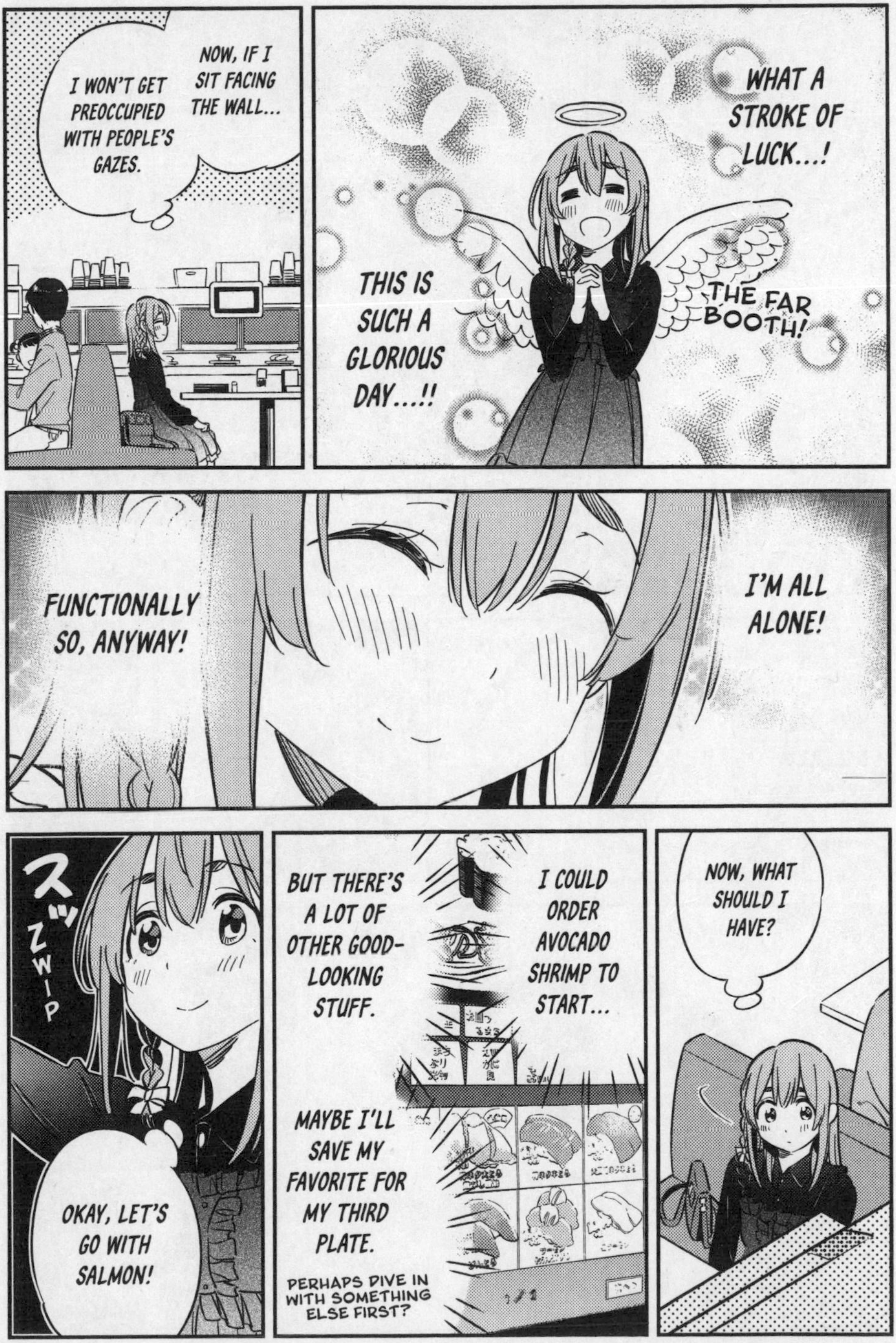
WHAT A STROKE OF LUCK...!
THE FAR BOOTH!
THIS IS SUCH A GLORIOUS DAY...!!
NOW, IF I SIT FACING THE WALL...
I WON'T GET PREOCCUPIED WITH PEOPLE'S GAZES.
I'M ALL ALONE!
FUNCTIONALLY SO, ANYWAY!
NOW, WHAT SHOULD I HAVE?
I COULD ORDER AVOCADO SHRIMP TO START...
BUT THERE'S A LOT OF OTHER GOOD-LOOKING STUFF.
MAYBE I'LL SAVE MY FAVORITE FOR MY THIRD PLATE.
PERHAPS DIVE IN WITH SOMETHING ELSE FIRST?
スッ
ZWIP
OKAY, LET'S GO WITH SALMON!

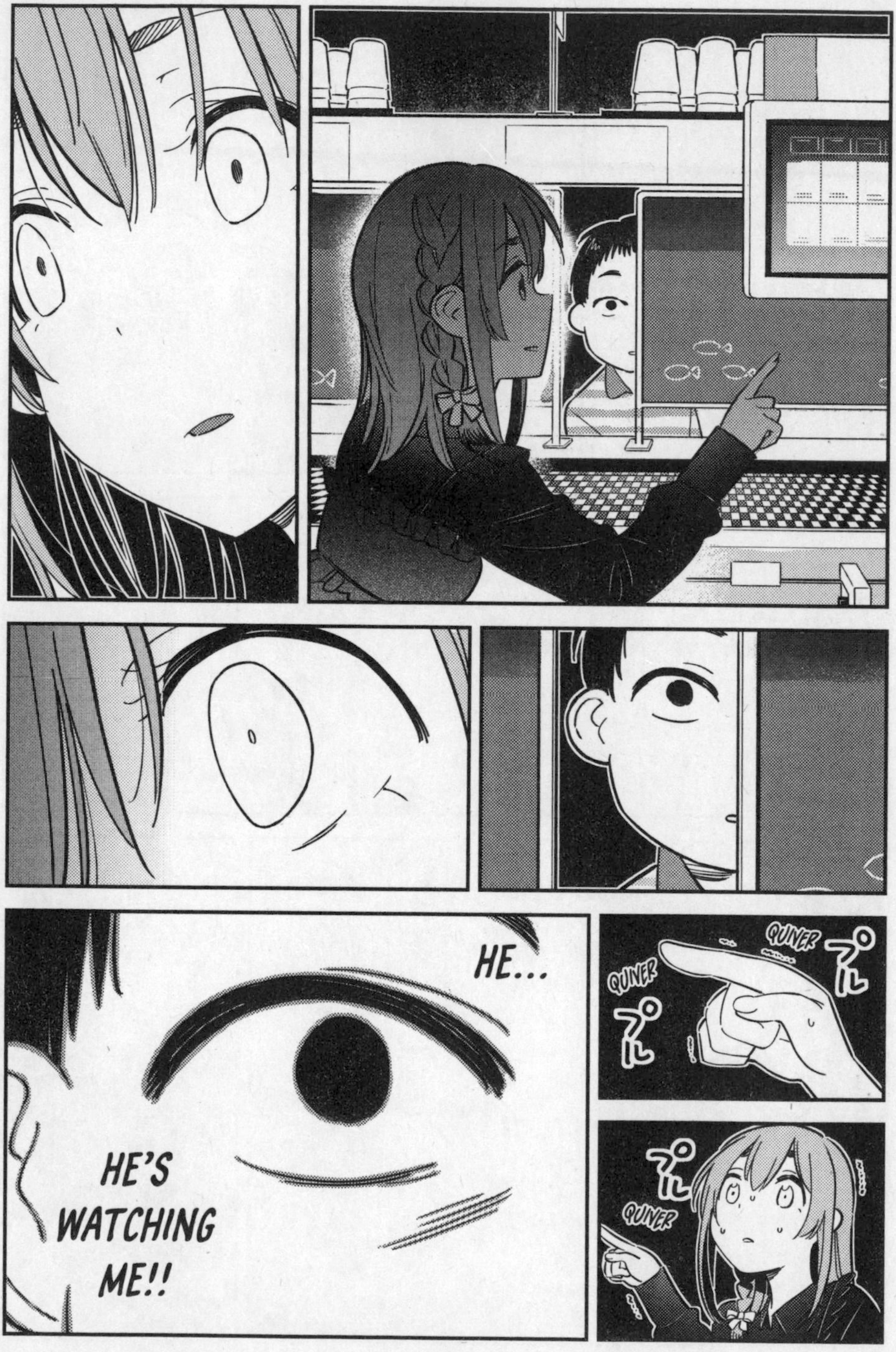
QUIVER
ぷル
QUIVER
ぷル
ぷル
QUIVER
HE...
HE'S WATCHING ME!!

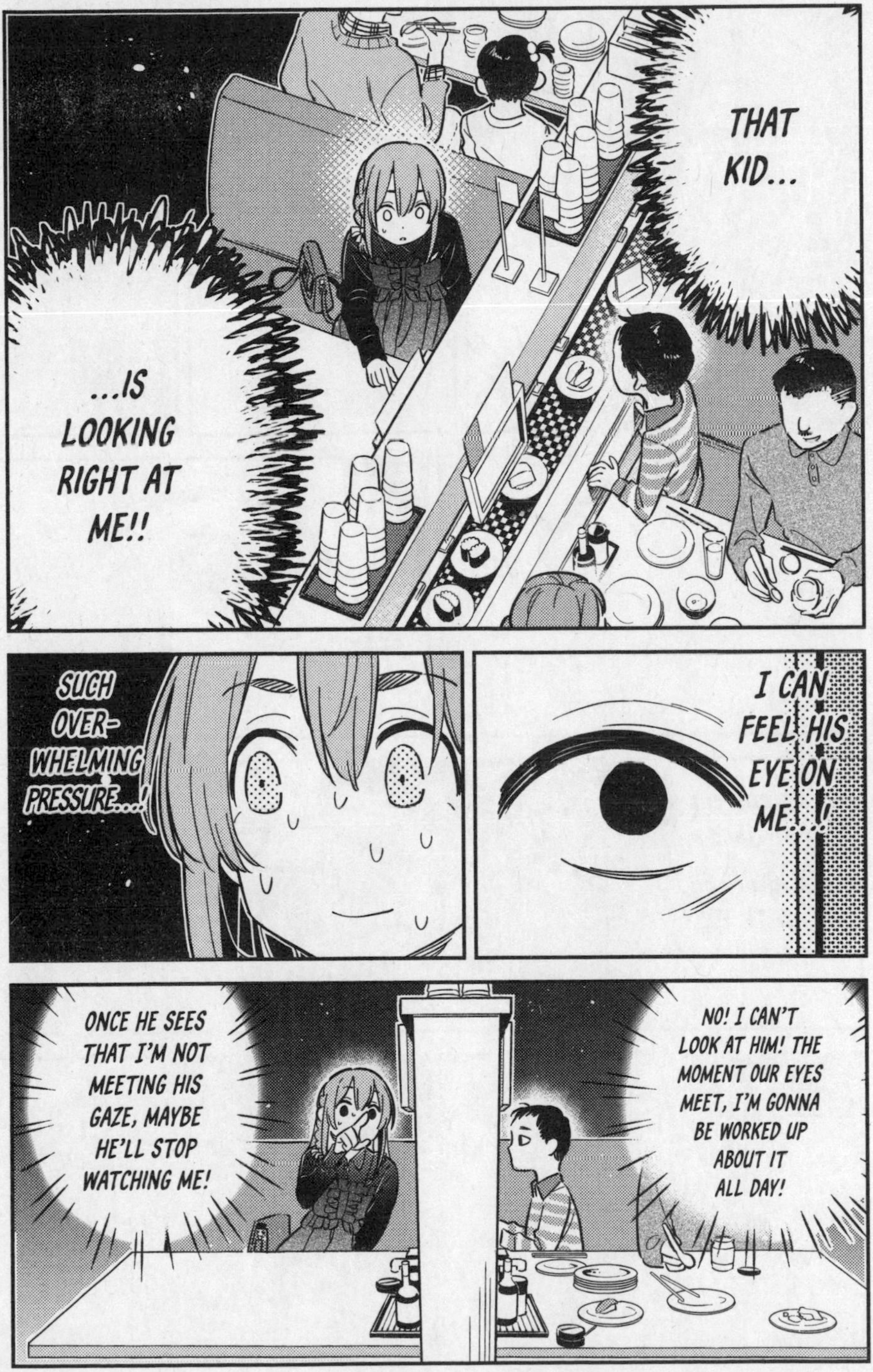
THAT KID...
...IS LOOKING RIGHT AT ME!!
I CAN FEEL HIS EYE ON ME...!
SUCH OVER-WHELMING PRESSURE...!
NO! I CAN'T LOOK AT HIM! THE MOMENT OUR EYES MEET, I'M GONNA BE WORKED UP ABOUT IT ALL DAY!
ONCE HE SEES THAT I'M NOT MEETING HIS GAZE, MAYBE HE'LL STOP WATCHING ME!

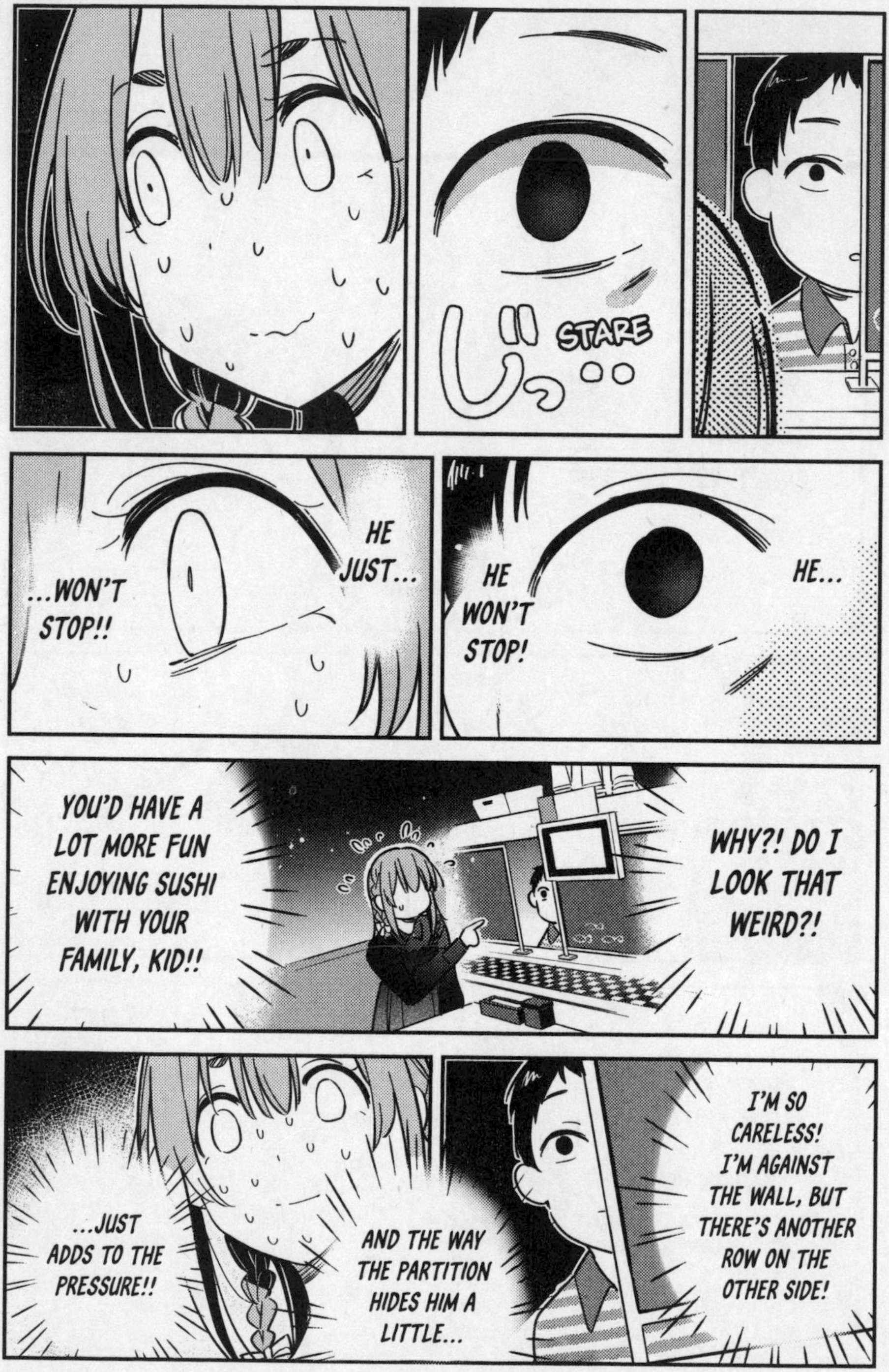
じっ
STARE
HE...
HE WON'T STOP!
HE JUST...
...WON'T STOP!!
WHY?! DO I LOOK THAT WEIRD?!
YOU'D HAVE A LOT MORE FUN ENJOYING SUSHI WITH YOUR FAMILY, KID!!
I'M SO CARELESS! I'M AGAINST THE WALL, BUT THERE'S ANOTHER ROW ON THE OTHER SIDE!
AND THE WAY THE PARTITION HIDES HIM A LITTLE...
...JUST ADDS TO THE PRESSURE!!

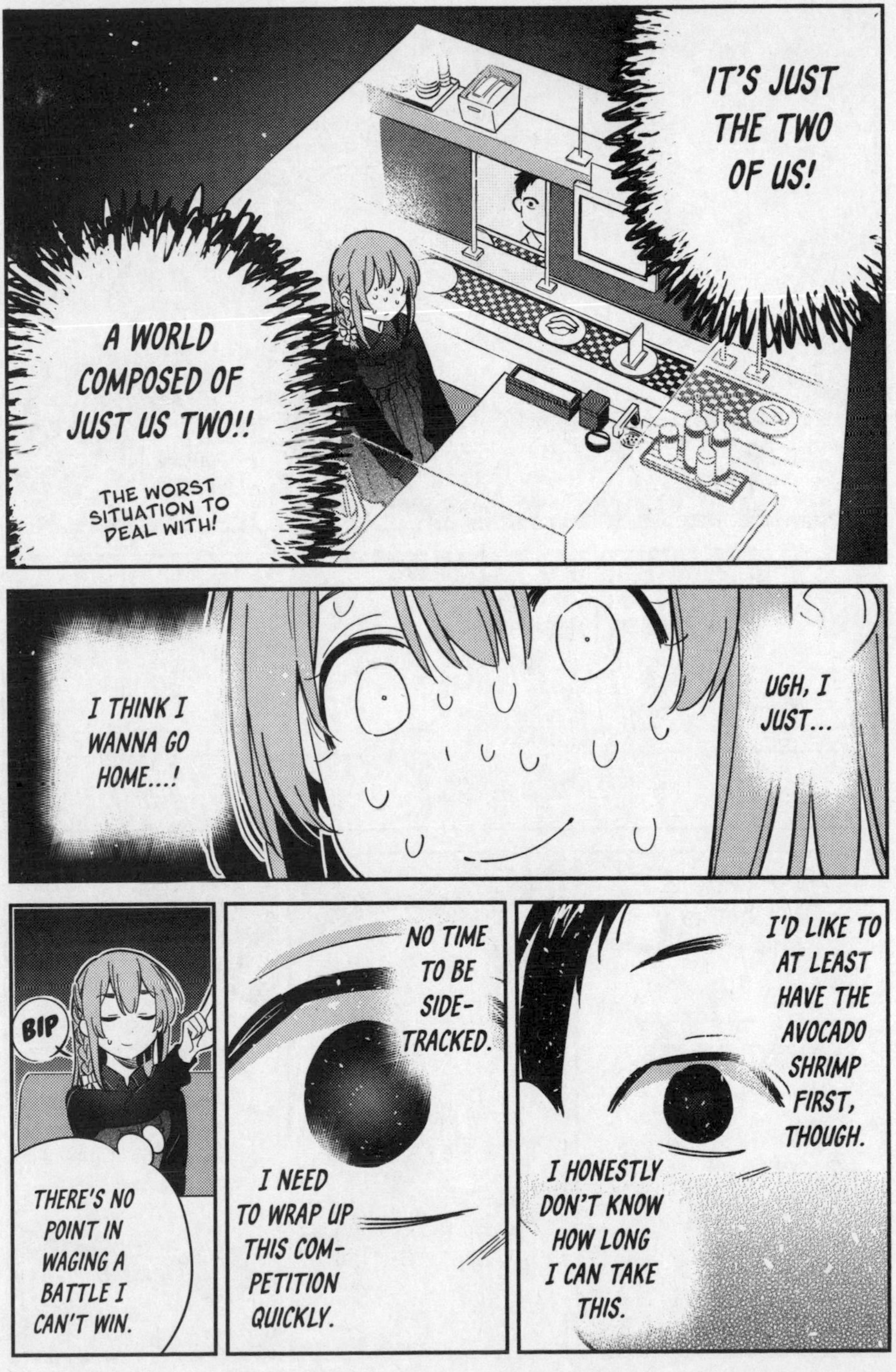
IT'S JUST THE TWO OF US!
A WORLD COMPOSED OF JUST US TWO!!
THE WORST SITUATION TO DEAL WITH!
UGH, I JUST...
I THINK I WANNA GO HOME...!
I'D LIKE TO AT LEAST HAVE THE AVOCADO SHRIMP FIRST, THOUGH.
I HONESTLY DON'T KNOW HOW LONG I CAN TAKE THIS.
NO TIME TO BE SIDE-TRACKED.
I NEED TO WRAP UP THIS COMPETITION QUICKLY.
BIP
THERE'S NO POINT IN WAGING A BATTLE I CAN'T WIN.

YOUR ORDER WILL BE ARRIVING SOON.
OH! HERE WE GO!
CUSTOMER ORDER
C...
CONGER EEL...?
THAT'S DEFINITELY CONGER EEL...
CUSTOMER
ZWIP
ぱっ
...AND NOT AVOCADO SHRIMP!!
I-I HIT THE WRONG BUTTON!
MY ORDER...
Your Orders
1
1 Grilled Conger Eel
2

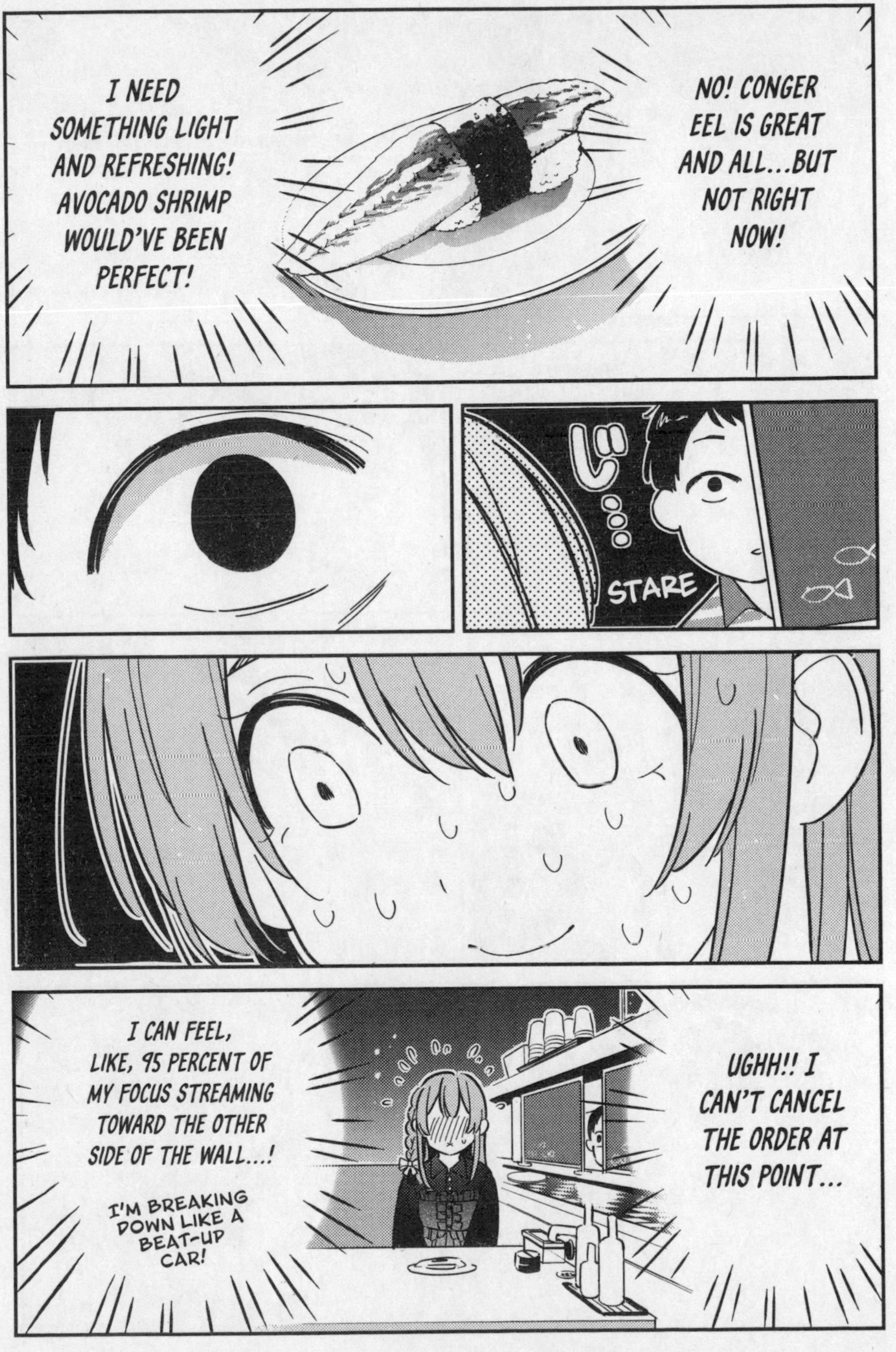
NO! CONGER EEL IS GREAT AND ALL...BUT NOT RIGHT NOW!
I NEED SOMETHING LIGHT AND REFRESHING! AVOCADO SHRIMP WOULD'VE BEEN PERFECT!
じ…
STARE
UGHH!! I CAN'T CANCEL THE ORDER AT THIS POINT...
I CAN FEEL, LIKE, 95 PERCENT OF MY FOCUS STREAMING TOWARD THE OTHER SIDE OF THE WALL...!
I'M BREAKING DOWN LIKE A BEAT-UP CAR!

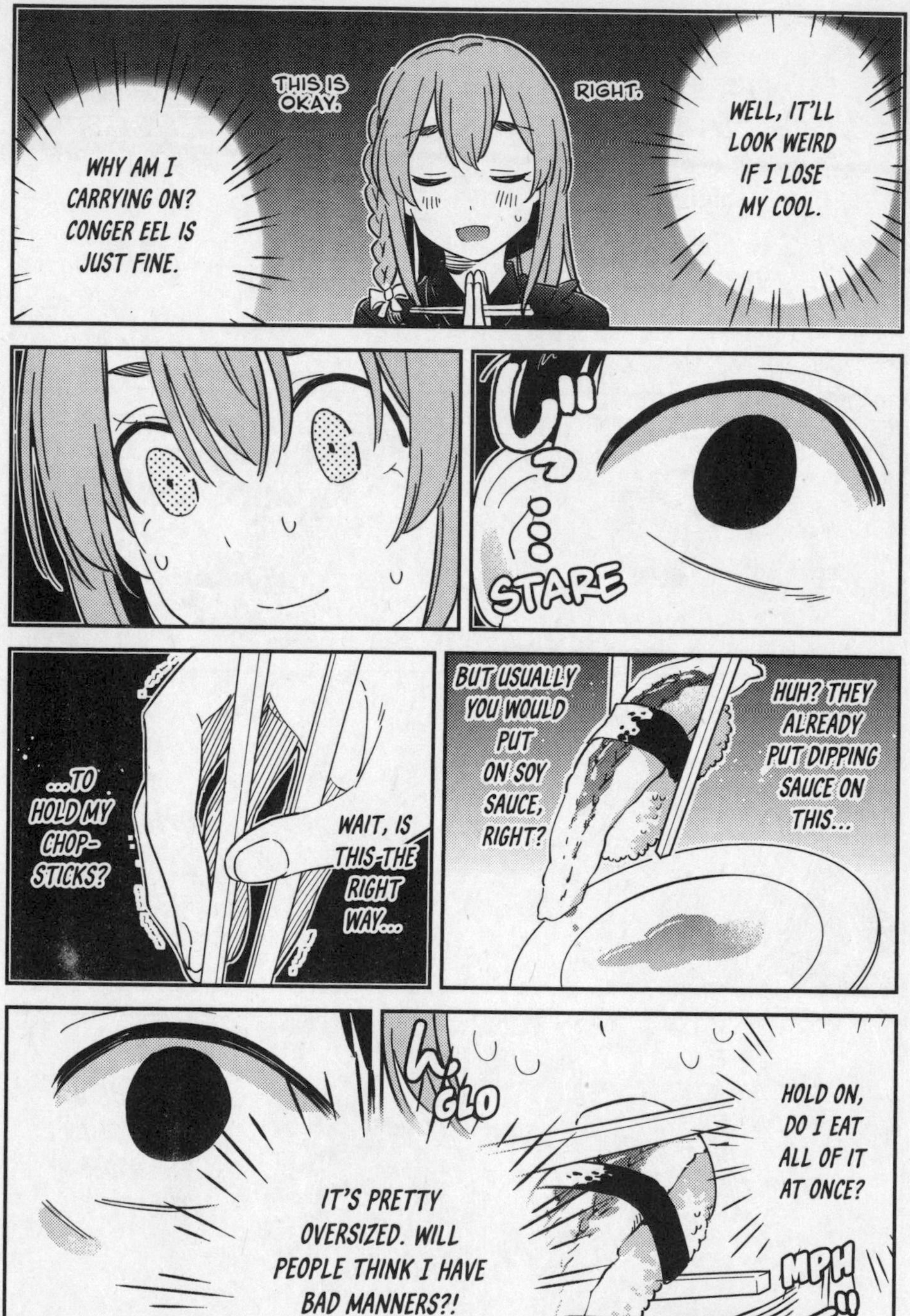
WELL, IT'LL LOOK WEIRD IF I LOSE MY COOL.
RIGHT.
THIS IS OKAY.
WHY AM I CARRYING ON? CONGER EEL IS JUST FINE.
STARE
HUH? THEY ALREADY PUT DIPPING SAUCE ON THIS...
BUT USUALLY YOU WOULD PUT ON SOY SAUCE, RIGHT?
WAIT, IS THIS THE RIGHT WAY...
...TO HOLD MY CHOP-STICKS?
HOLD ON, DO I EAT ALL OF IT AT ONCE?
MPH
IT'S PRETTY OVERSIZED. WILL PEOPLE THINK I HAVE BAD MANNERS?!
GLO

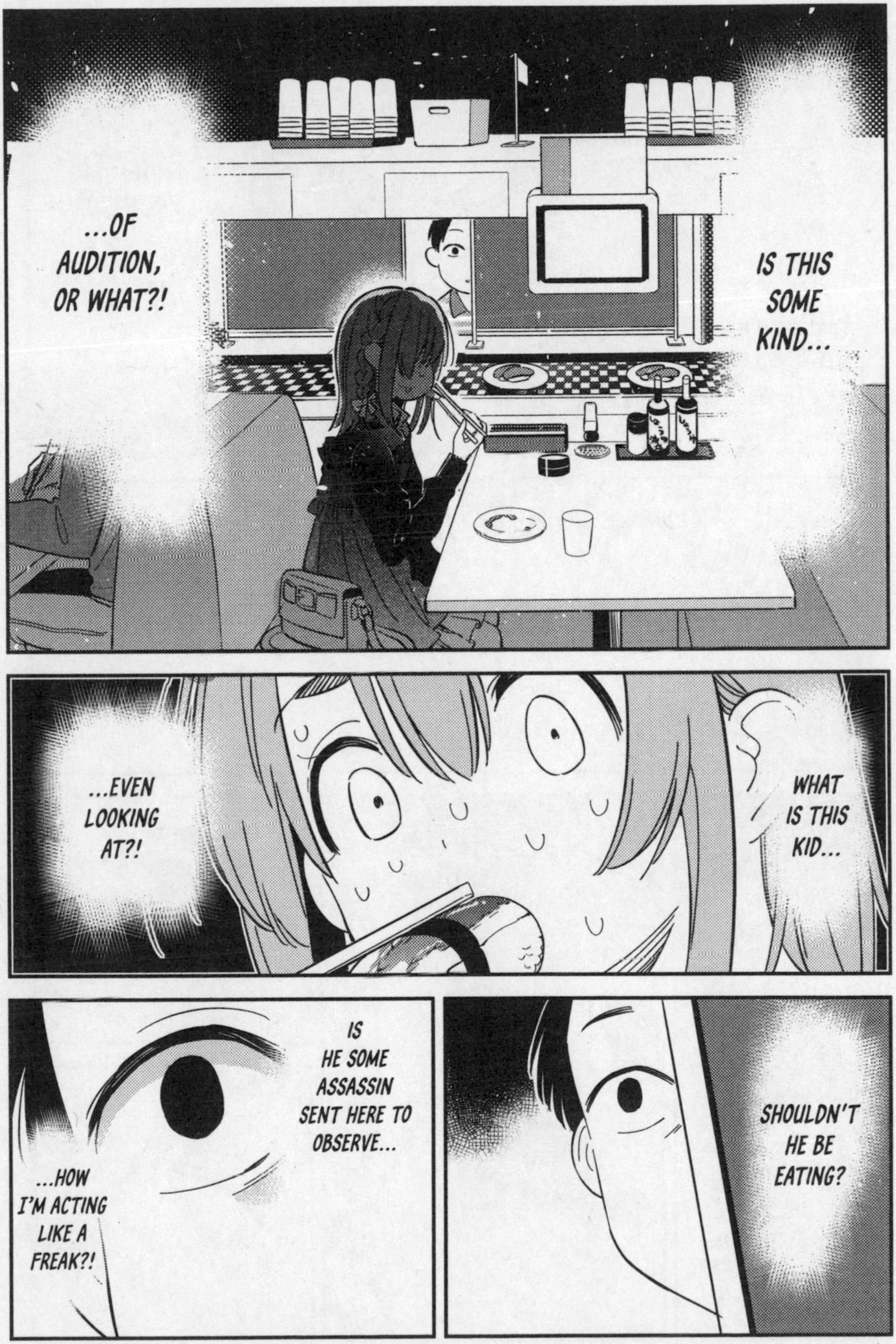
IS THIS SOME KIND...
...OF AUDITION, OR WHAT?!
WHAT IS THIS KID...
...EVEN LOOKING AT?!
SHOULDN'T HE BE EATING?
IS HE SOME ASSASSIN SENT HERE TO OBSERVE...
...HOW I'M ACTING LIKE A FREAK?!

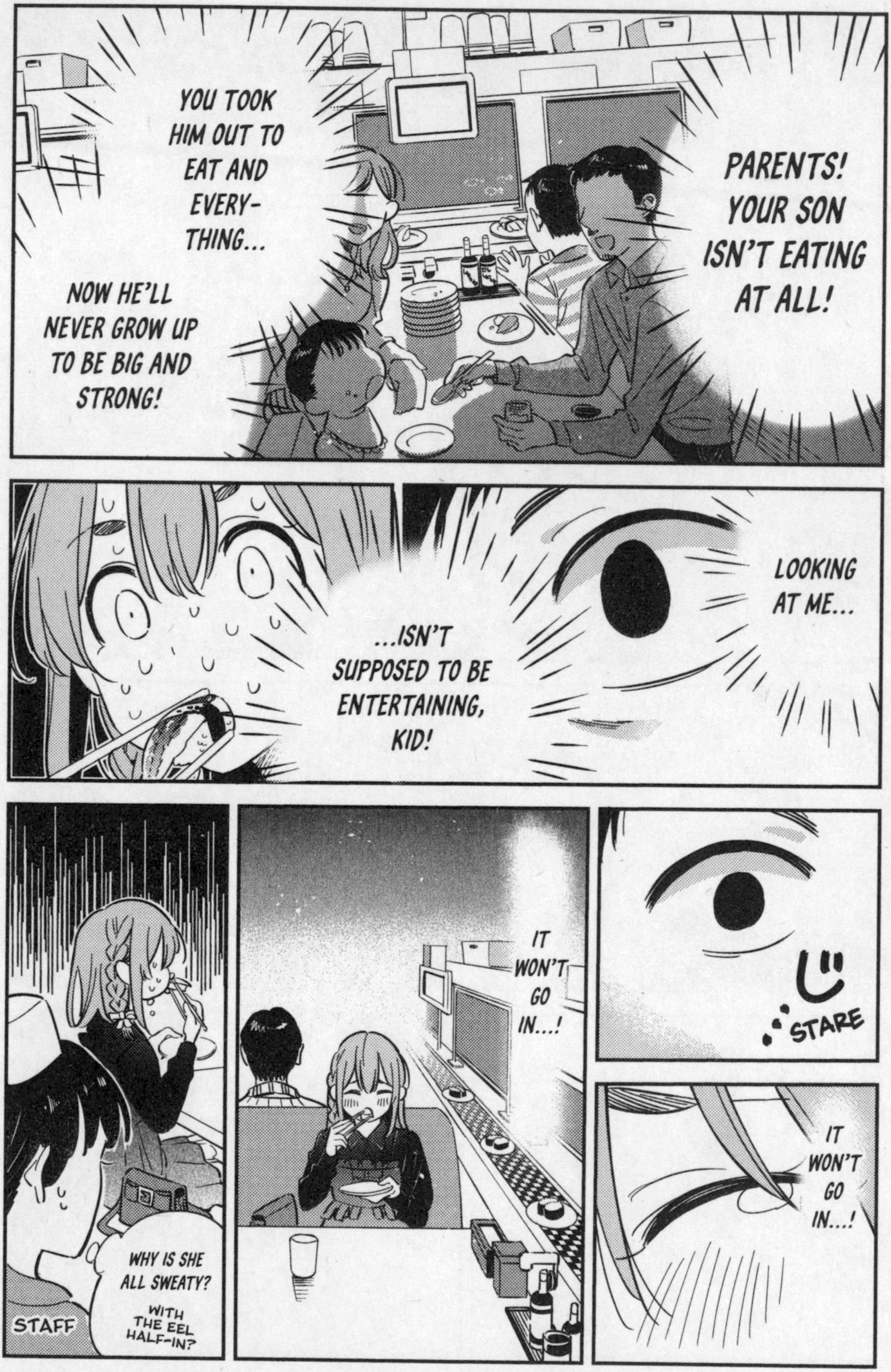
PARENTS! YOUR SON ISN'T EATING AT ALL!
YOU TOOK HIM OUT TO EAT AND EVERY-THING...
NOW HE'LL NEVER GROW UP TO BE BIG AND STRONG!
LOOKING AT ME...
...ISN'T SUPPOSED TO BE ENTERTAINING, KID!
じ
STARE
IT WON'T GO IN...!
IT WON'T GO IN...!
WHY IS SHE ALL SWEATY?
WITH THE EEL HALF-IN?
STAFF

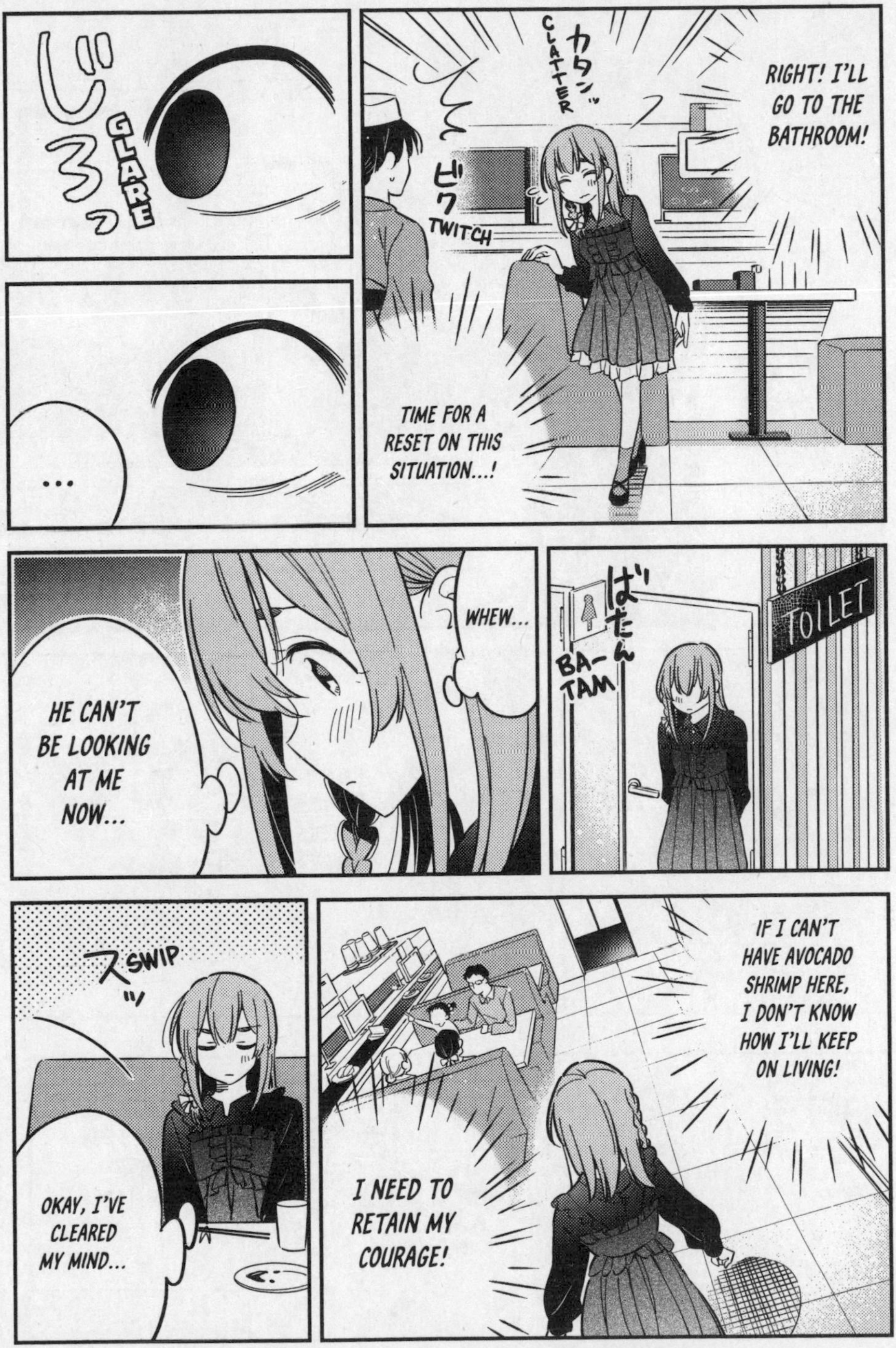
RIGHT! I'LL GO TO THE BATHROOM!
カタンッ
CLATTER
ビク
TWITCH
TIME FOR A RESET ON THIS SITUATION...!
じろっ
GLARE
...
ばたん
BA-TAM
TOILET
WHEW...
HE CAN'T BE LOOKING AT ME NOW...
IF I CAN'T HAVE AVOCADO SHRIMP HERE, I DON'T KNOW HOW I'LL KEEP ON LIVING!
I NEED TO RETAIN MY COURAGE!
スッ
SWIP
OKAY, I'VE CLEARED MY MIND...

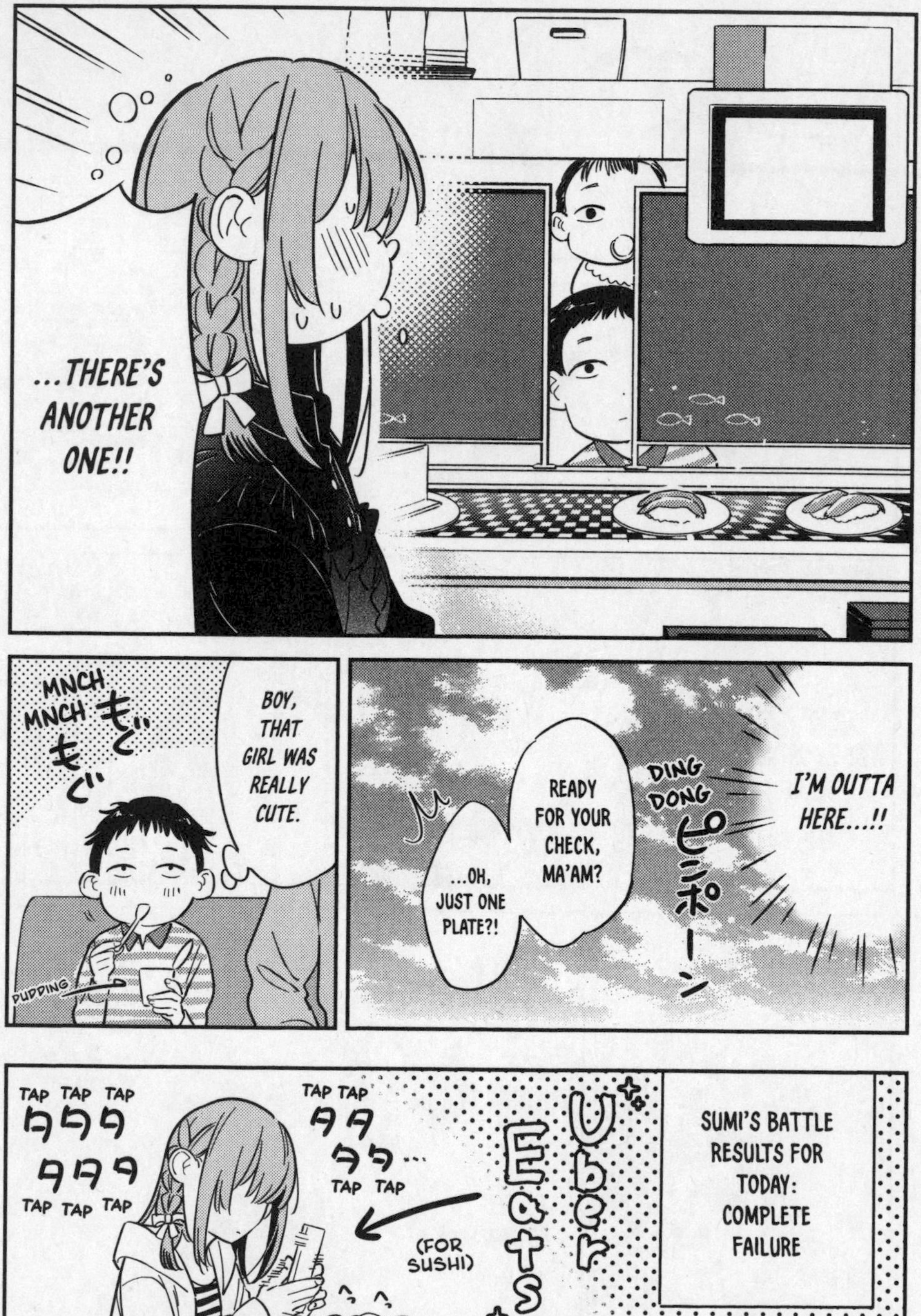
...THERE'S ANOTHER ONE!!
I'M OUTTA HERE...!!
DING DONG
ピンポーン
READY FOR YOUR CHECK, MA'AM?
...OH, JUST ONE PLATE?!
BOY, THAT GIRL WAS REALLY CUTE.
MNCH MNCH
もぐもぐ
PUDDING
SUMI'S BATTLE RESULTS FOR TODAY: COMPLETE FAILURE
Uber Eats
(FOR SUSHI)
TAP TAP
タタタタ...
TAP TAP
TAP TAP TAP
タタタ
タタタ
TAP TAP TAP

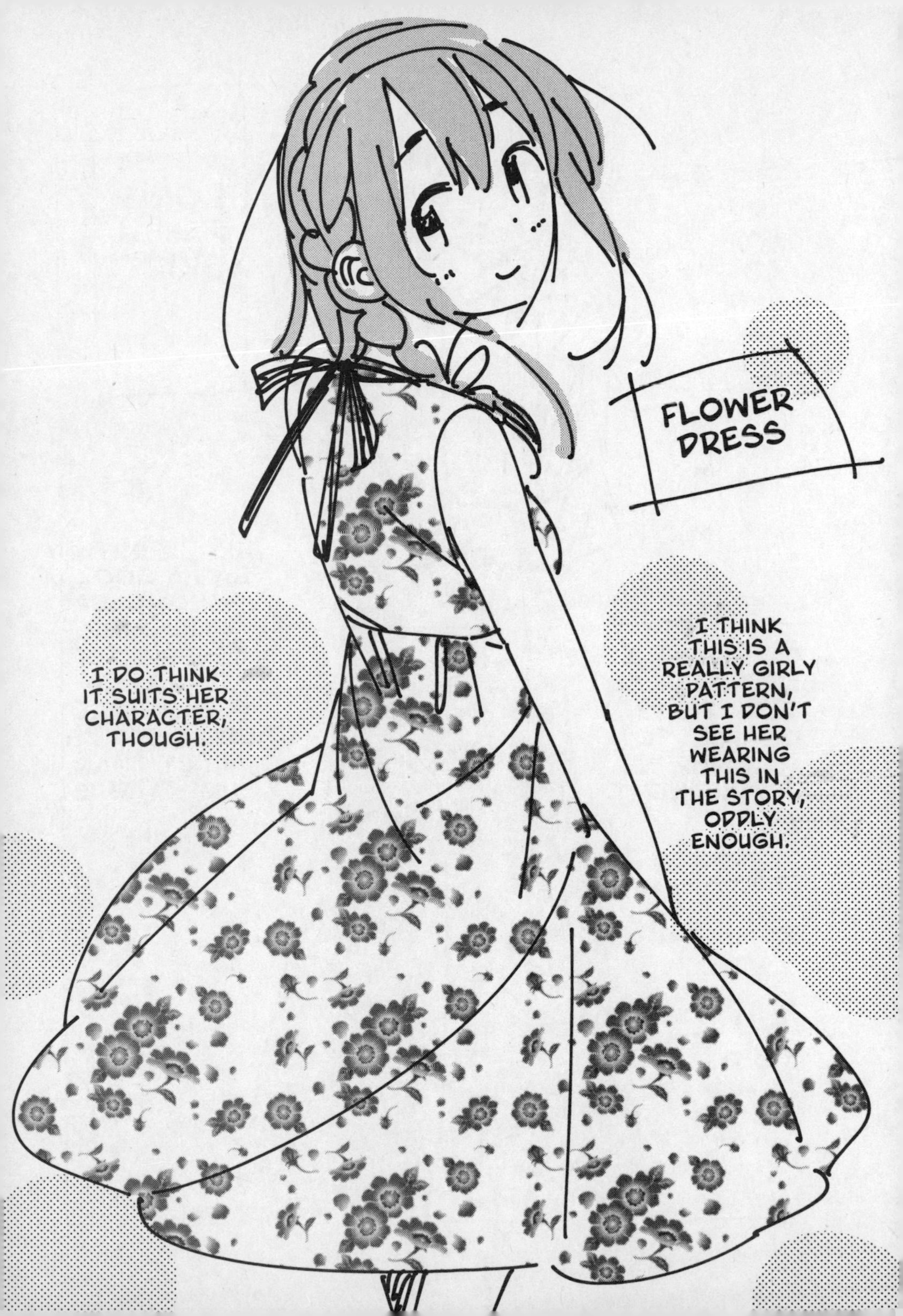
FLOWER DRESS
I THINK THIS IS A REALLY GIRLY PATTERN, BUT I DON'T SEE HER WEARING THIS IN THE STORY, ODDLY ENOUGH.
I DO THINK IT SUITS HER CHARACTER, THOUGH.

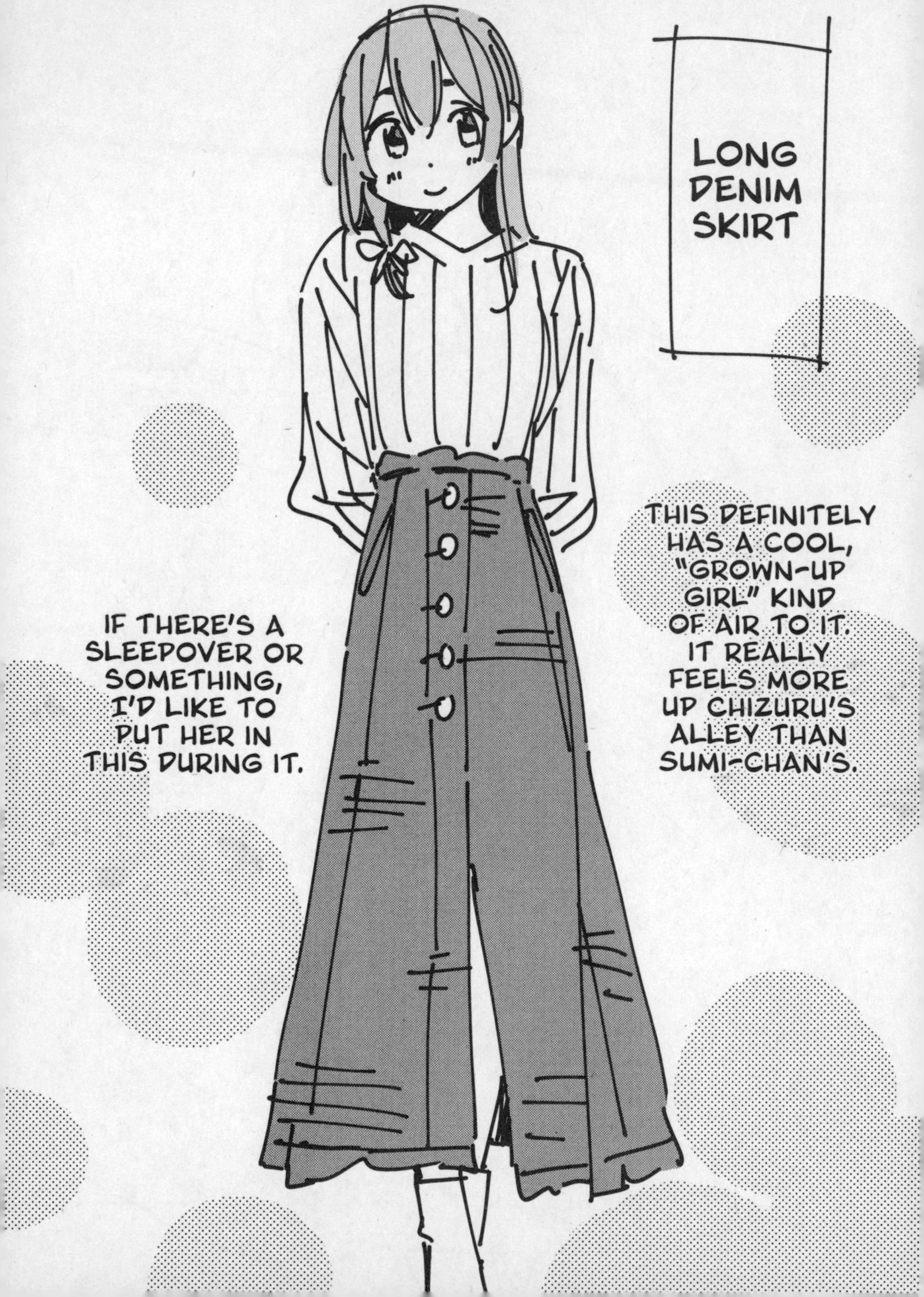
LONG DENIM SKIRT
THIS DEFINITELY HAS A COOL, "GROWN-UP GIRL" KIND OF AIR TO IT. IT REALLY FEELS MORE UP CHIZURU'S ALLEY THAN SUMI-CHAN'S.
IF THERE'S A SLEEPOVER OR SOMETHING, I'D LIKE TO PUT HER IN THIS DURING IT.

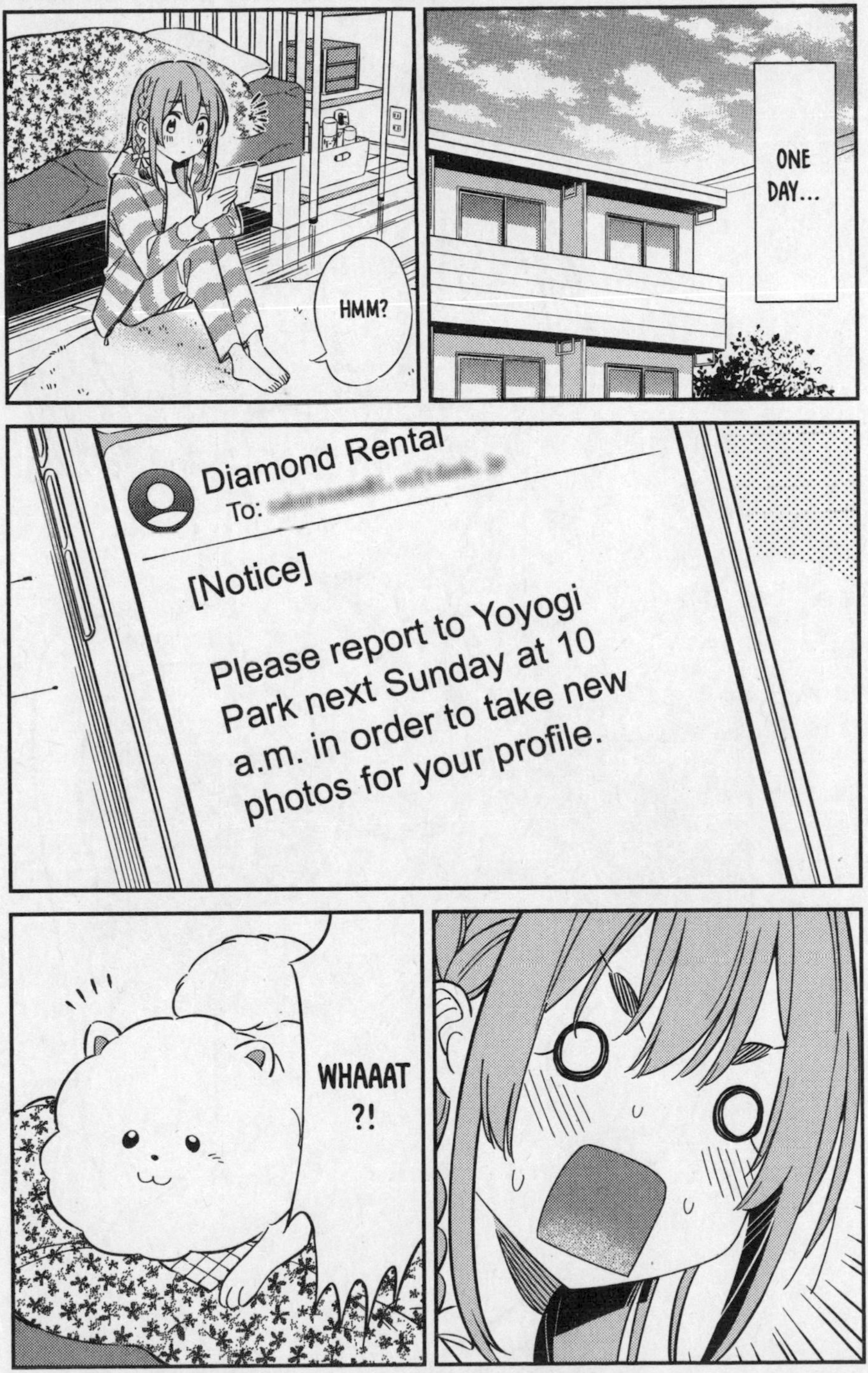
ONE DAY...
HMM?
Diamond Rental
To:
[Notice]
Please report to Yoyogi Park next Sunday at 10 a.m. in order to take new photos for your profile.
WHAAAT ?!

RATING 11 SUMI AND THE PHOTO SESSION

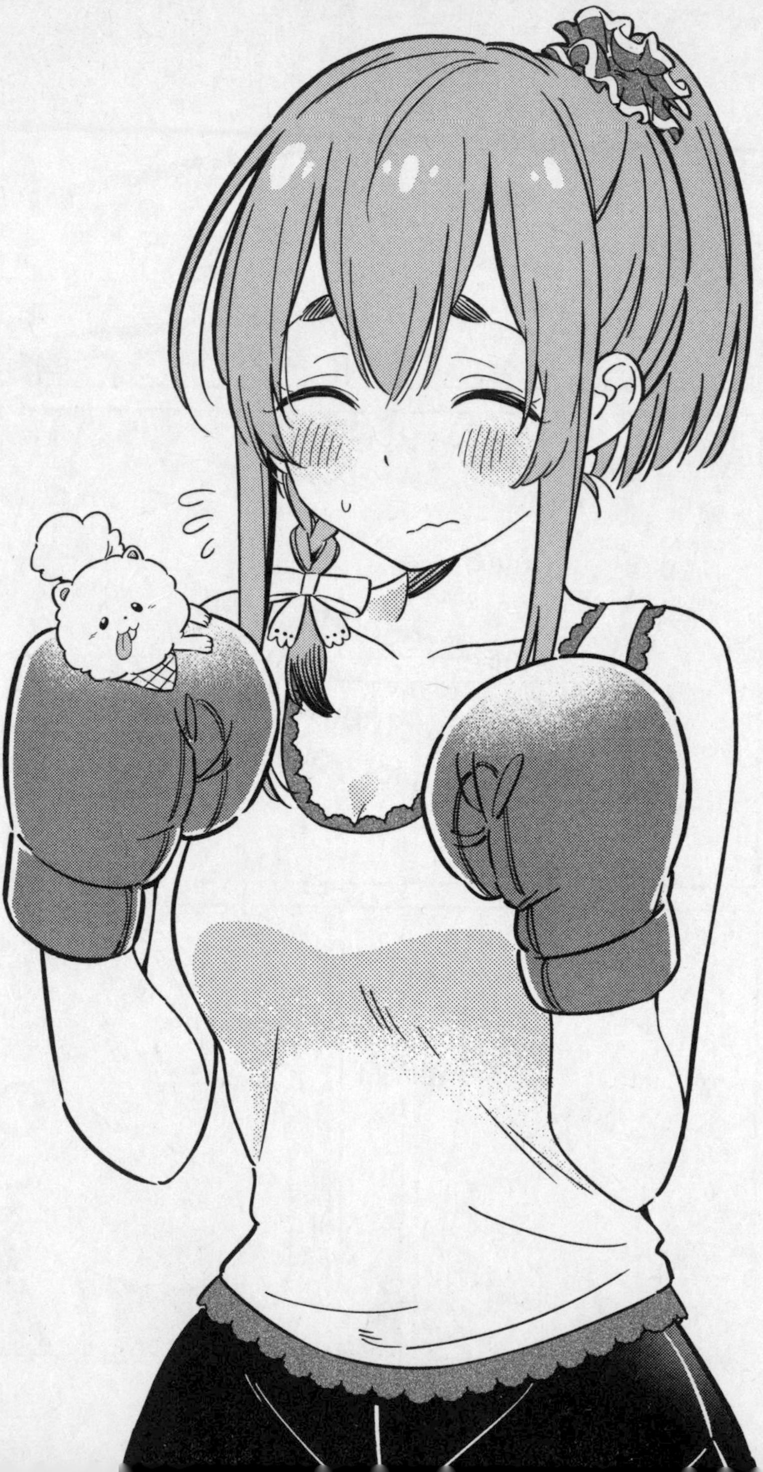

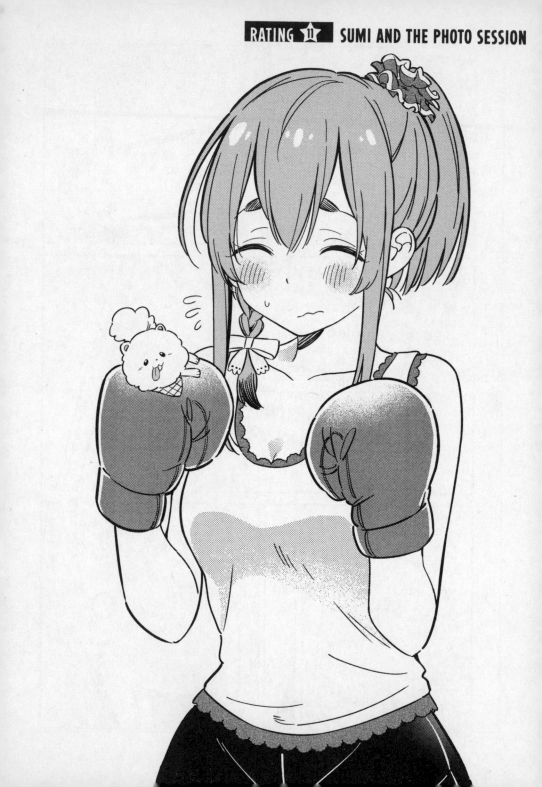

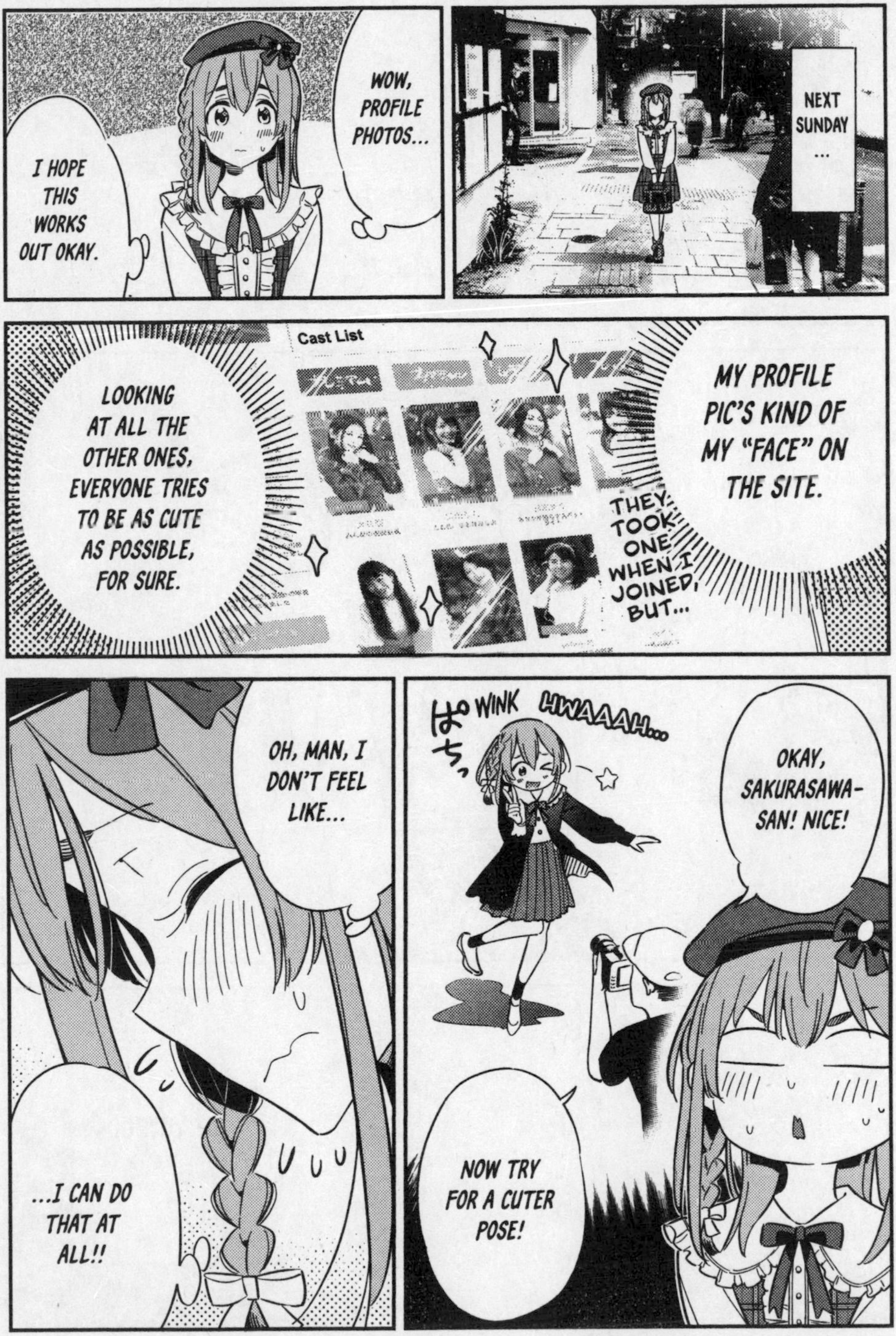
NEXT SUNDAY ...
WOW, PROFILE PHOTOS...
I HOPE THIS WORKS OUT OKAY.
MY PROFILE PIC'S KIND OF MY "FACE" ON THE SITE.
THEY TOOK ONE WHEN I JOINED, BUT...
Cast List
LOOKING AT ALL THE OTHER ONES, EVERYONE TRIES TO BE AS CUTE AS POSSIBLE, FOR SURE.
OKAY, SAKURASAWA-SAN! NICE!
HWAAAH...
WINK
ぱちっ
NOW TRY FOR A CUTER POSE!
OH, MAN, I DON'T FEEL LIKE...
...I CAN DO THAT AT ALL!!

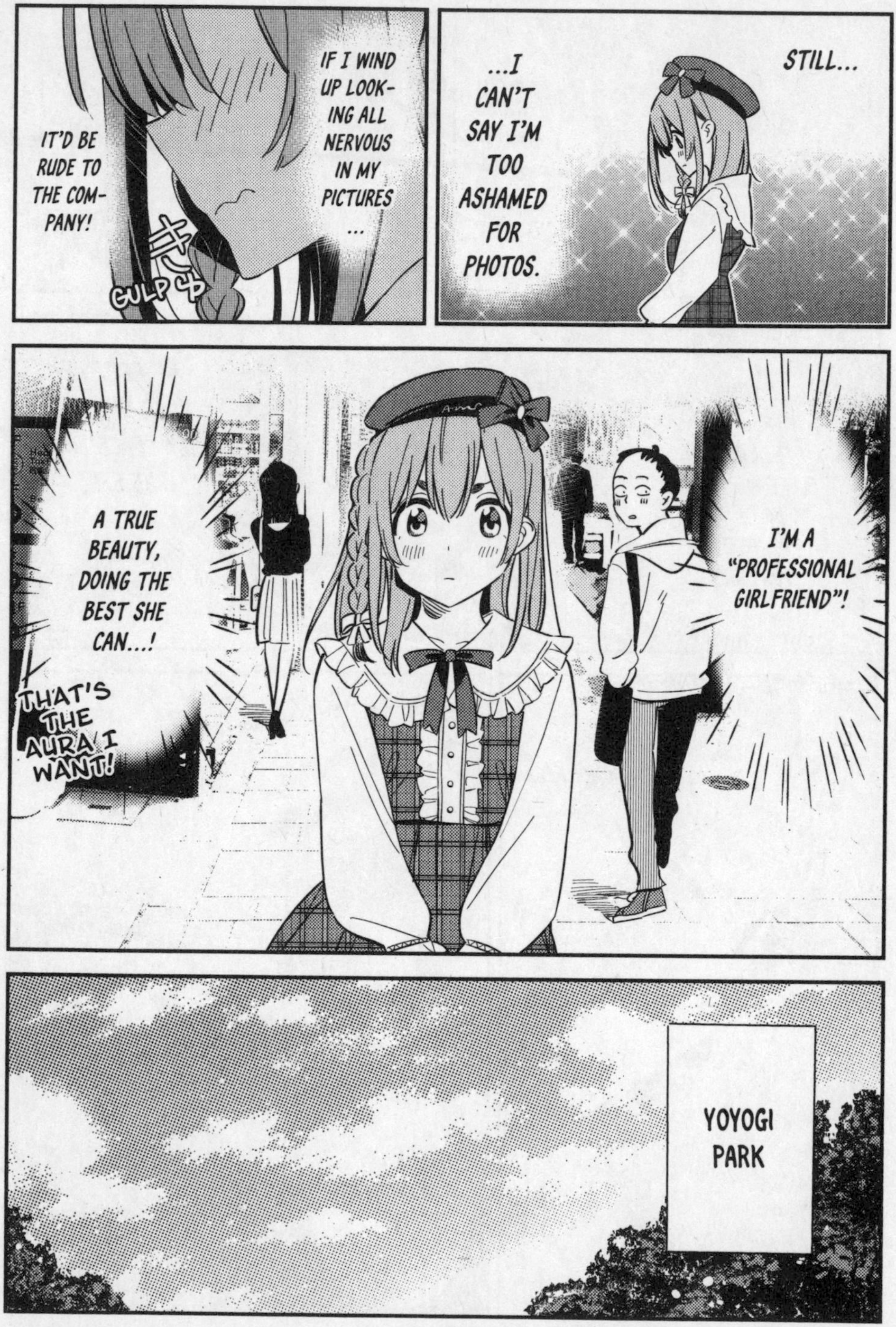
STILL...
...I CAN'T SAY I'M TOO ASHAMED FOR PHOTOS.
IF I WIND UP LOOKING ALL NERVOUS IN MY PICTURES...
IT'D BE RUDE TO THE COMPANY!
GULP
I'M A "PROFESSIONAL GIRLFRIEND"!
A TRUE BEAUTY, DOING THE BEST SHE CAN...!
THAT'S THE AURA I WANT!
YOYOGI PARK

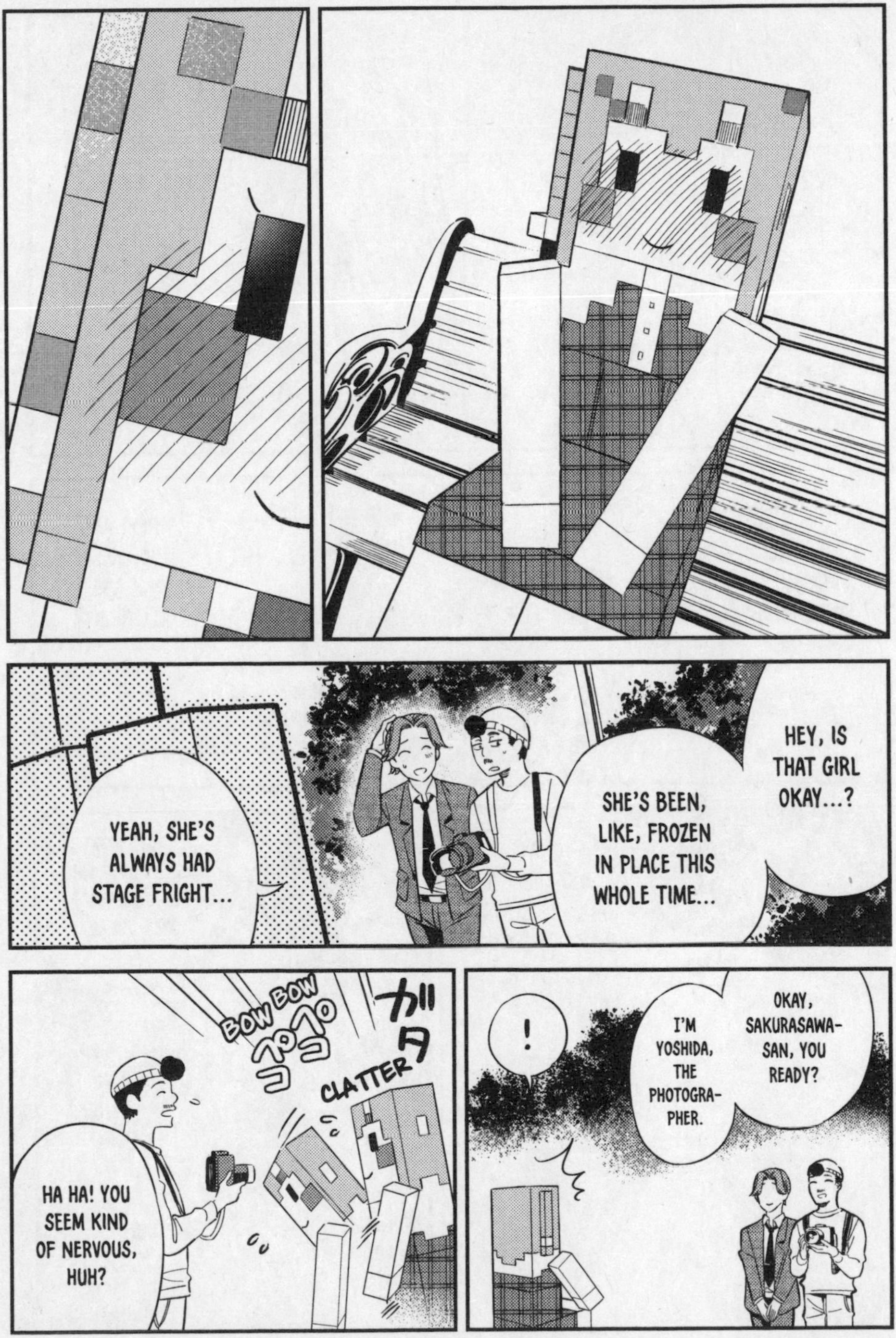

HEY, IS THAT GIRL OKAY...?
SHE'S BEEN, LIKE, FROZEN IN PLACE THIS WHOLE TIME...
YEAH, SHE'S ALWAYS HAD STAGE FRIGHT...
OKAY, SAKURASAWA-SAN, YOU READY?
I'M YOSHIDA, THE PHOTOGRA-PHER.
!
ガタ
CLATTER
ペコペコ
BOW BOW
HA HA! YOU SEEM KIND OF NERVOUS, HUH?

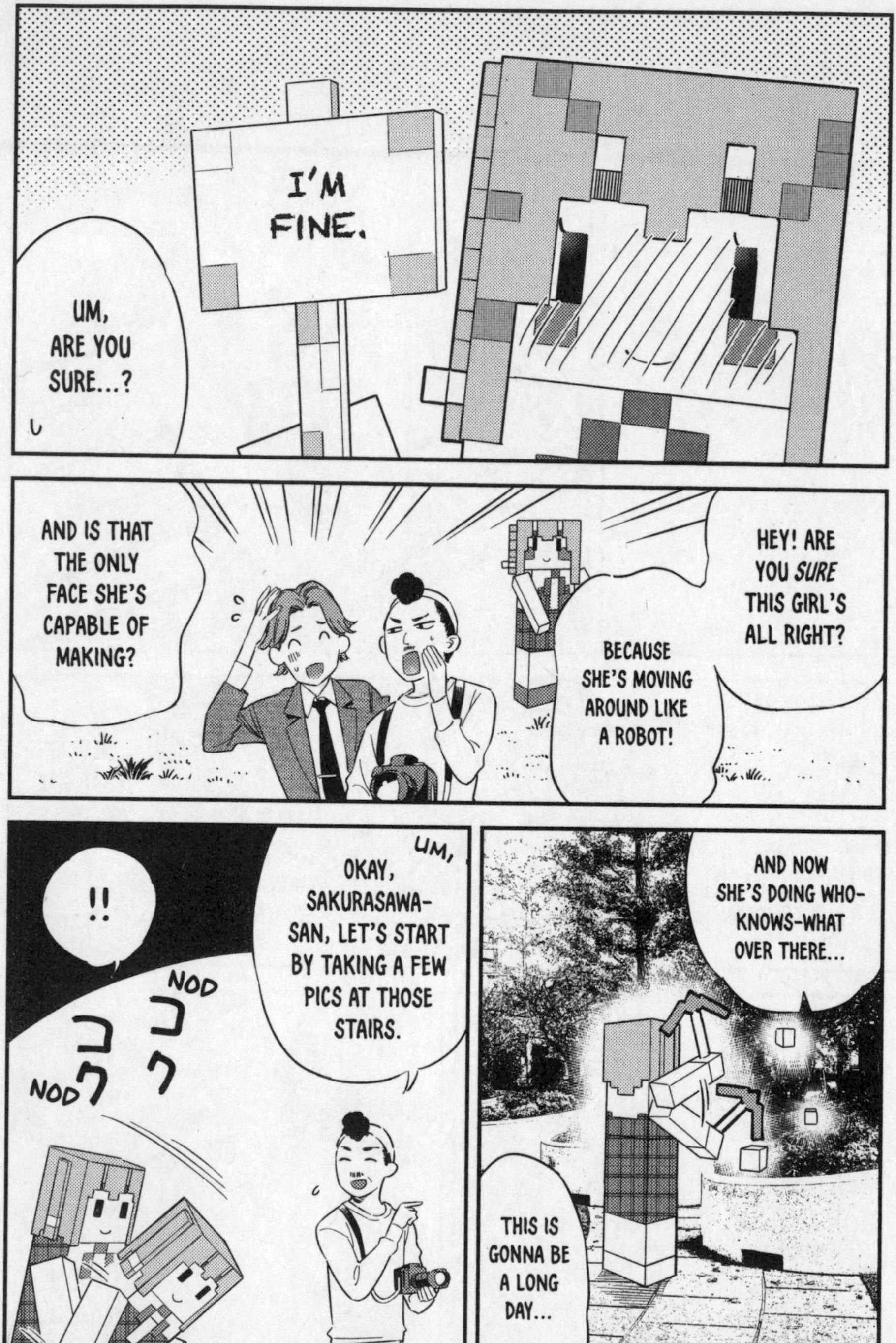
I'M FINE.
UM, ARE YOU SURE...?
HEY! ARE YOU *SURE* THIS GIRL'S ALL RIGHT?
BECAUSE SHE'S MOVING AROUND LIKE A ROBOT!
AND IS THAT THE ONLY FACE SHE'S CAPABLE OF MAKING?
AND NOW SHE'S DOING WHO-KNOWS-WHAT OVER THERE...
THIS IS GONNA BE A LONG DAY...
UM,
OKAY, SAKURASAWA-SAN, LET'S START BY TAKING A FEW PICS AT THOSE STAIRS.
!!
コク NOD
コク NOD

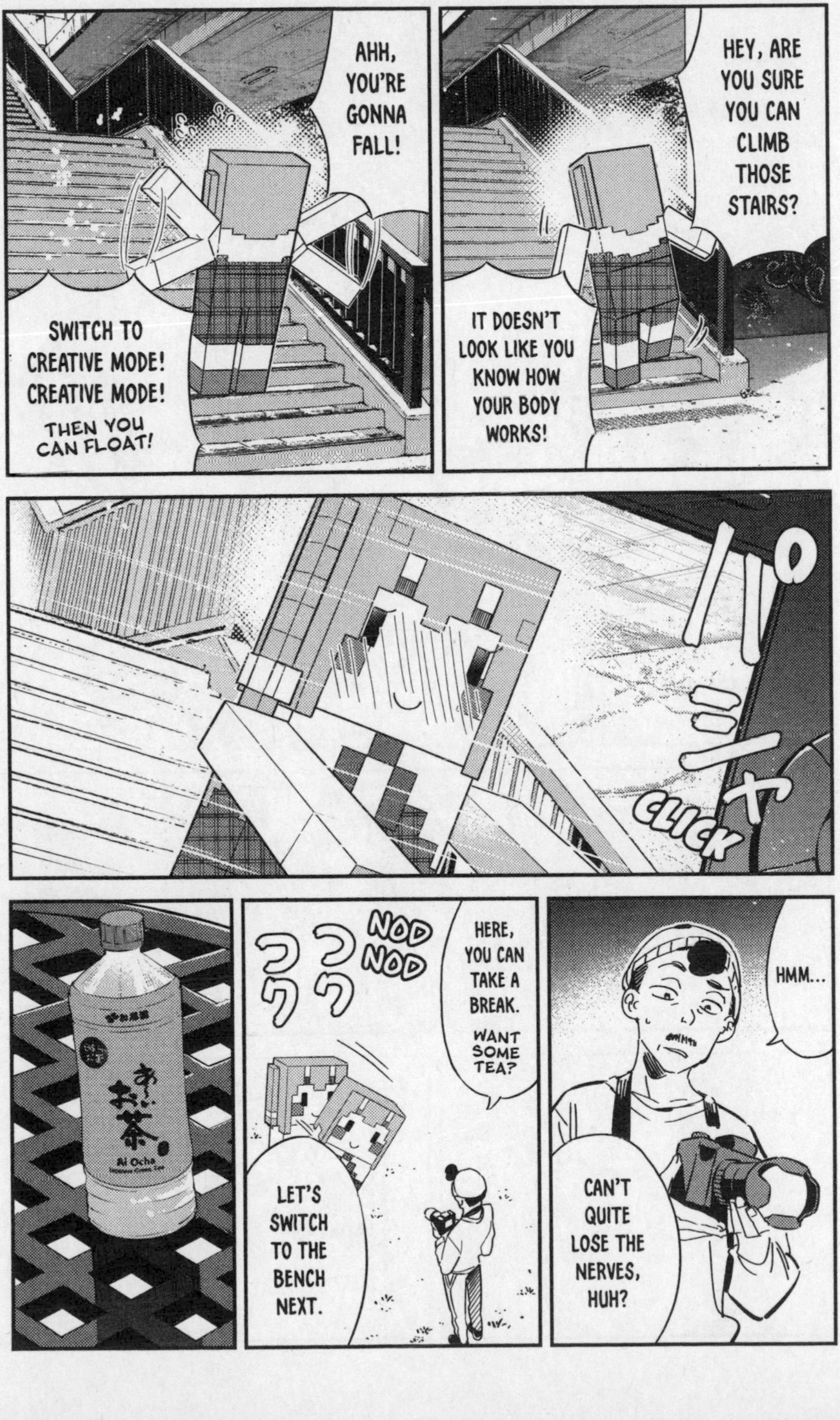
HEY, ARE YOU SURE YOU CAN CLIMB THOSE STAIRS?
IT DOESN'T LOOK LIKE YOU KNOW HOW YOUR BODY WORKS!
AHH, YOU'RE GONNA FALL!
SWITCH TO CREATIVE MODE! CREATIVE MODE!
THEN YOU CAN FLOAT!
パシャ
CLICK
HMM...
CAN'T QUITE LOSE THE NERVES, HUH?
HERE, YOU CAN TAKE A BREAK.
WANT SOME TEA?
コクコク
NOD NOD
LET'S SWITCH TO THE BENCH NEXT.
Ai Ocha

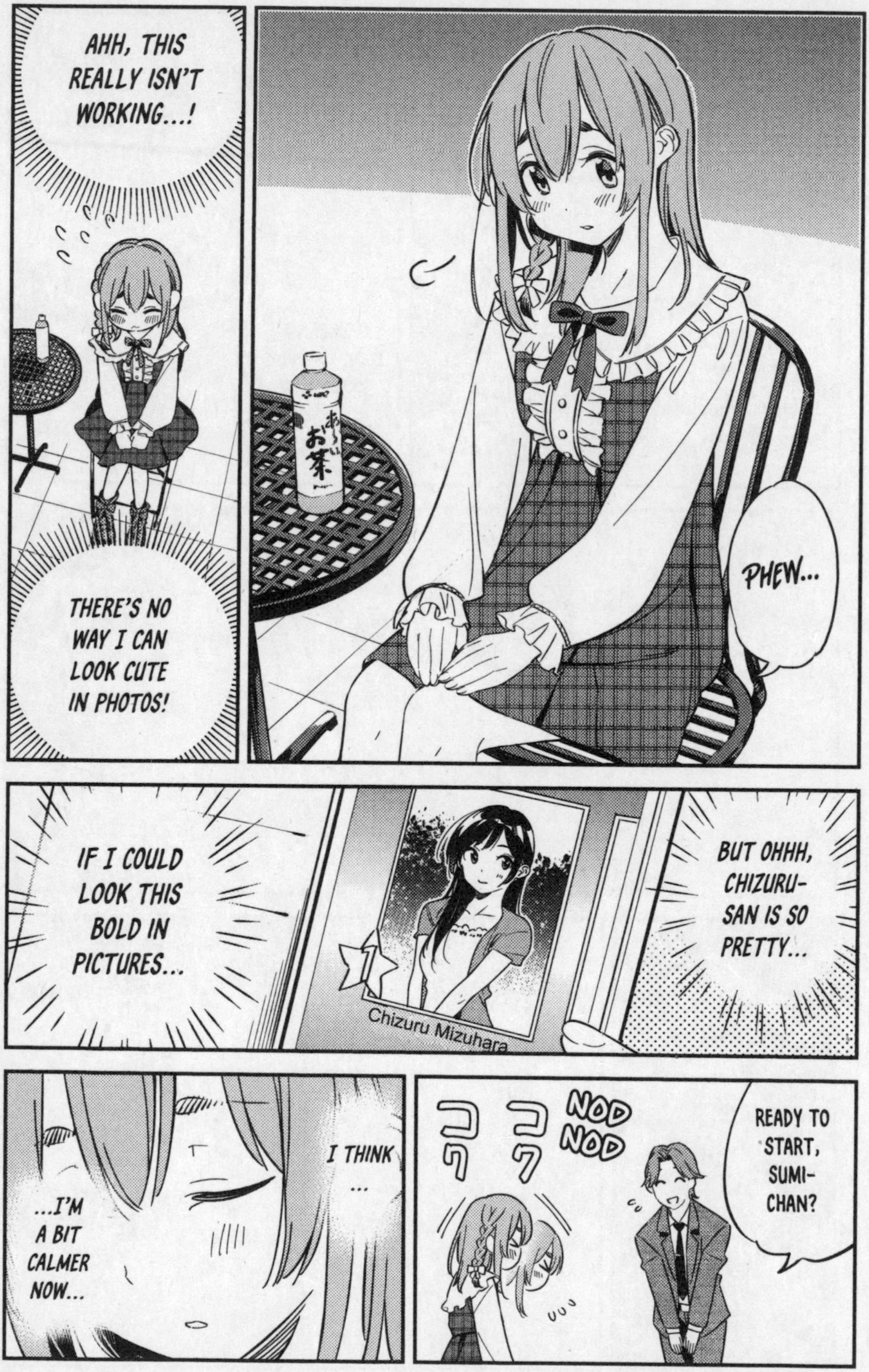
PHEW...
AHH, THIS REALLY ISN'T WORKING...!
THERE'S NO WAY I CAN LOOK CUTE IN PHOTOS!
BUT OHHH, CHIZURU-SAN IS SO PRETTY...
IF I COULD LOOK THIS BOLD IN PICTURES...
Chizuru Mizuhara
READY TO START, SUMI-CHAN?
コク コク
NOD NOD
I THINK ...
...I'M A BIT CALMER NOW...

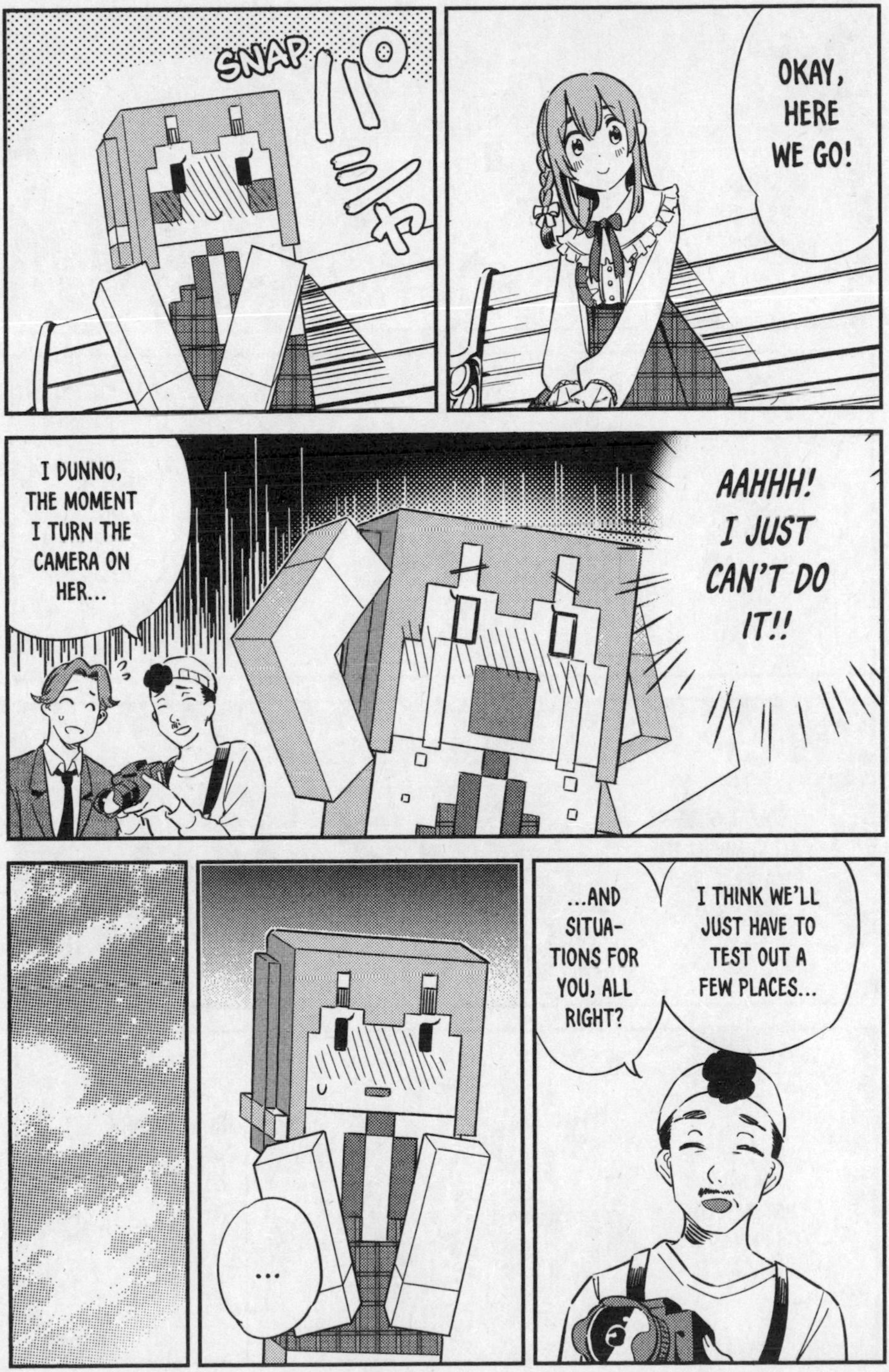
OKAY, HERE WE GO!
SNAP
パシャ
AAHHH! I JUST CAN'T DO IT!!
I DUNNO, THE MOMENT I TURN THE CAMERA ON HER...
I THINK WE'LL JUST HAVE TO TEST OUT A FEW PLACES...
...AND SITUA-TIONS FOR YOU, ALL RIGHT?
...

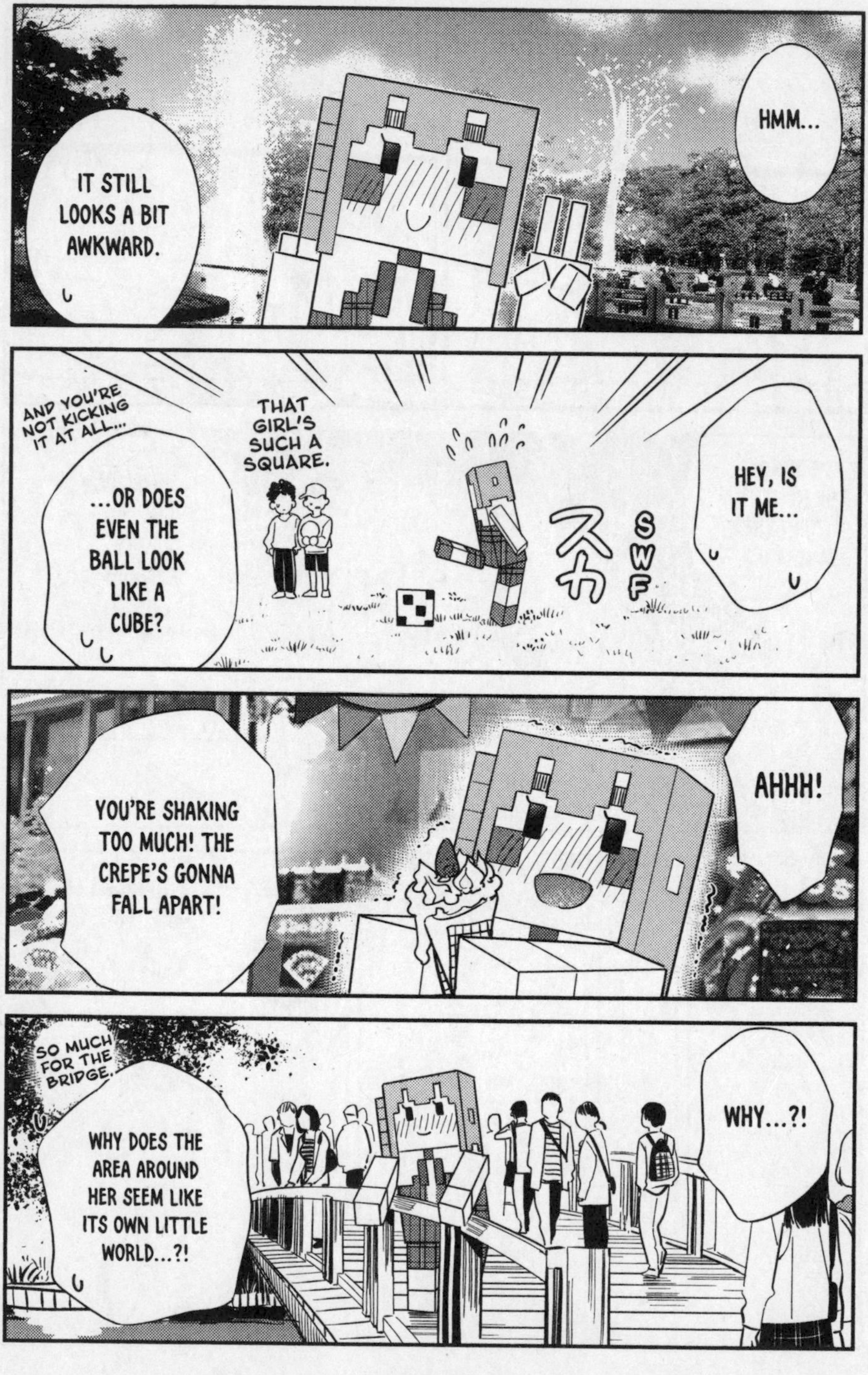
HMM...
IT STILL LOOKS A BIT AWKWARD.
HEY, IS IT ME...
スカ
SWF
THAT GIRL'S SUCH A SQUARE.
AND YOU'RE NOT KICKING IT AT ALL...
...OR DOES EVEN THE BALL LOOK LIKE A CUBE?
AHHH!
YOU'RE SHAKING TOO MUCH! THE CREPE'S GONNA FALL APART!
WHY...?!
SO MUCH FOR THE BRIDGE.
WHY DOES THE AREA AROUND HER SEEM LIKE ITS OWN LITTLE WORLD...?!

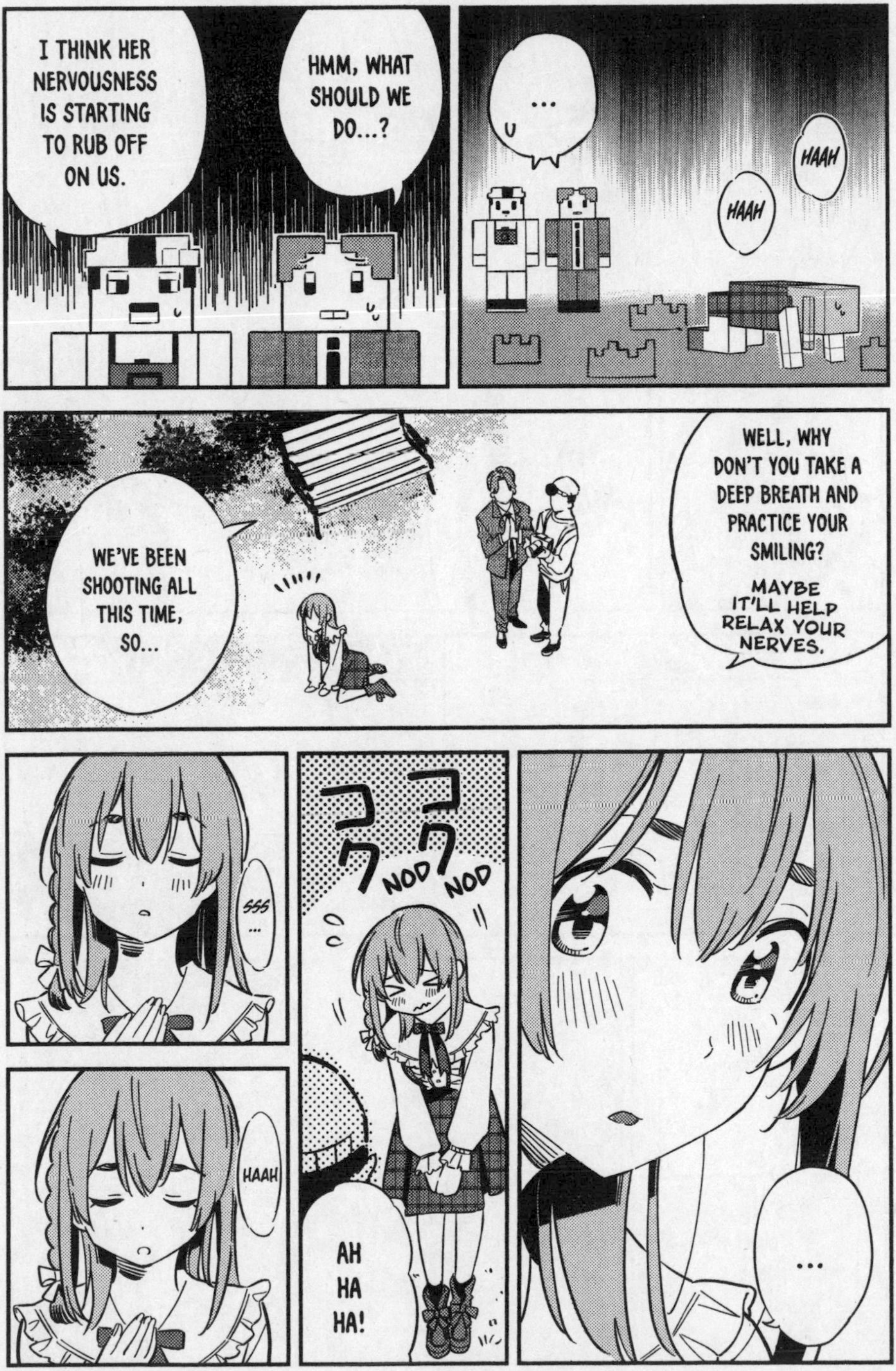
HAAH
HAAH
...
HMM, WHAT SHOULD WE DO...?
I THINK HER NERVOUSNESS IS STARTING TO RUB OFF ON US.
WELL, WHY DON'T YOU TAKE A DEEP BREATH AND PRACTICE YOUR SMILING?
MAYBE IT'LL HELP RELAX YOUR NERVES.
WE'VE BEEN SHOOTING ALL THIS TIME, SO...
...
コク コク
NOD NOD
AH HA HA!
SSS...
HAAH

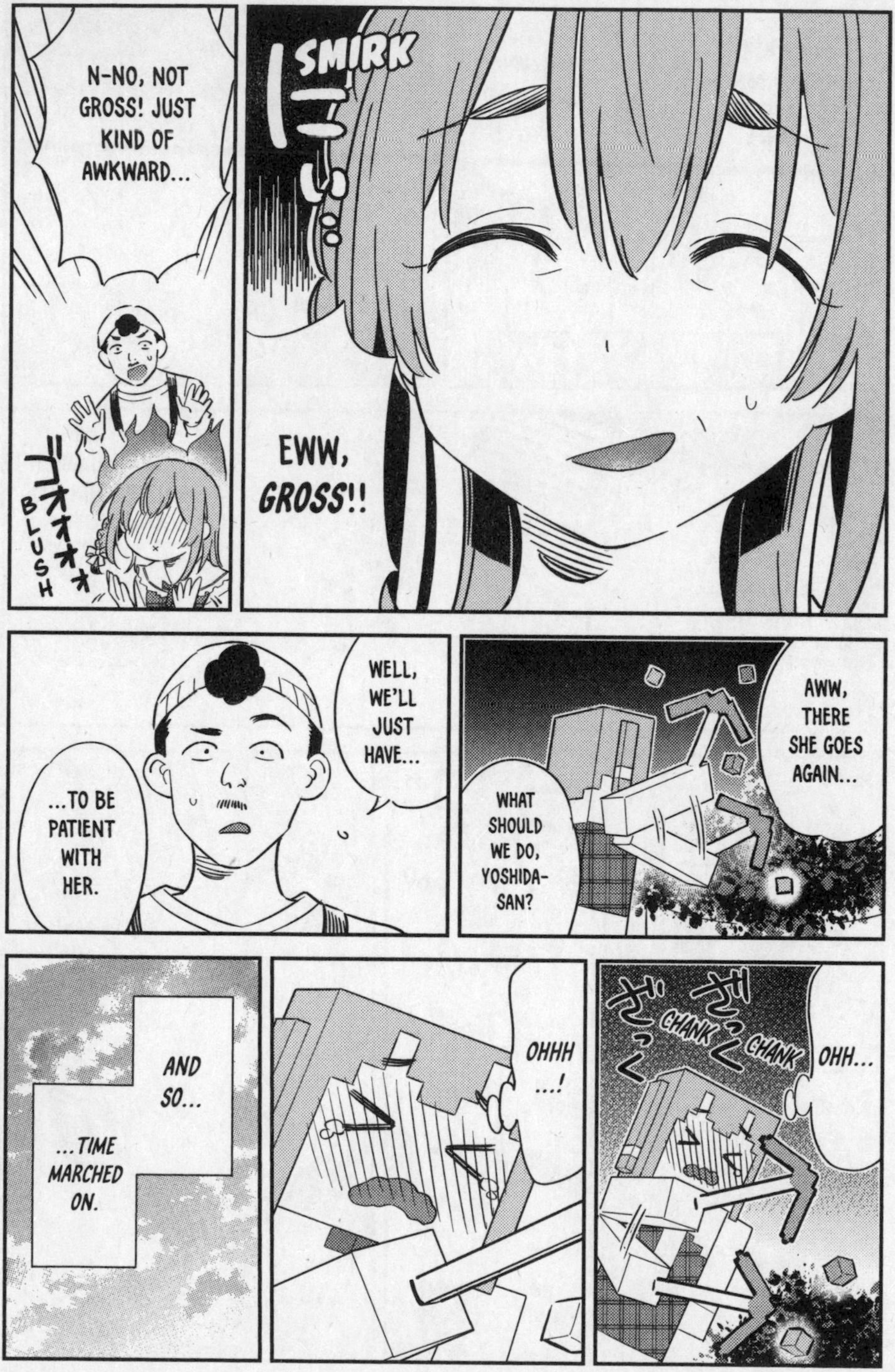
SMIRK
EWW, *GROSS*!!
N-NO, NOT GROSS! JUST KIND OF AWKWARD...
ゴオオオオ
BLUSH
AWW, THERE SHE GOES AGAIN...
WHAT SHOULD WE DO, YOSHIDA-SAN?
WELL, WE'LL JUST HAVE...
...TO BE PATIENT WITH HER.
ざっく ざっく
CHANK CHANK
OHH...
OHHH ...!
AND SO...
...TIME MARCHED ON.

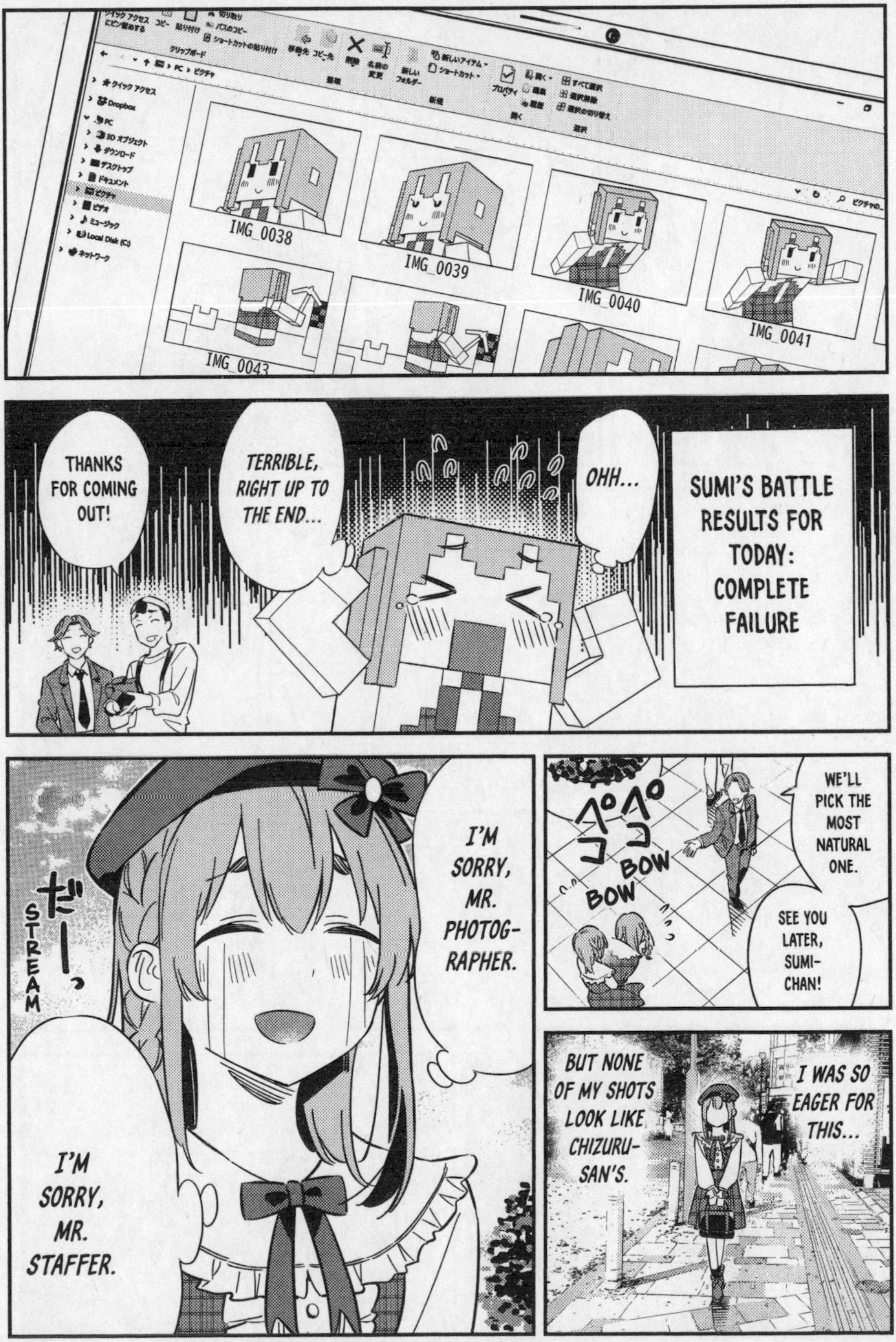
Dropbox
PC
Local Disk (C:)
IMG_0038
IMG_0039
IMG_0040
IMG_0041
IMG_0043
SUMI'S BATTLE RESULTS FOR TODAY: COMPLETE FAILURE
OHH...
TERRIBLE, RIGHT UP TO THE END...
THANKS FOR COMING OUT!
WE'LL PICK THE MOST NATURAL ONE.
SEE YOU LATER, SUMI-CHAN!
ペコペコ
BOW BOW
I WAS SO EAGER FOR THIS...
BUT NONE OF MY SHOTS LOOK LIKE CHIZURU-SAN'S.
I'M SORRY, MR. PHOTOGRAPHER.
だー
STREAM
I'M SORRY, MR. STAFFER.

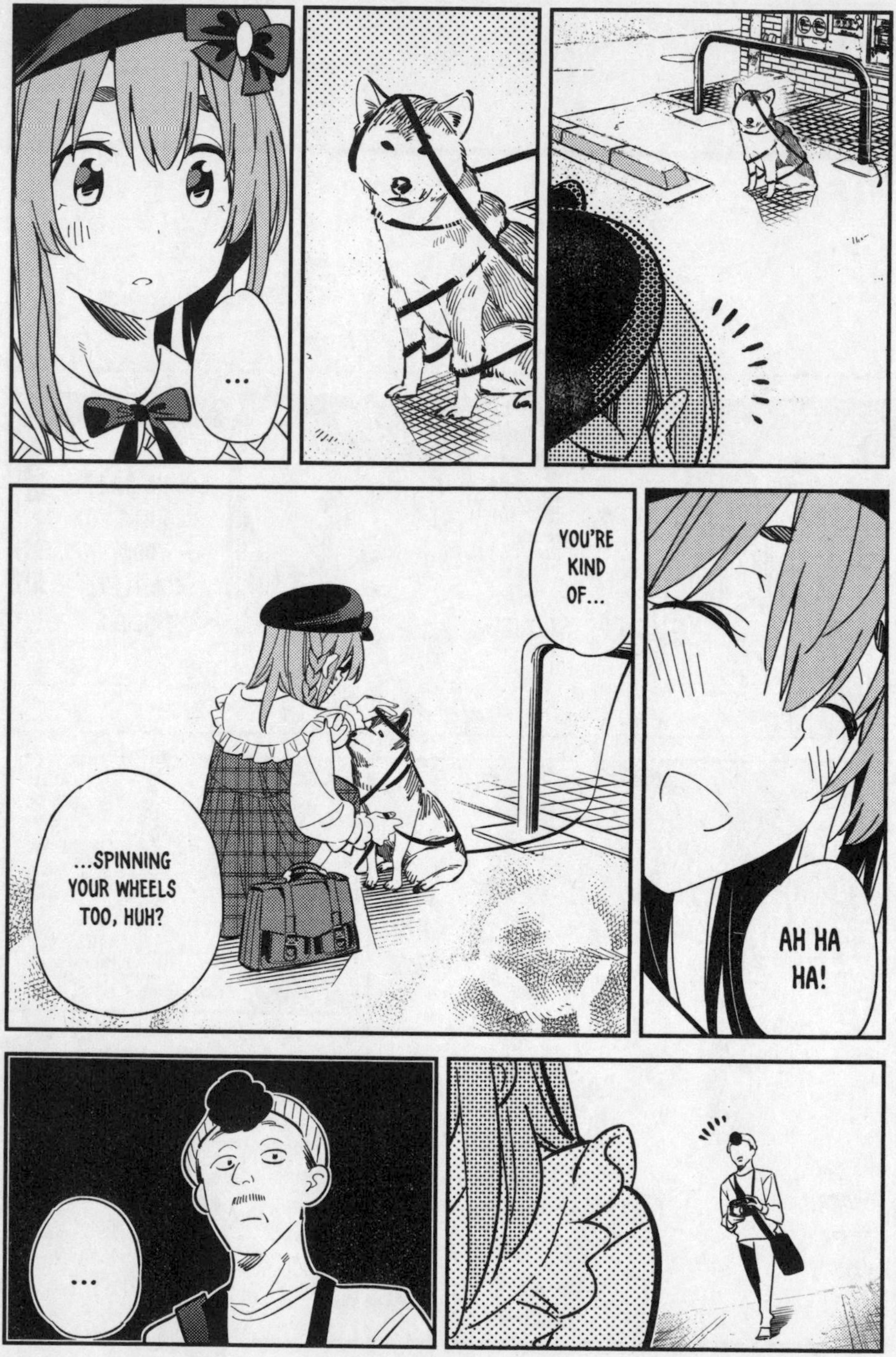
...
AH HA HA!
YOU'RE KIND OF...
...SPINNING YOUR WHEELS TOO, HUH?
...

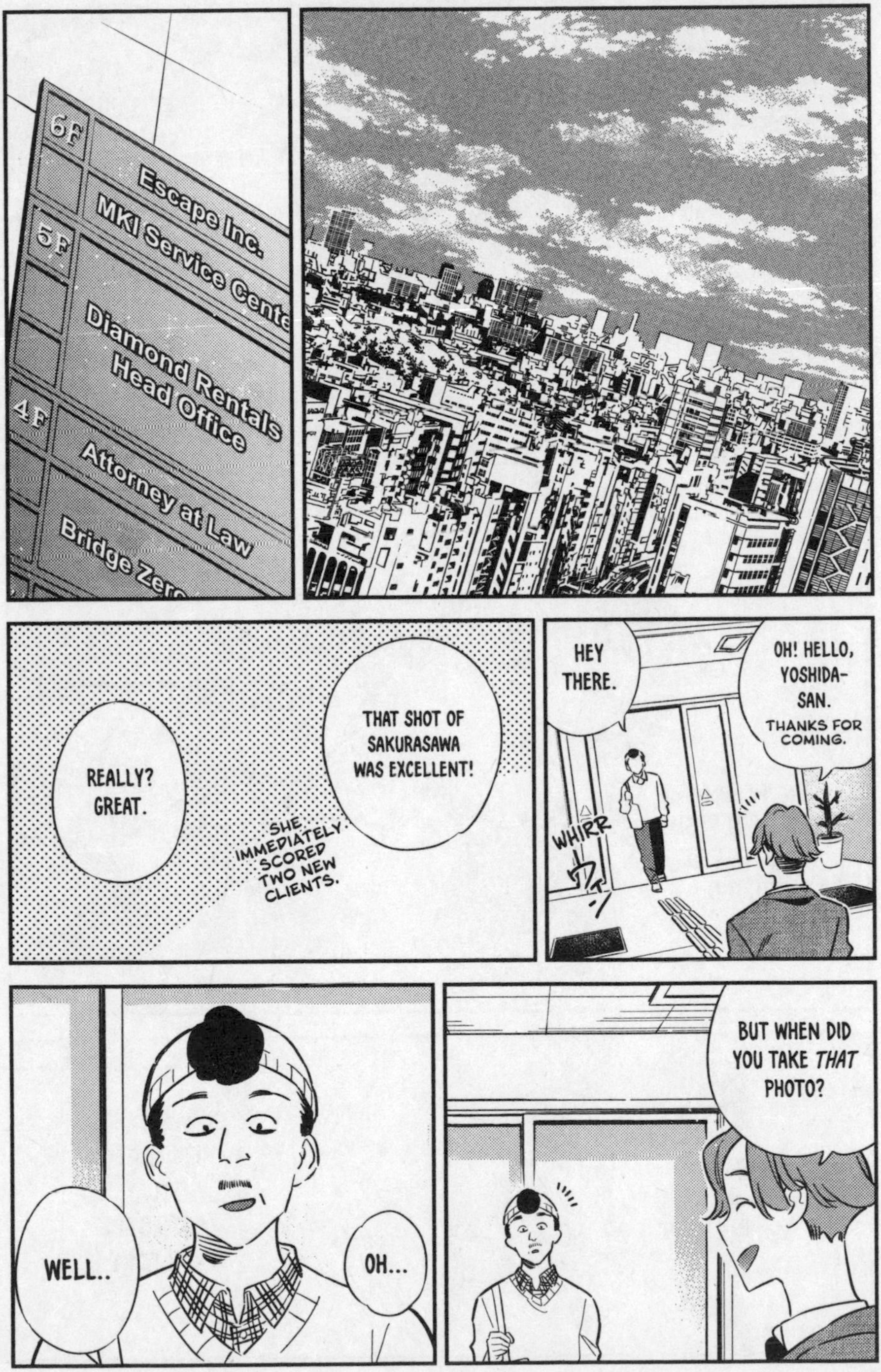
6F
Escape Inc.
MKI Service Cente
5F
Diamond Rentals
Head Office
4F
Attorney at Law
Bridge Zer
OH! HELLO, YOSHIDA-SAN.
THANKS FOR COMING.
HEY THERE.
WHIRR
THAT SHOT OF SAKURASAWA WAS EXCELLENT!
SHE IMMEDIATELY SCORED TWO NEW CLIENTS.
REALLY? GREAT.
BUT WHEN DID YOU TAKE *THAT* PHOTO?
OH...
WELL..

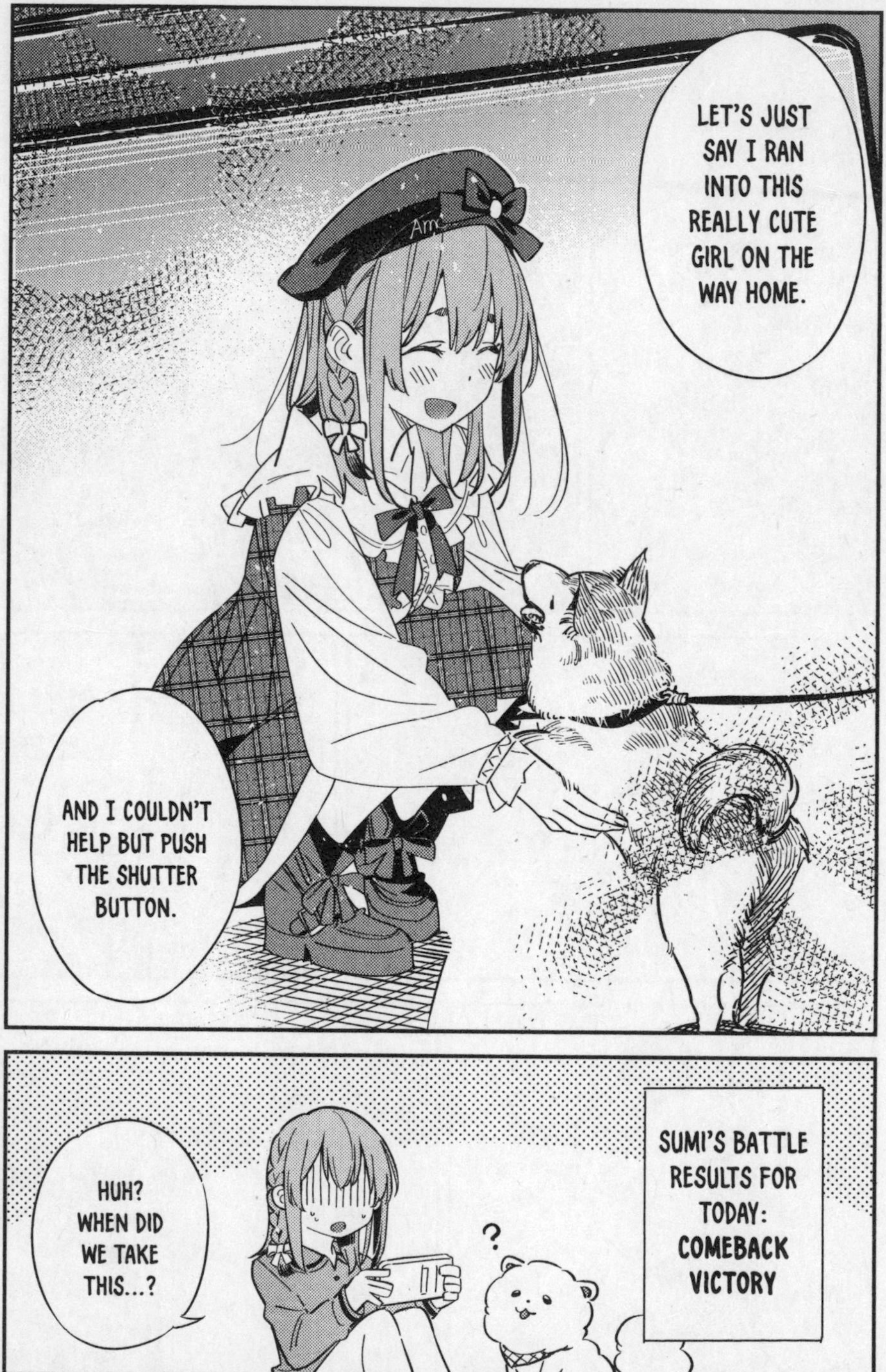
LET'S JUST SAY I RAN INTO THIS REALLY CUTE GIRL ON THE WAY HOME.
AND I COULDN'T HELP BUT PUSH THE SHUTTER BUTTON.
SUMI'S BATTLE RESULTS FOR TODAY: COMEBACK VICTORY
HUH? WHEN DID WE TAKE THIS...?

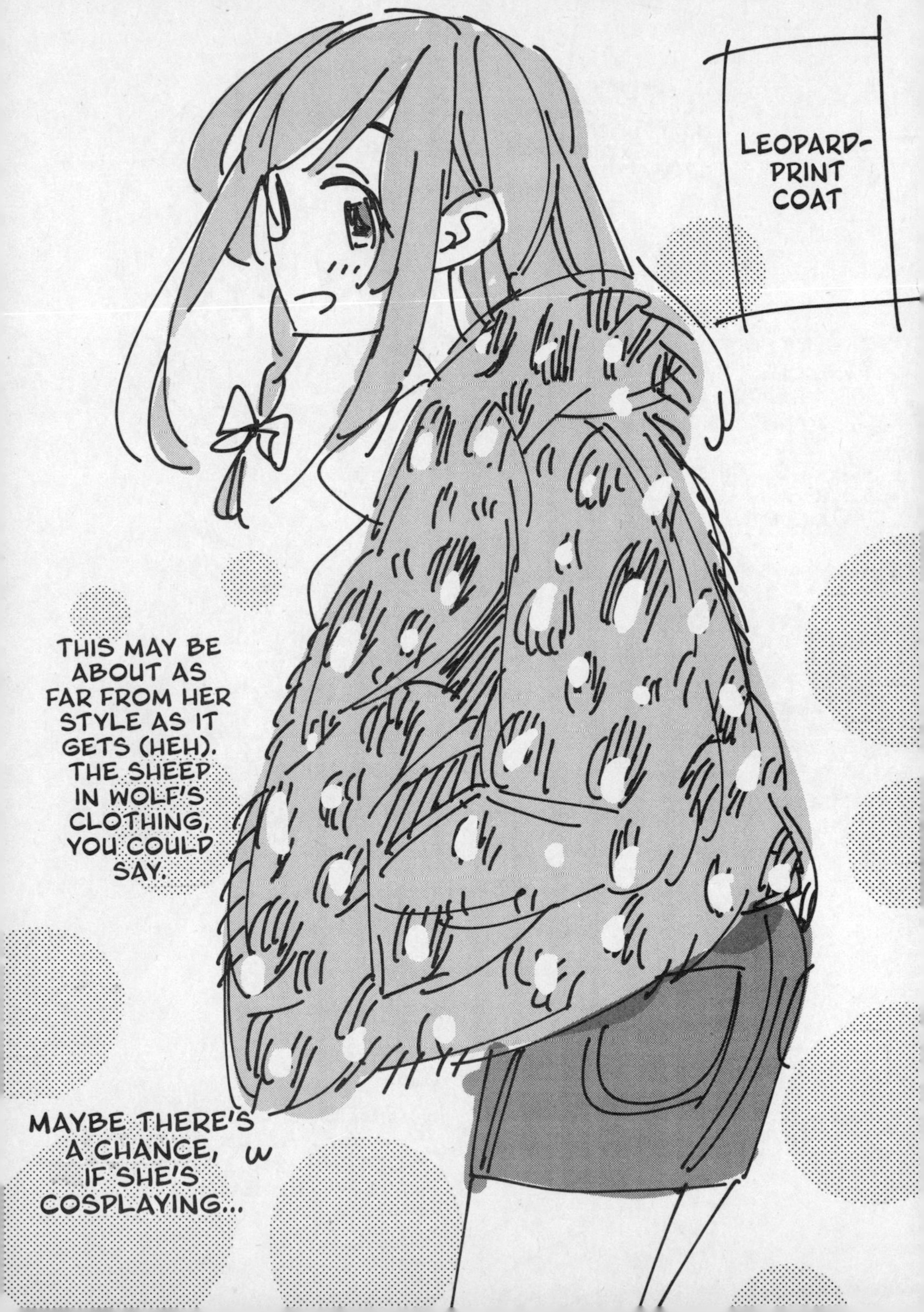
LEOPARD-PRINT COAT
THIS MAY BE ABOUT AS FAR FROM HER STYLE AS IT GETS (HEH). THE SHEEP IN WOLF'S CLOTHING, YOU COULD SAY.
MAYBE THERE'S A CHANCE, IF SHE'S COSPLAYING... w

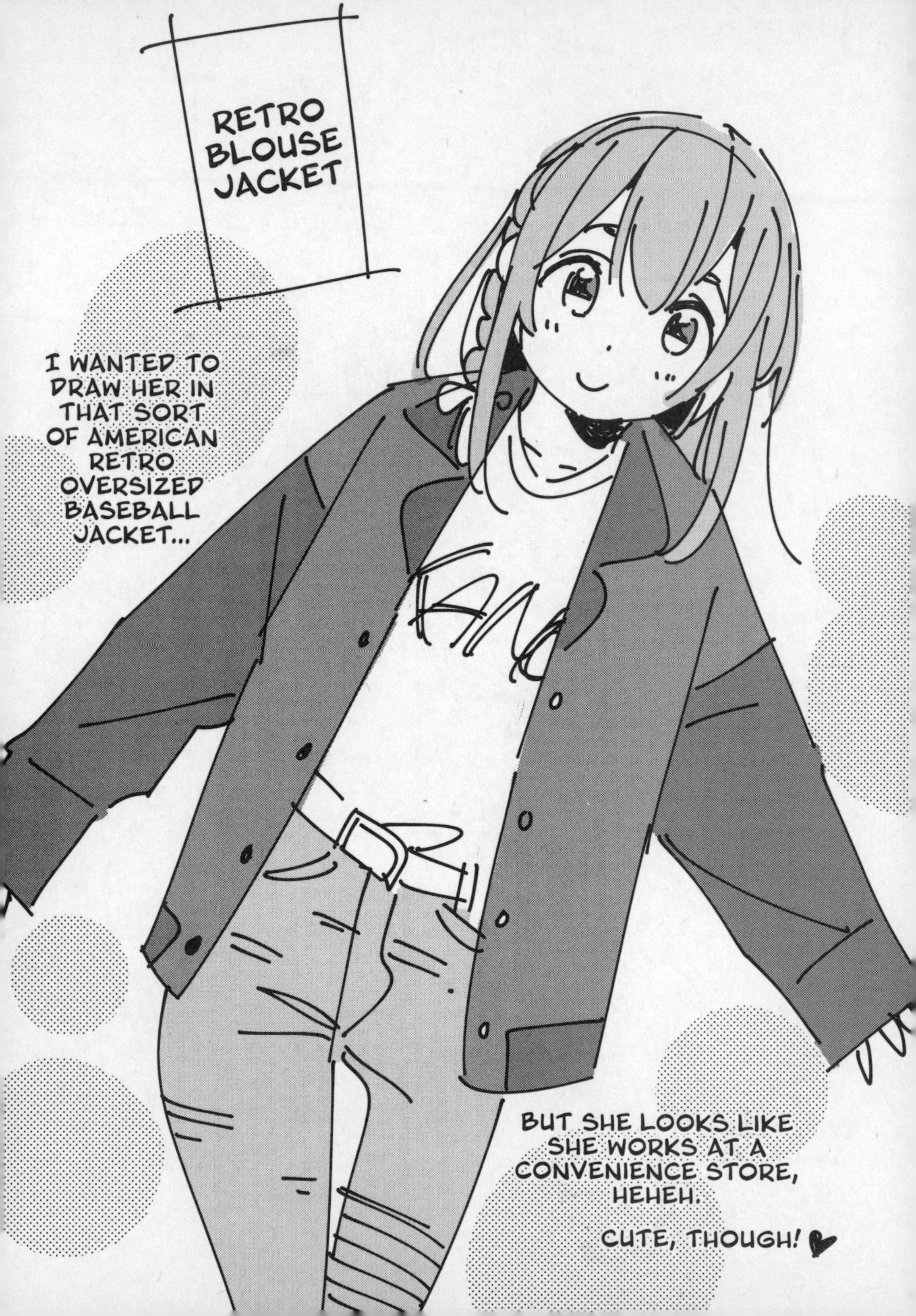
RETRO BLOUSE JACKET
I WANTED TO DRAW HER IN THAT SORT OF AMERICAN RETRO OVERSIZED BASEBALL JACKET...
BUT SHE LOOKS LIKE SHE WORKS AT A CONVENIENCE STORE, HEHEH.
CUTE, THOUGH! ♥

RATING 12 SUMI AND HER DOG WALK

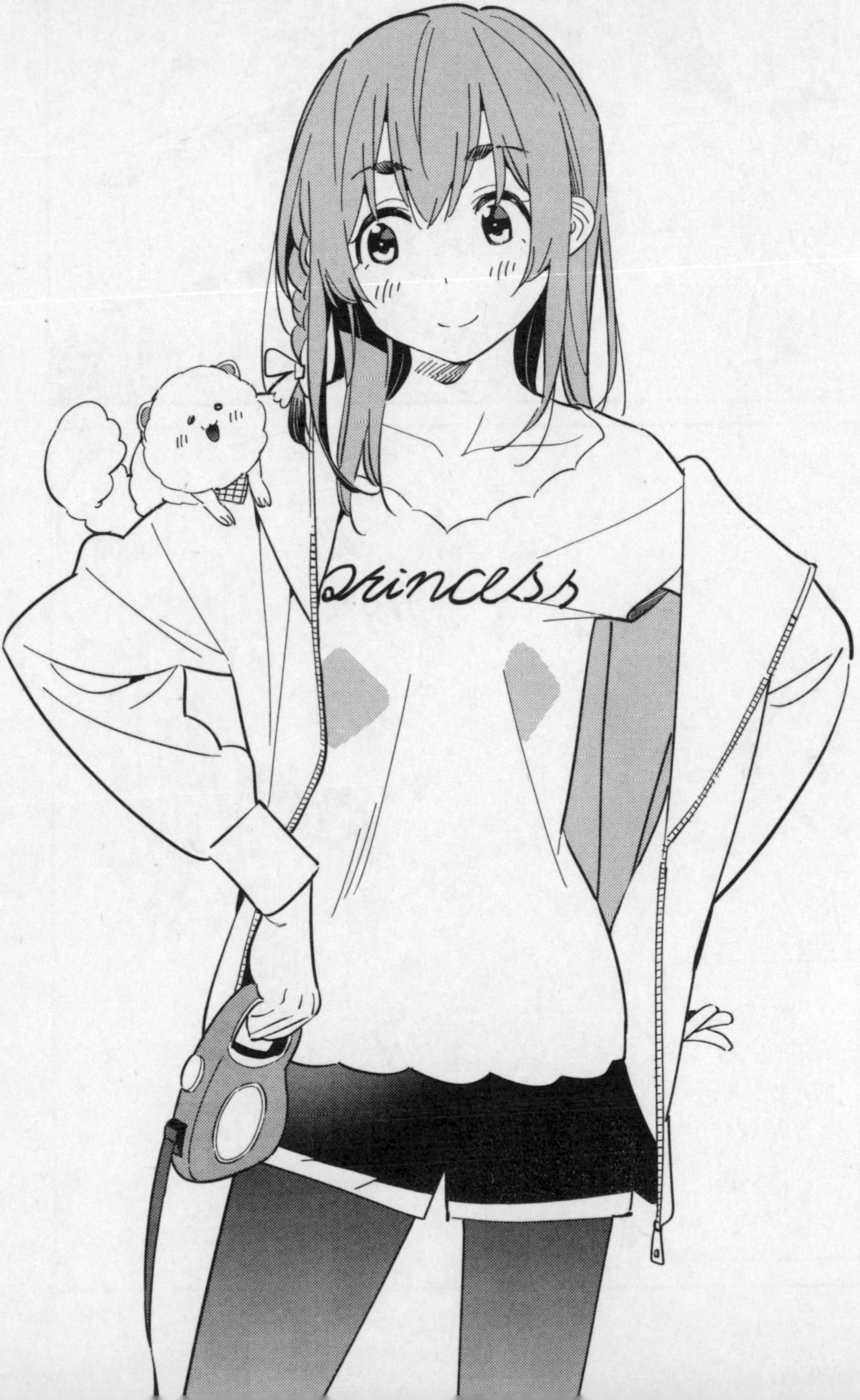
princess

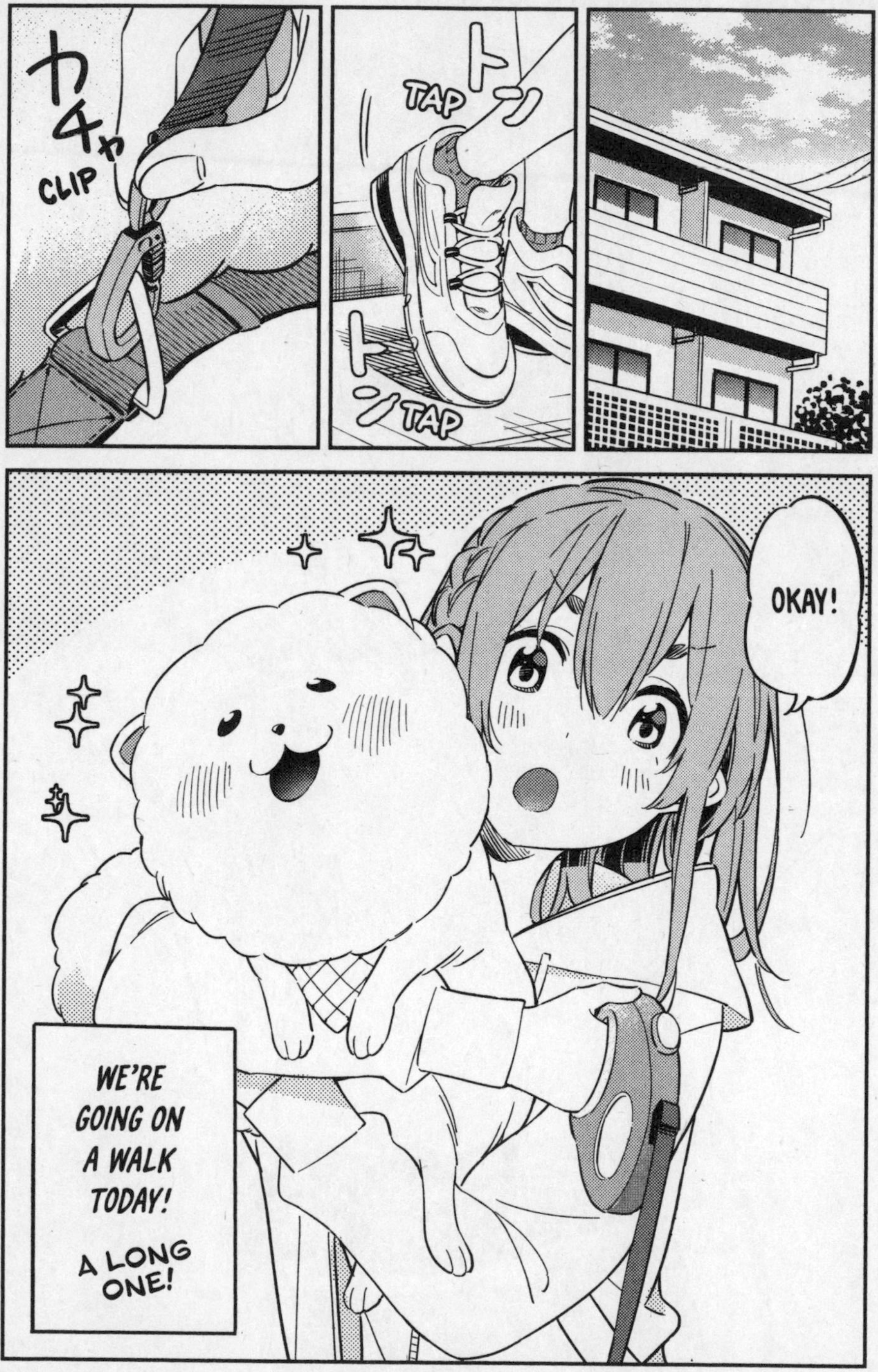
トーン
TAP
トン
TAP
カチャ
CLIP
OKAY!
WE'RE GOING ON A WALK TODAY!
A LONG ONE!

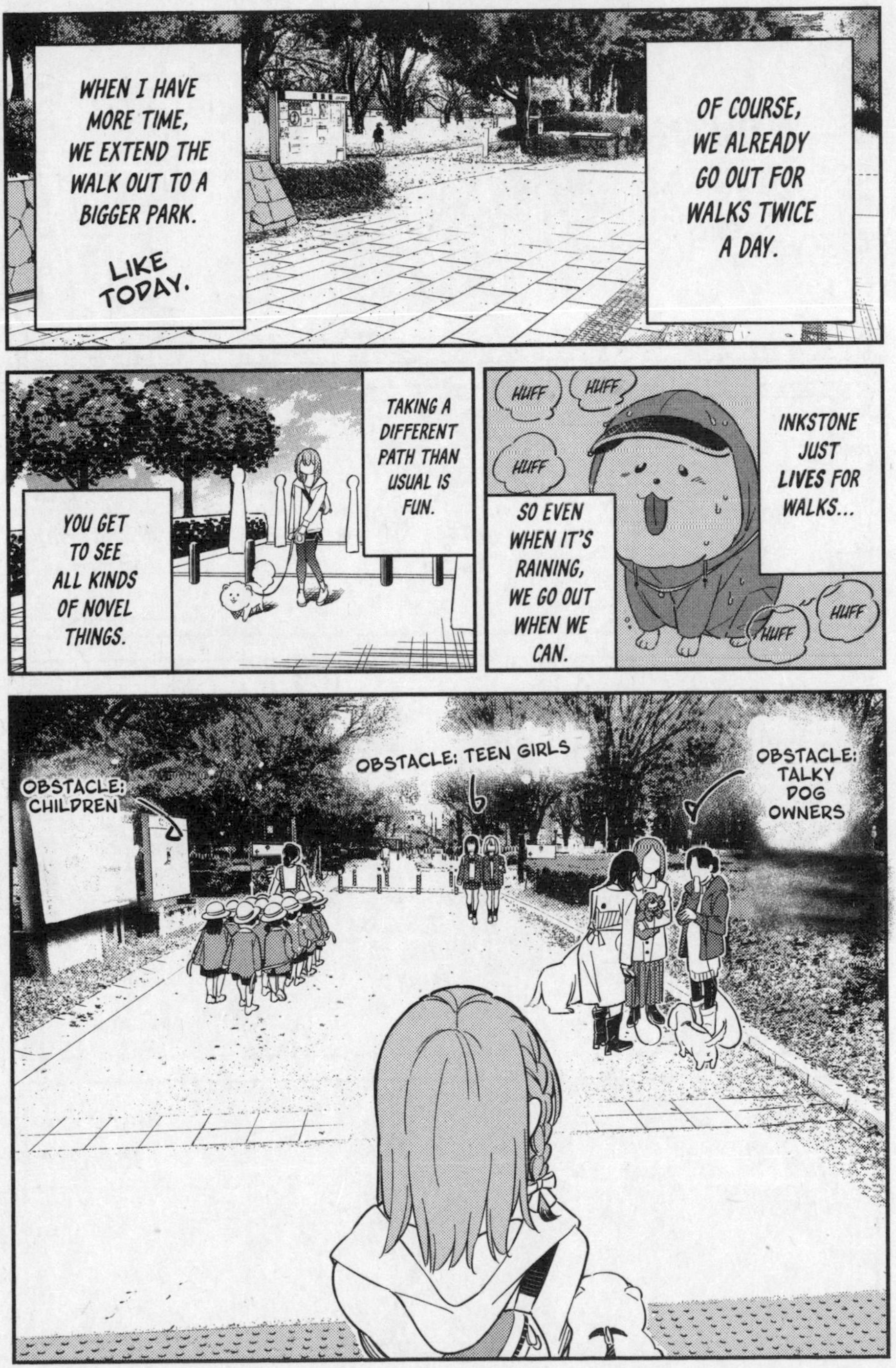
OF COURSE, WE ALREADY GO OUT FOR WALKS TWICE A DAY.
WHEN I HAVE MORE TIME, WE EXTEND THE WALK OUT TO A BIGGER PARK.
LIKE TODAY.
INKSTONE JUST LIVES FOR WALKS...
HUFF
HUFF
HUFF
SO EVEN WHEN IT'S RAINING, WE GO OUT WHEN WE CAN.
HUFF
HUFF
TAKING A DIFFERENT PATH THAN USUAL IS FUN.
YOU GET TO SEE ALL KINDS OF NOVEL THINGS.
OBSTACLE: TALKY DOG OWNERS
OBSTACLE: TEEN GIRLS
OBSTACLE: CHILDREN

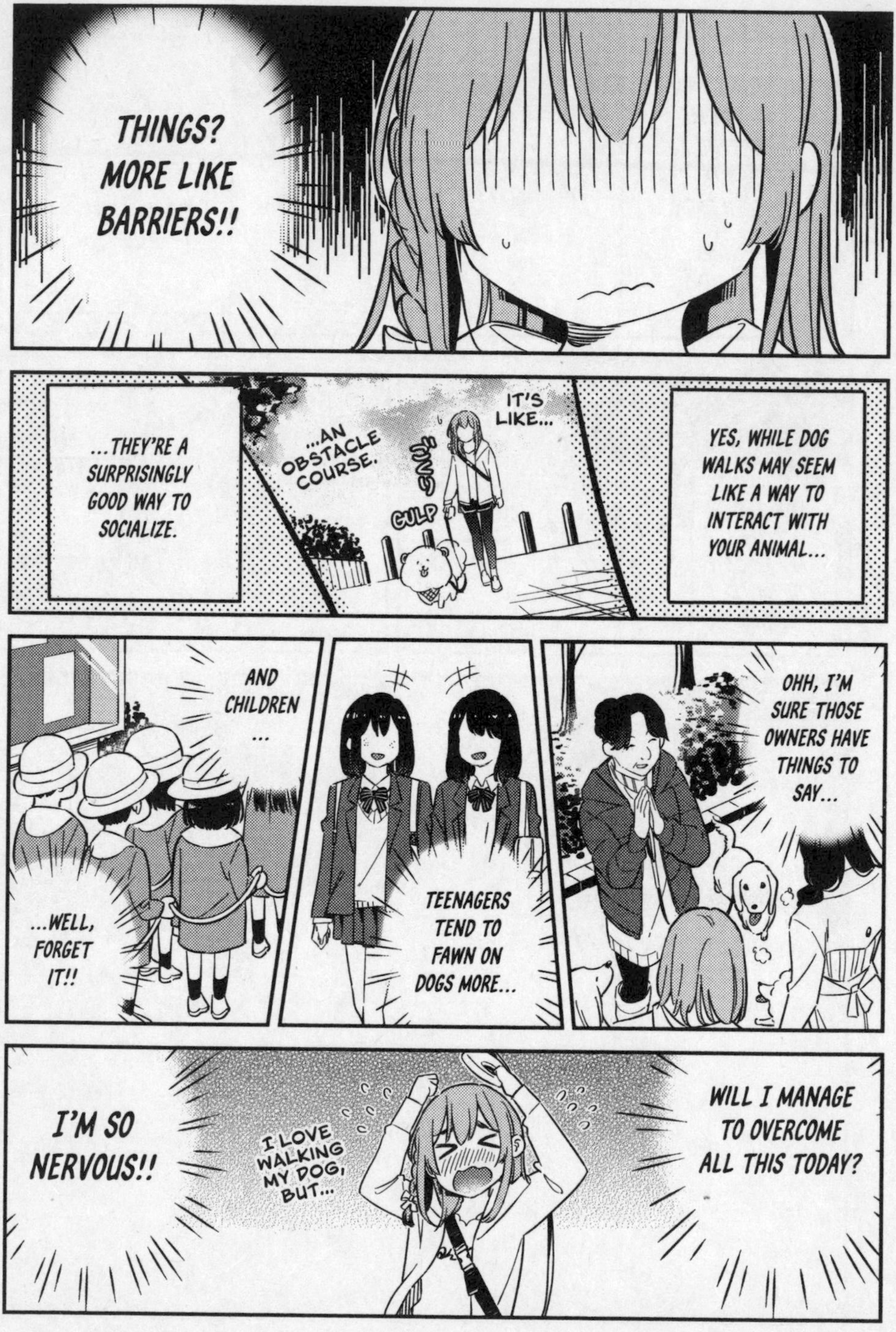
THINGS? MORE LIKE BARRIERS!!
YES, WHILE DOG WALKS MAY SEEM LIKE A WAY TO INTERACT WITH YOUR ANIMAL...
IT'S LIKE...
...AN OBSTACLE COURSE.
GULP
...THEY'RE A SURPRISINGLY GOOD WAY TO SOCIALIZE.
OHH, I'M SURE THOSE OWNERS HAVE THINGS TO SAY...
TEENAGERS TEND TO FAWN ON DOGS MORE...
AND CHILDREN ...
...WELL, FORGET IT!!
WILL I MANAGE TO OVERCOME ALL THIS TODAY?
I LOVE WALKING MY DOG, BUT...
I'M SO NERVOUS!!

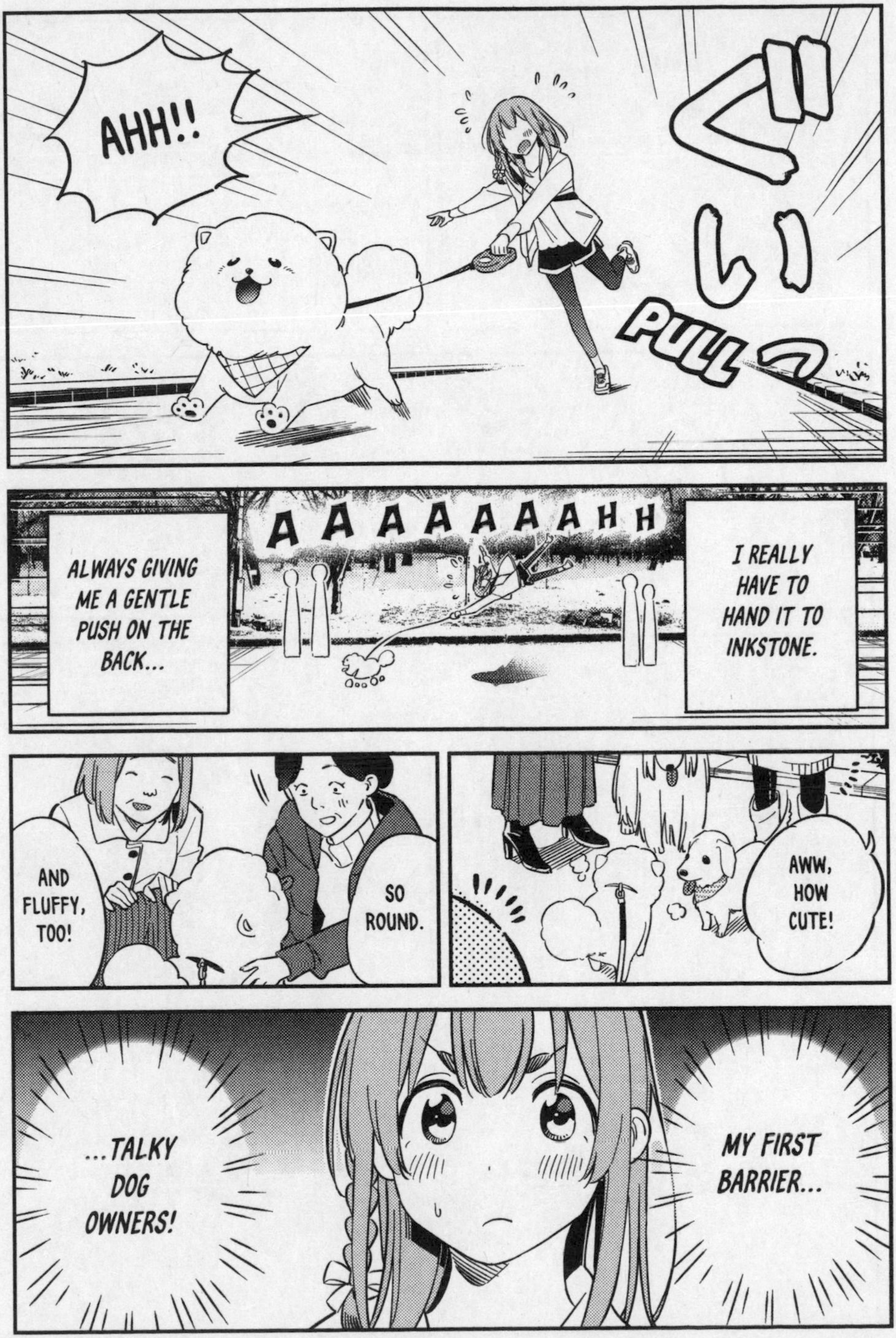
ぐいっ
PULL
AHH!!
I REALLY HAVE TO HAND IT TO INKSTONE.
AAAAAAAHH
ALWAYS GIVING ME A GENTLE PUSH ON THE BACK...
AWW, HOW CUTE!
SO ROUND.
AND FLUFFY, TOO!
MY FIRST BARRIER...
...TALKY DOG OWNERS!

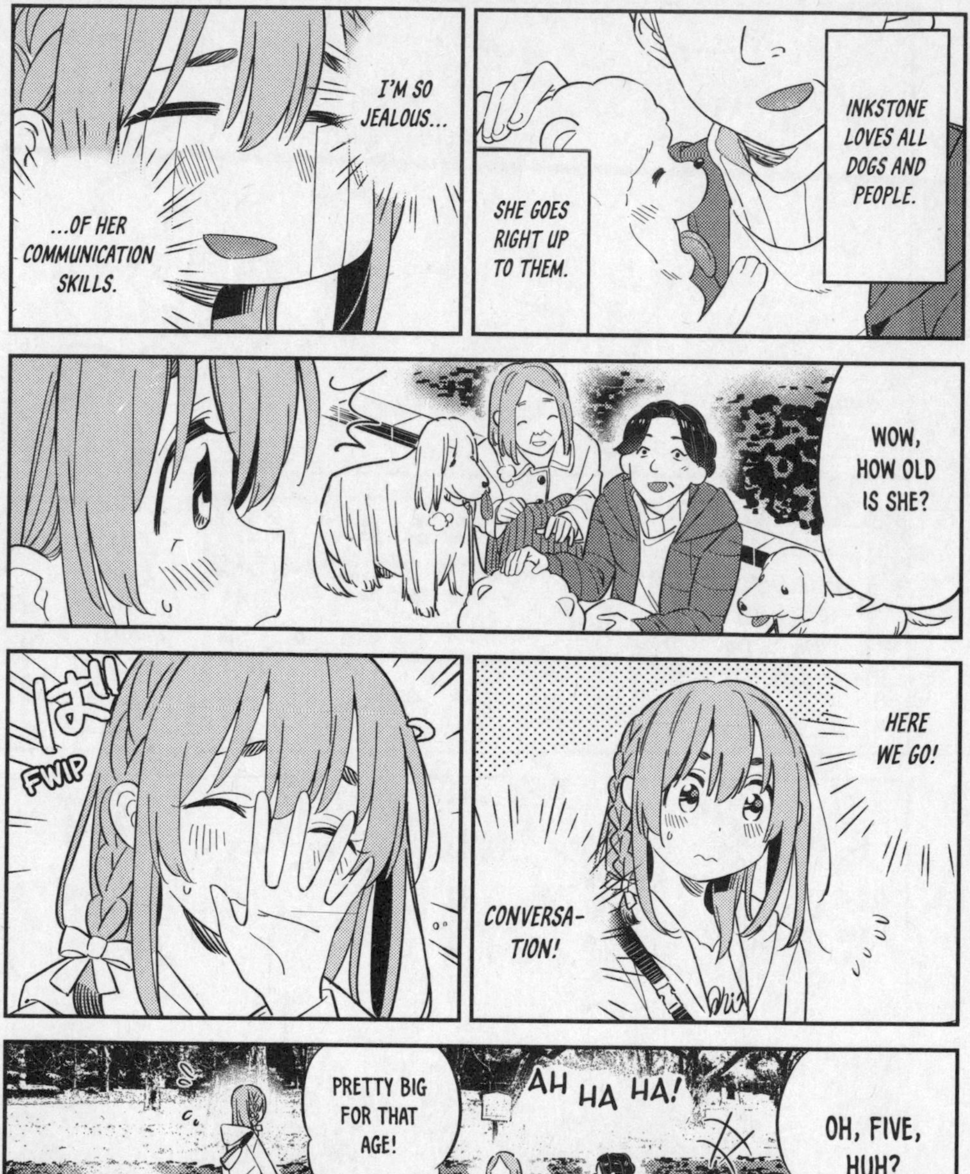
INKSTONE LOVES ALL DOGS AND PEOPLE.
SHE GOES RIGHT UP TO THEM.
I'M SO JEALOUS...
...OF HER COMMUNICATION SKILLS.
WOW, HOW OLD IS SHE?
HERE WE GO!
CONVERSATION!
FWIP
OH, FIVE, HUH?
AH HA HA!
PRETTY BIG FOR THAT AGE!
WOW, SHE'S FRIENDLY!

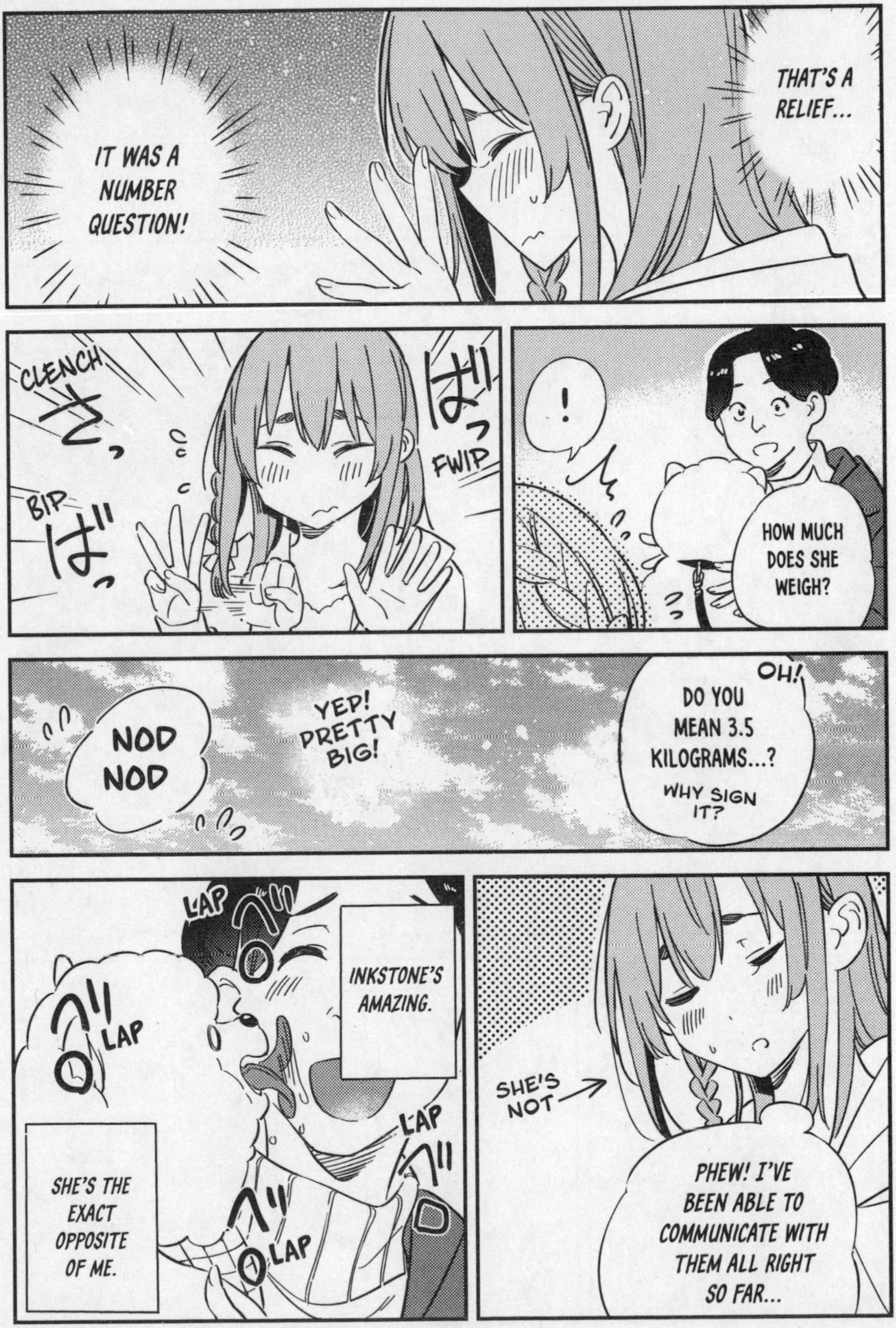
THAT'S A RELIEF...
IT WAS A NUMBER QUESTION!
!
HOW MUCH DOES SHE WEIGH?
ぱっ
FWIP
CLENCH
さっ
BIP
ばっ
OH!
DO YOU MEAN 3.5 KILOGRAMS...?
WHY SIGN IT?
YEP! PRETTY BIG!
NOD NOD
SHE'S NOT
PHEW! I'VE BEEN ABLE TO COMMUNICATE WITH THEM ALL RIGHT SO FAR...
INKSTONE'S AMAZING.
LAP
LAP
LAP
SHE'S THE EXACT OPPOSITE OF ME.
LAP

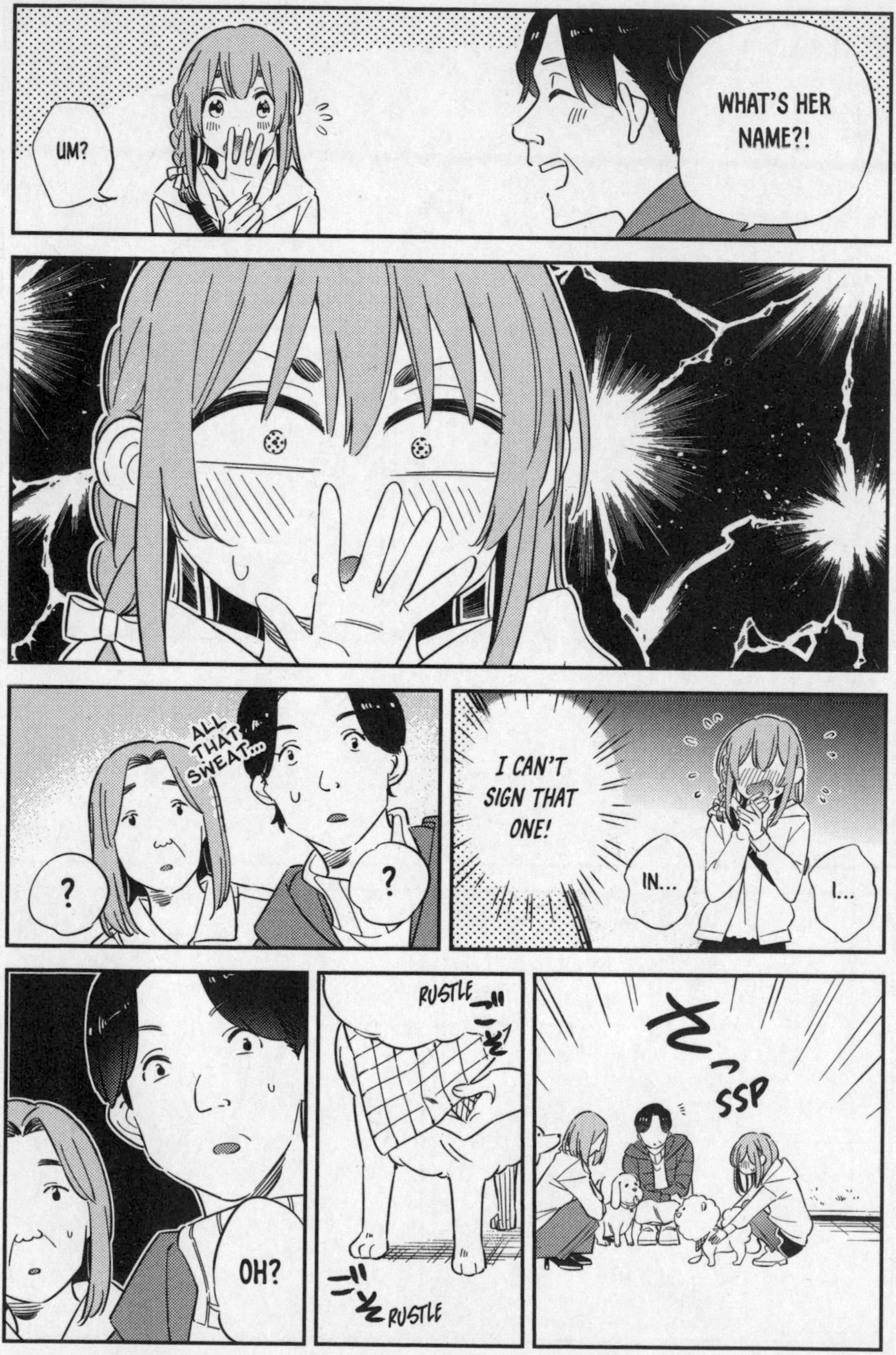

WHAT'S HER NAME?!
UM?
I...
IN...
I CAN'T SIGN THAT ONE!
ALL THAT SWEAT...
?
?
さっ
SSP
RUSTLE
ごそ
ごそ
RUSTLE
OH?

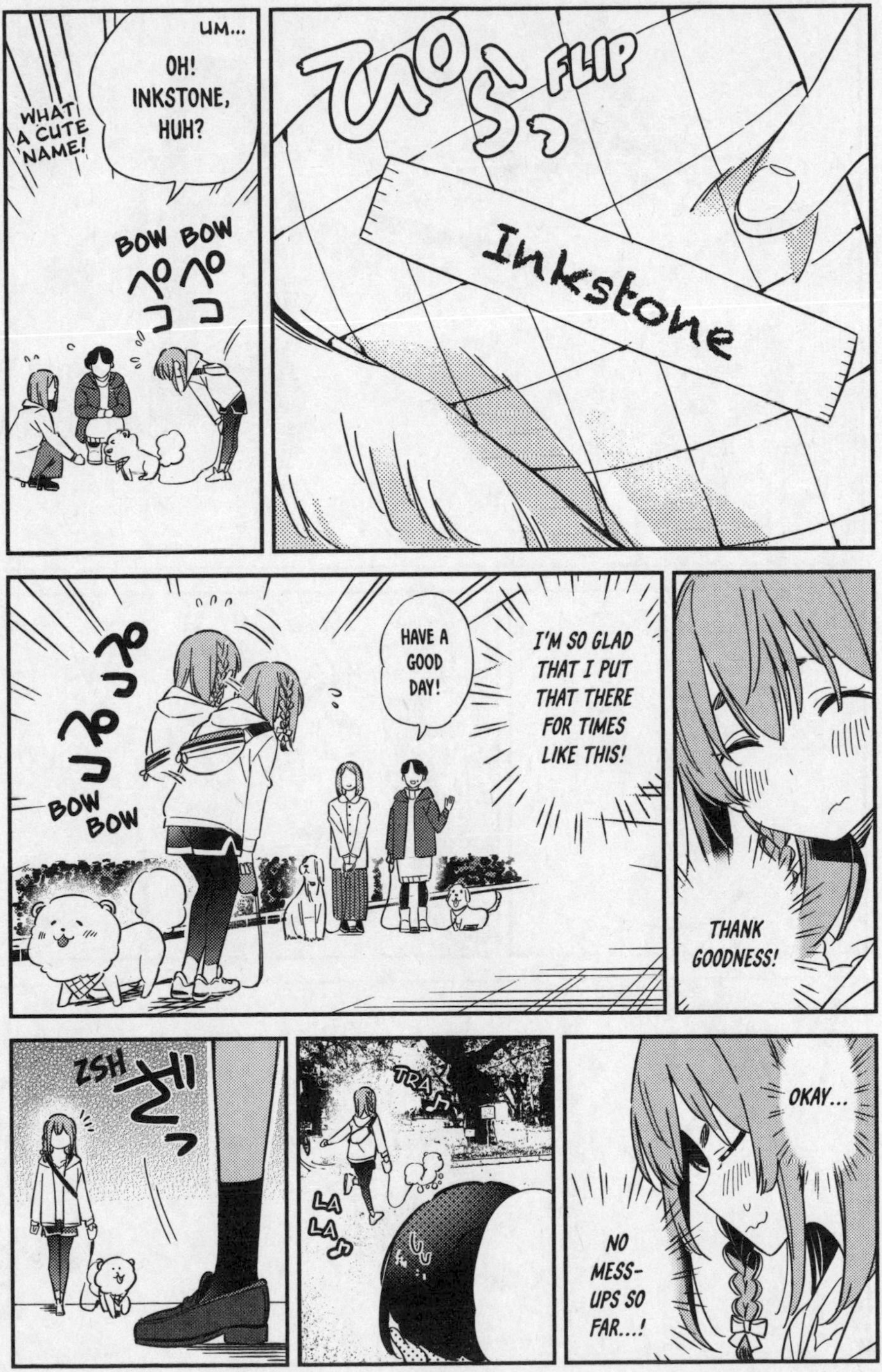
FLIP
Inkstone
UM...
OH! INKSTONE, HUH?
WHAT A CUTE NAME!
BOW BOW
THANK GOODNESS!
I'M SO GLAD THAT I PUT THAT THERE FOR TIMES LIKE THIS!
HAVE A GOOD DAY!
BOW BOW
OKAY...
NO MESS-UPS SO FAR...!
TRA
LA LA
ZSH

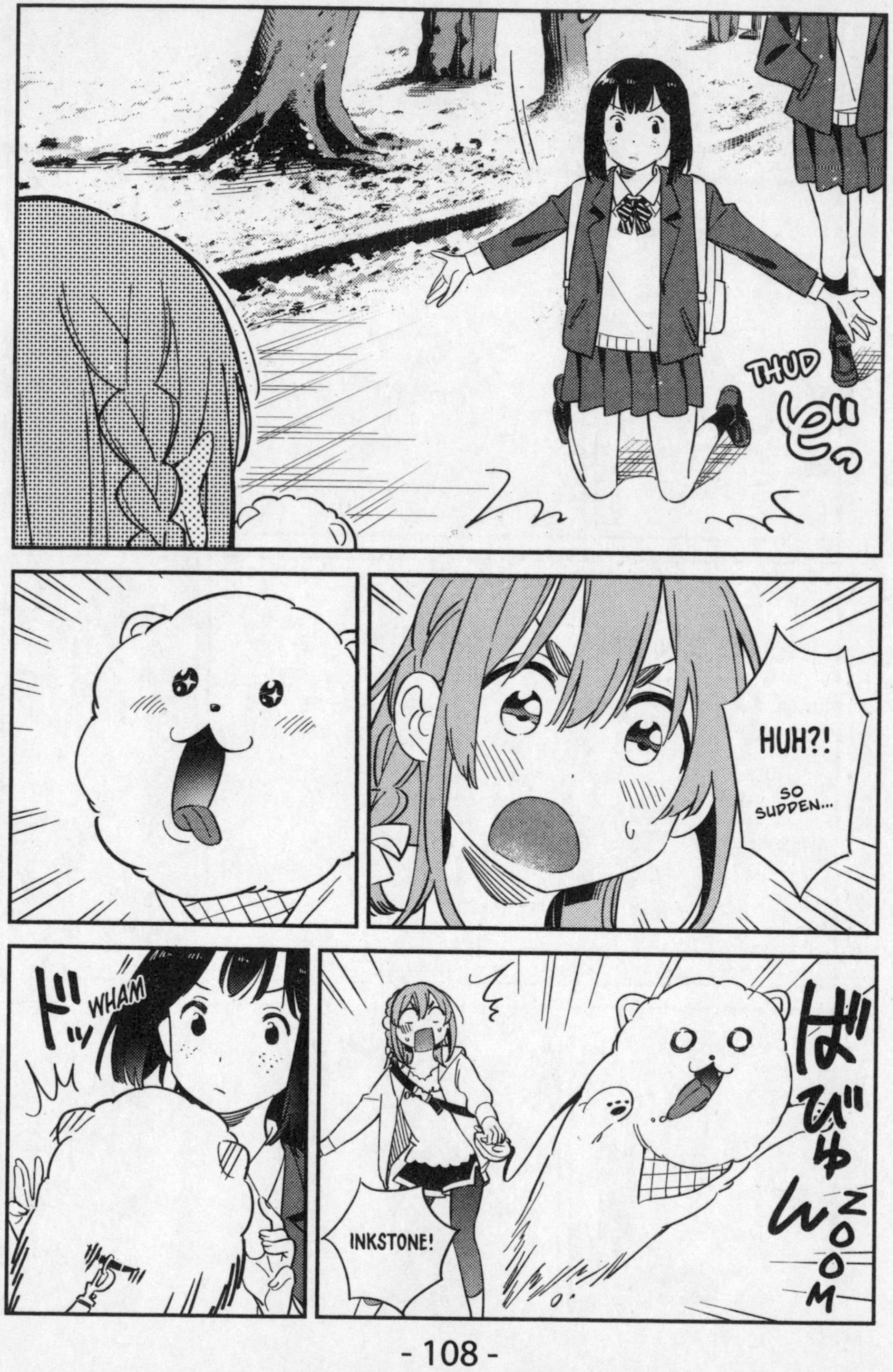
THUD
どっ
HUH?!
SO SUDDEN...
ばびゅん
ZOOM
INKSTONE!
ドッ
WHAM

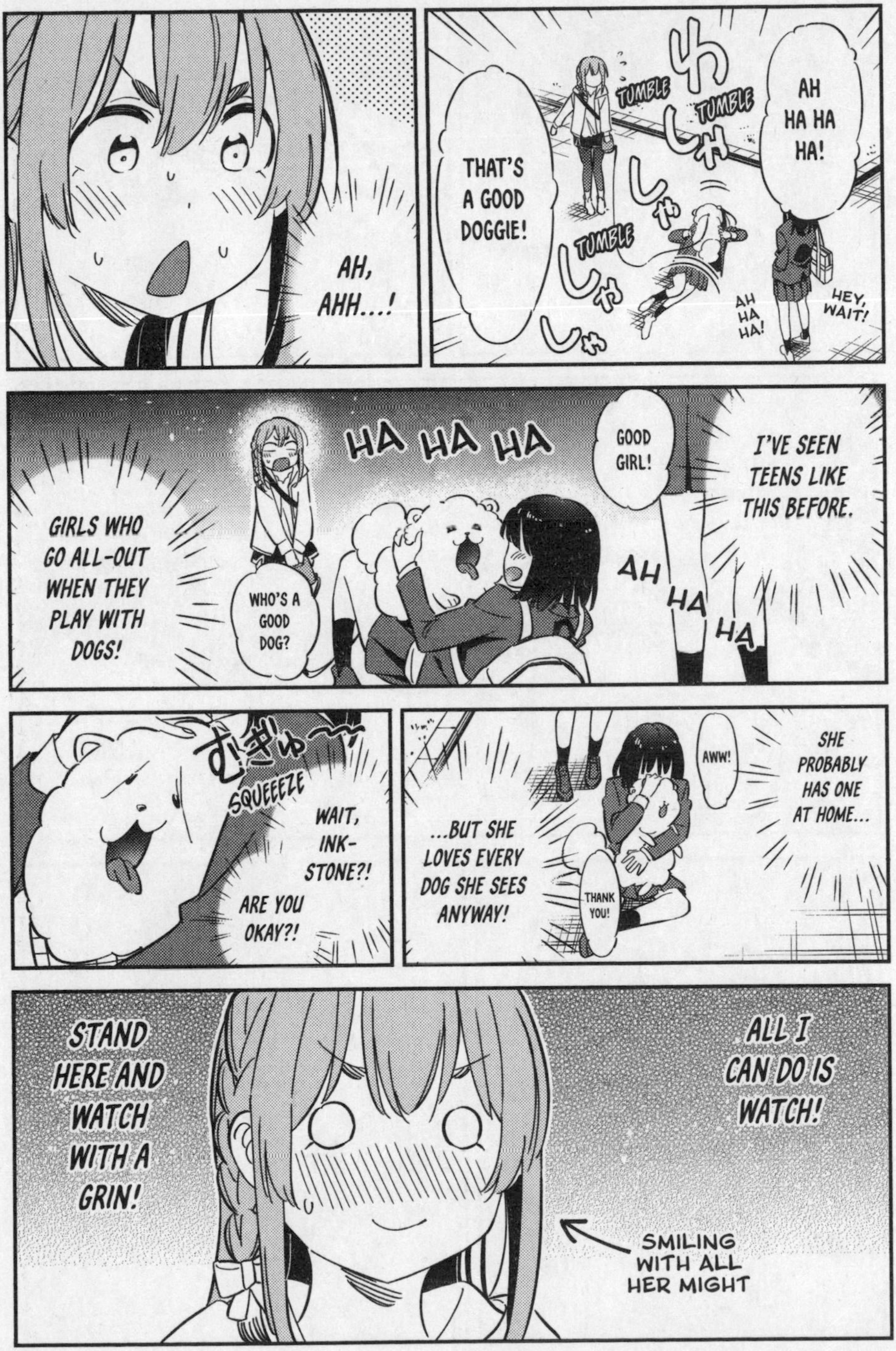
AH HA HA HA!
HEY, WAIT!
AH HA HA!
TUMBLE
TUMBLE
TUMBLE
THAT'S A GOOD DOGGIE!
AH, AHH...!
I'VE SEEN TEENS LIKE THIS BEFORE.
GOOD GIRL!
AH HA HA
HA HA HA
WHO'S A GOOD DOG?
GIRLS WHO GO ALL-OUT WHEN THEY PLAY WITH DOGS!
SHE PROBABLY HAS ONE AT HOME...
AWW!
THANK YOU!
...BUT SHE LOVES EVERY DOG SHE SEES ANYWAY!
SQUEEEZE
WAIT, INK-STONE?!
ARE YOU OKAY?!
ALL I CAN DO IS WATCH!
SMILING WITH ALL HER MIGHT
STAND HERE AND WATCH WITH A GRIN!

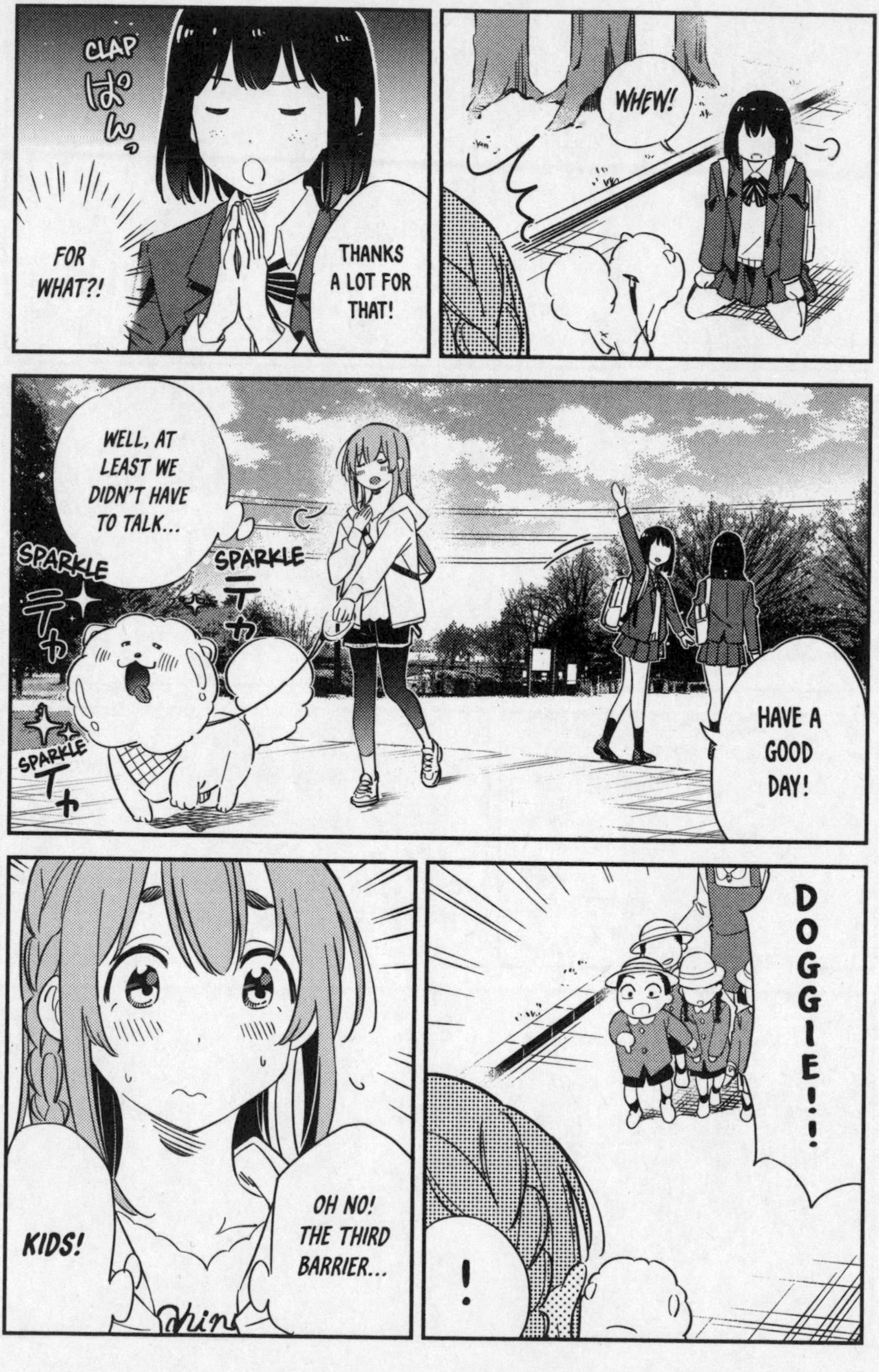
WHEW!
CLAP
ぱんっ
THANKS A LOT FOR THAT!
FOR WHAT?!
HAVE A GOOD DAY!
WELL, AT LEAST WE DIDN'T HAVE TO TALK...
SPARKLE
テカ
SPARKLE
テカ
SPARKLE
テカ
DOGGIE!!!
!
OH NO! THE THIRD BARRIER...
KIDS!

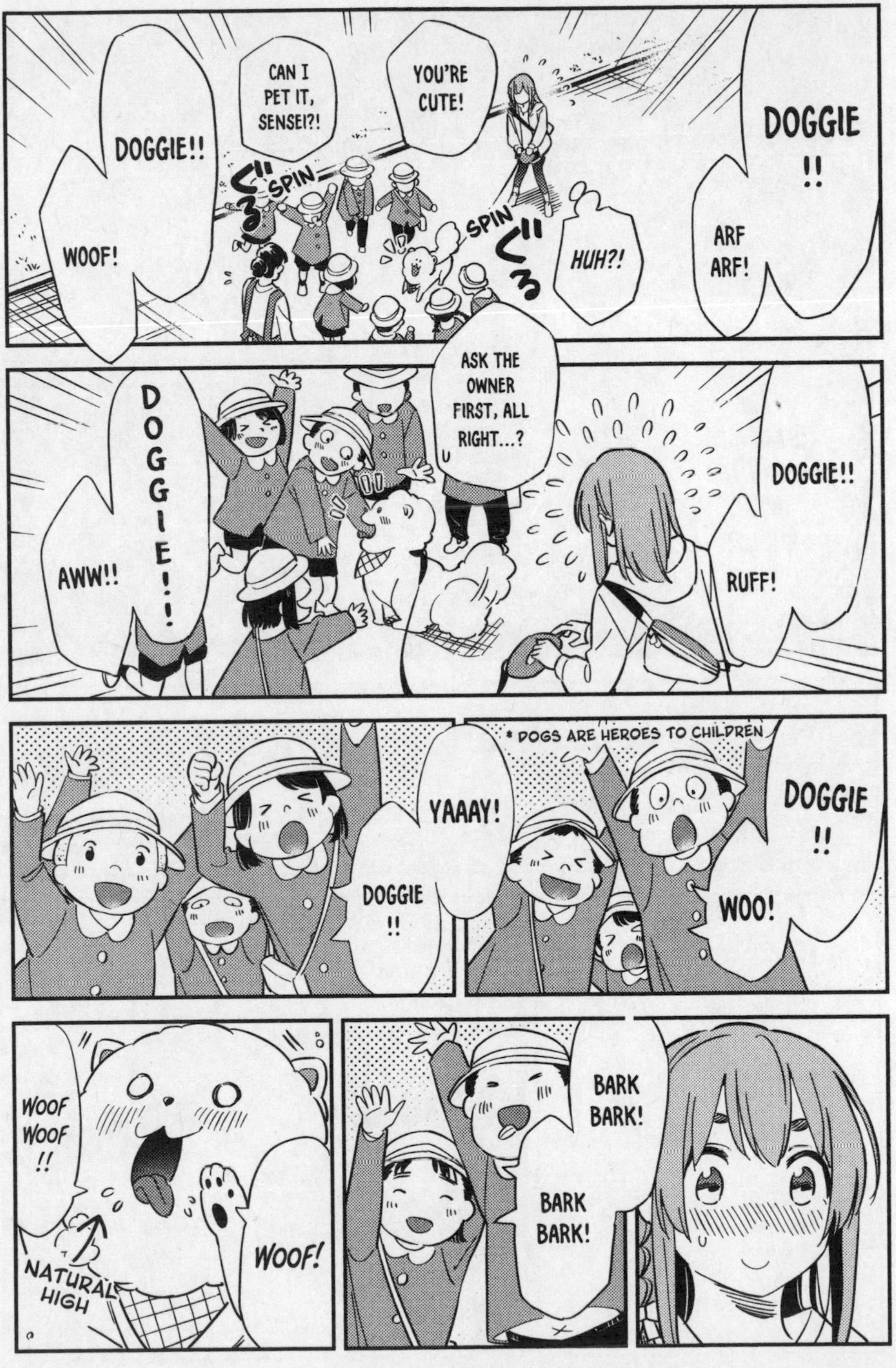
DOGGIE!!
ARF ARF!
HUH?!
SPIN
ぐる
YOU'RE CUTE!
CAN I PET IT, SENSEI?!
SPIN
ぐる
DOGGIE!!
WOOF!
DOGGIE!!
RUFF!
ASK THE OWNER FIRST, ALL RIGHT...?
DOGGIE!!!
AWW!!
* DOGS ARE HEROES TO CHILDREN
DOGGIE!!
WOO!
YAAAY!
DOGGIE!!
BARK BARK!
BARK BARK!
WOOF WOOF!!
WOOF!
NATURAL HIGH

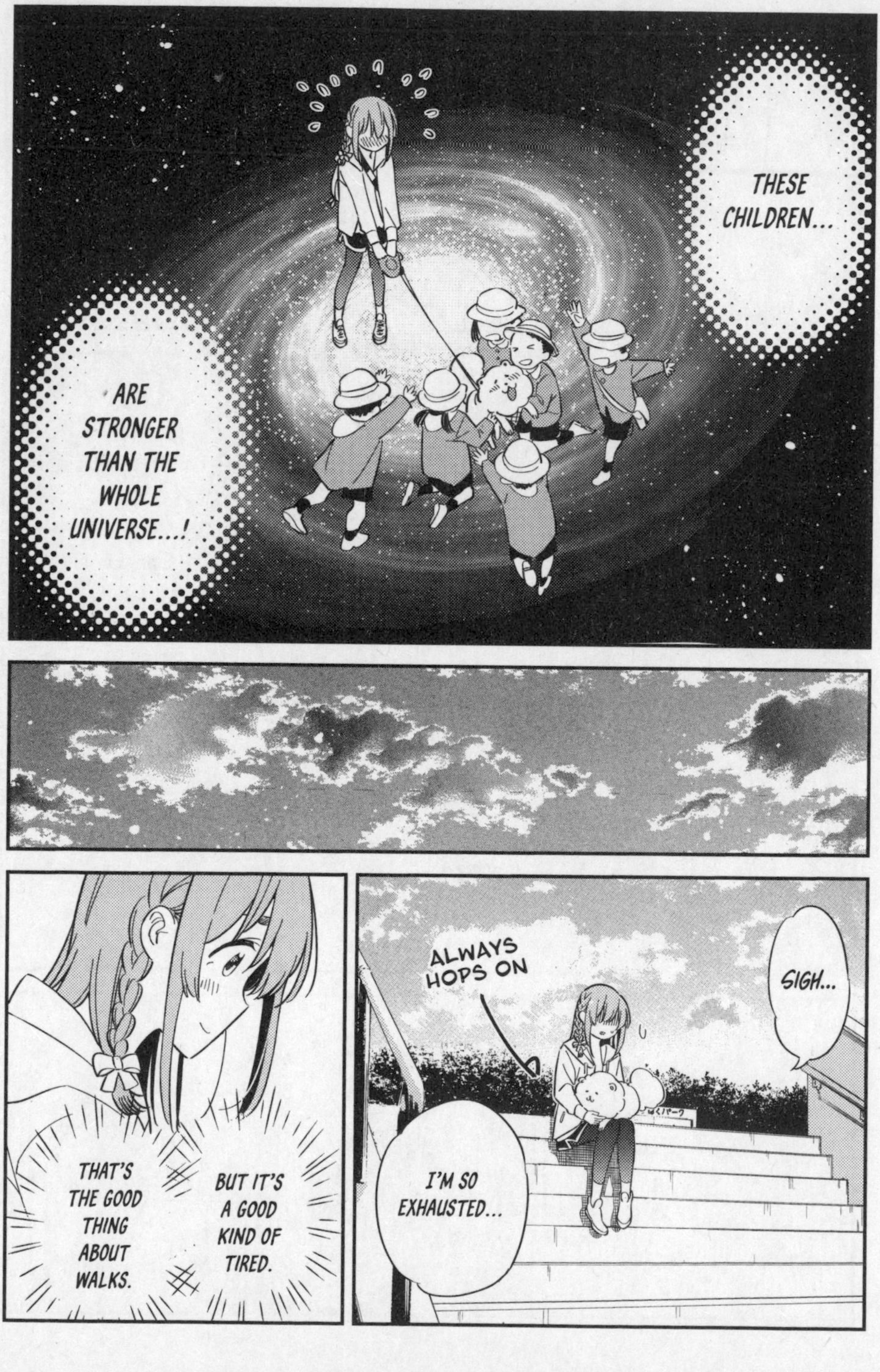
THESE CHILDREN...
ARE STRONGER THAN THE WHOLE UNIVERSE...!
SIGH...
ALWAYS HOPS ON
I'M SO EXHAUSTED...
BUT IT'S A GOOD KIND OF TIRED.
THAT'S THE GOOD THING ABOUT WALKS.

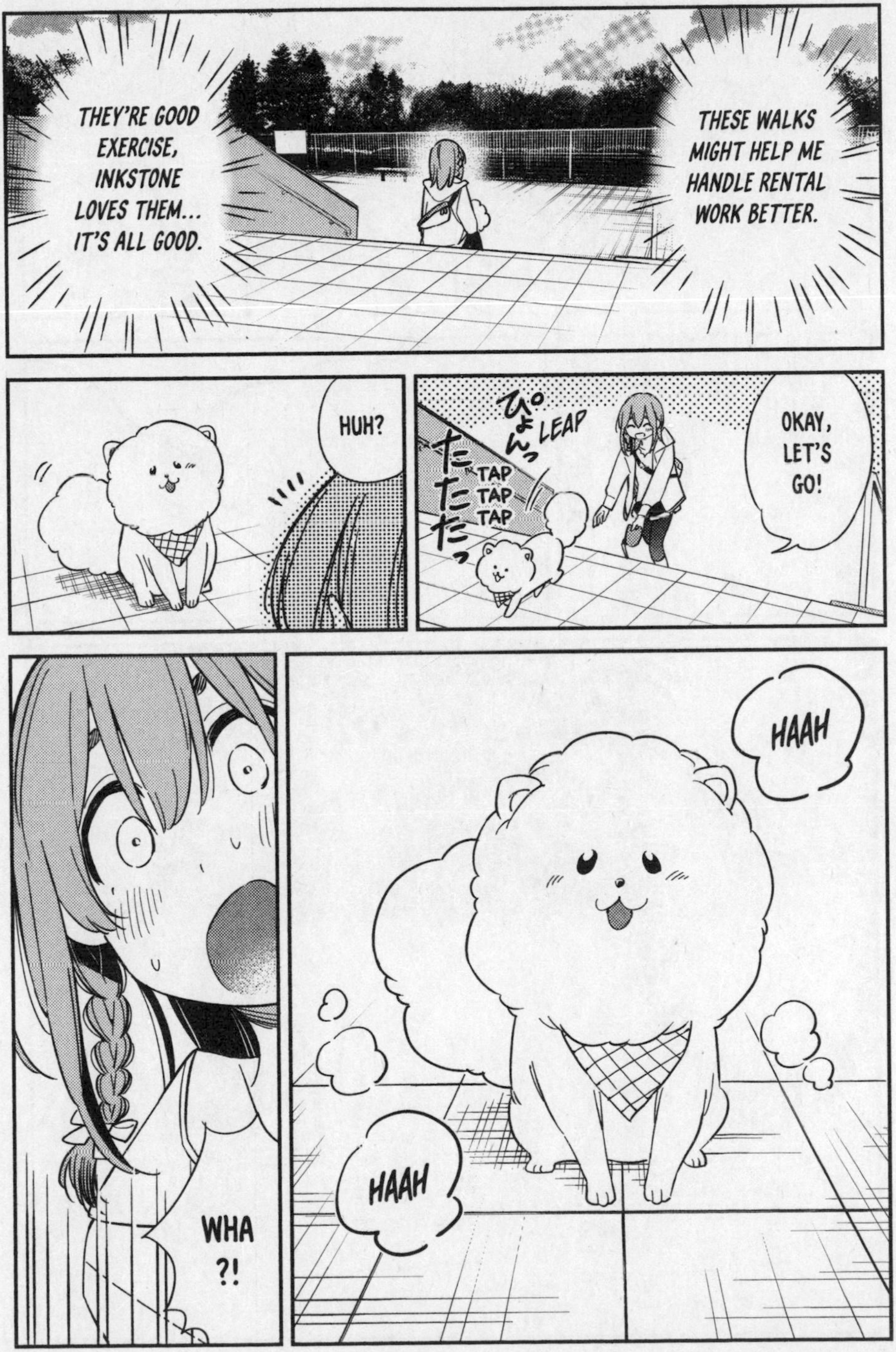
THESE WALKS MIGHT HELP ME HANDLE RENTAL WORK BETTER.
THEY'RE GOOD EXERCISE, INKSTONE LOVES THEM... IT'S ALL GOOD.
OKAY, LET'S GO!
ぴょんっ LEAP
たたたっ TAP TAP TAP
HUH?
HAAH
HAAH
WHA ?!

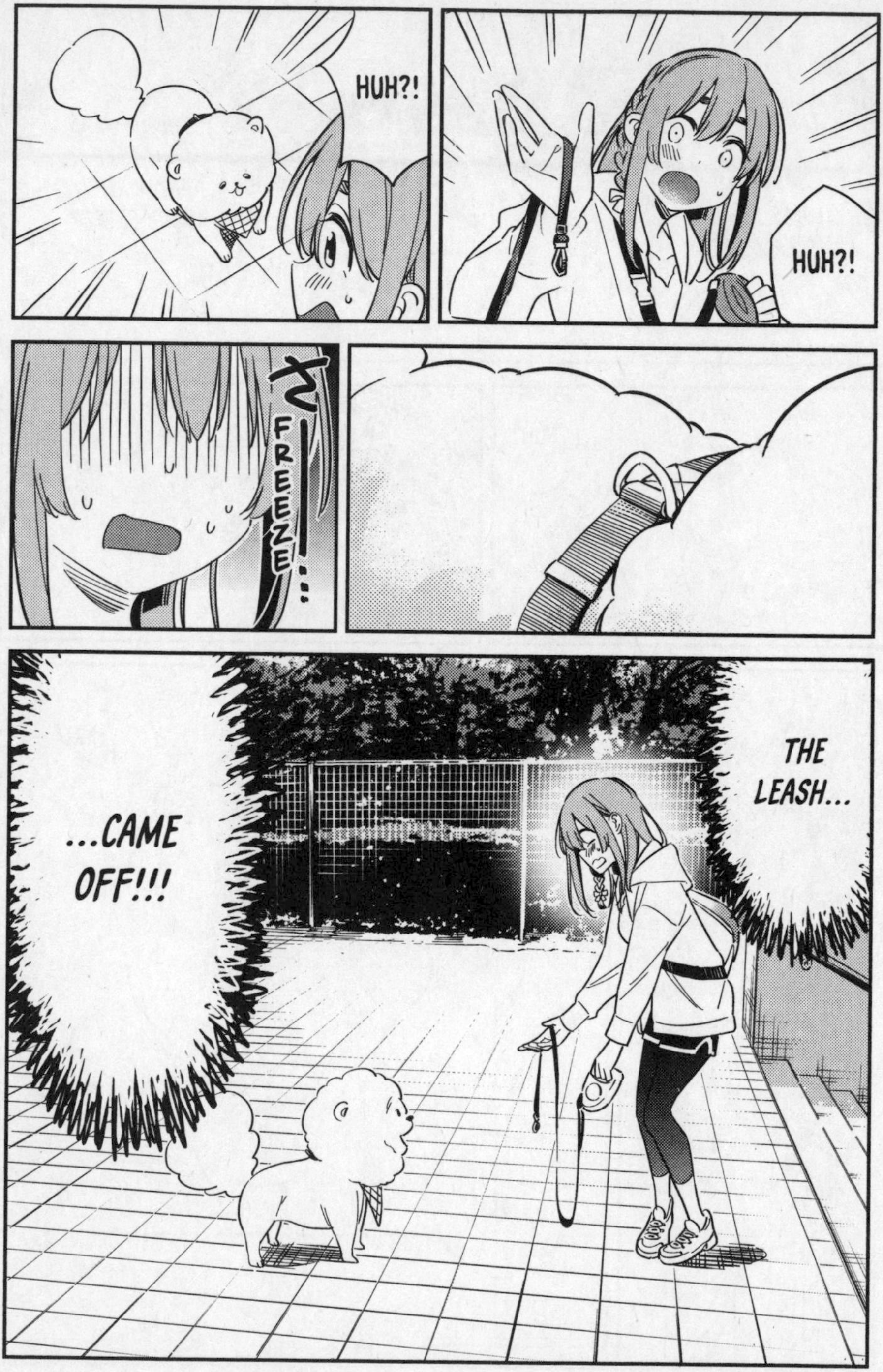
HUH?!
HUH?!
さ
FREEZE...
THE LEASH...
...CAME OFF!!!

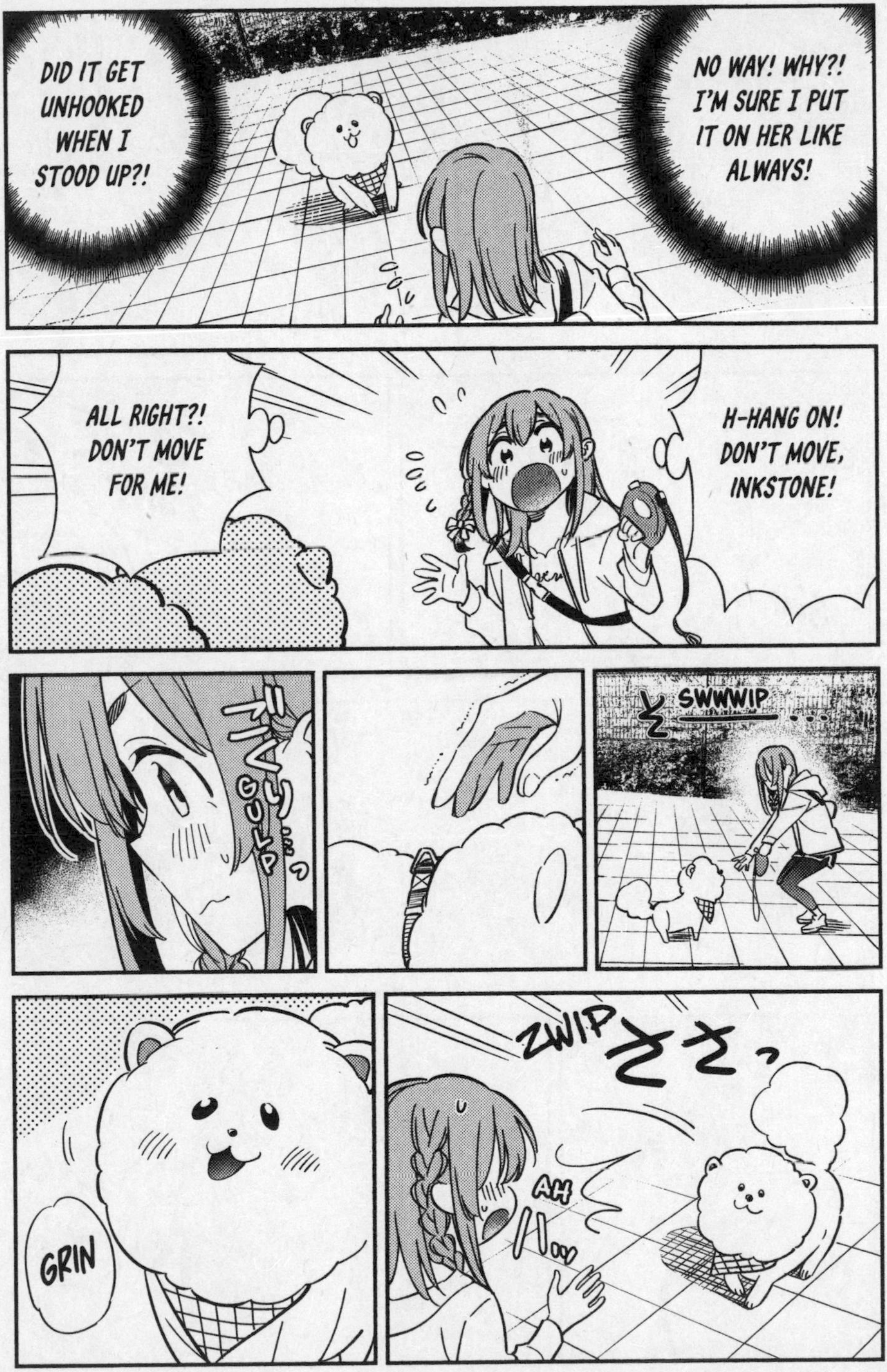
NO WAY! WHY?! I'M SURE I PUT IT ON HER LIKE ALWAYS!
DID IT GET UNHOOKED WHEN I STOOD UP?!
H-HANG ON! DON'T MOVE, INKSTONE!
ALL RIGHT?! DON'T MOVE FOR ME!
SWWWIP
GULP
ZWIP
AH
GRIN

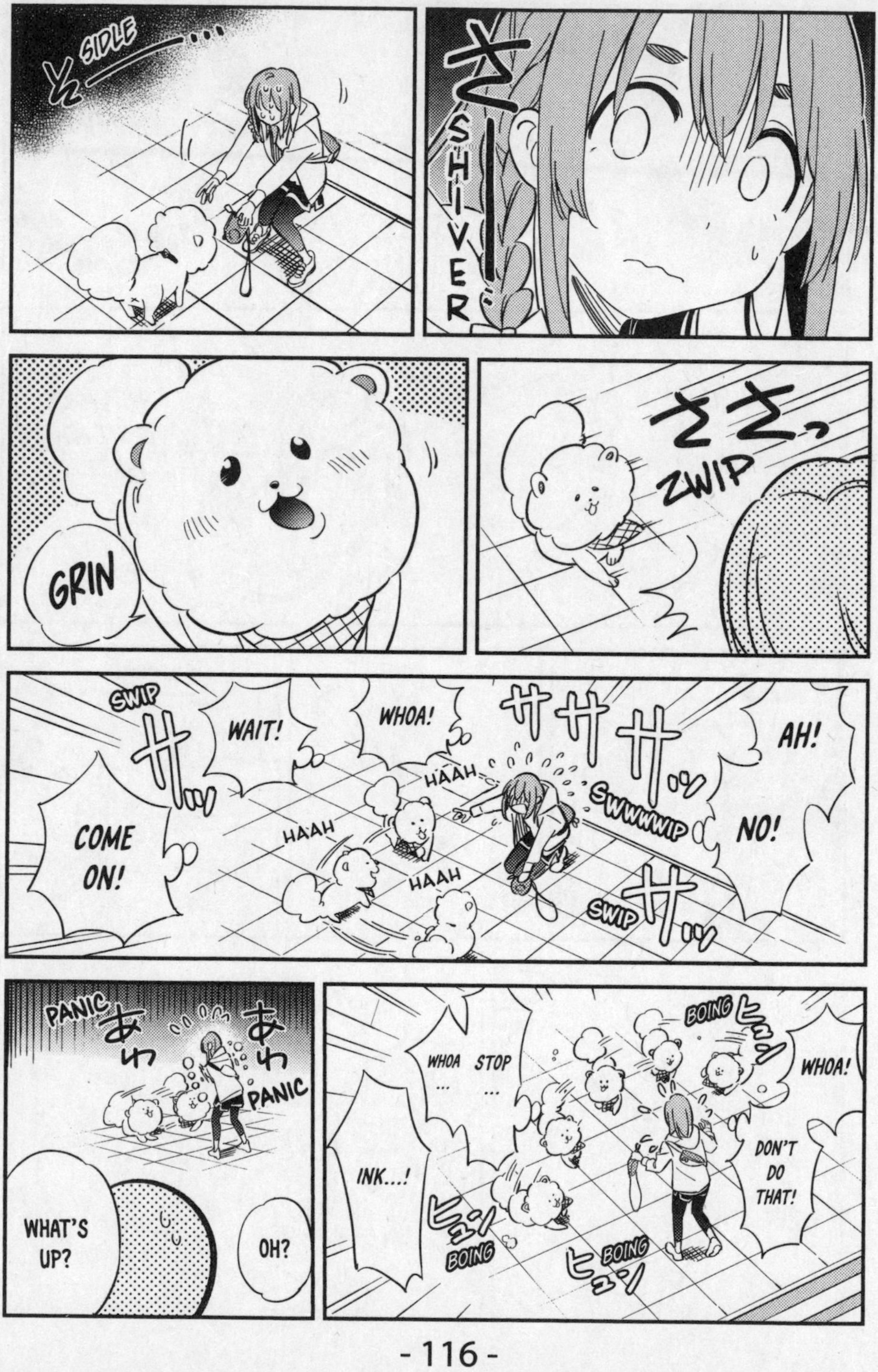
さ
SHIVER
SIDLE
そ
ささっ
ZWIP
GRIN
AH!
サササッ
NO!
SWWWWIP
SWIP
サッ
HAAH
WHOA!
WAIT!
SWIP
サッ
HAAH
HAAH
COME ON!
BOING
ヒュン
WHOA!
WHOA STOP ... ...
DON'T DO THAT!
INK...!
ヒュン
BOING
ヒュン
BOING
あわ あわ
PANIC
PANIC
OH?
WHAT'S UP?

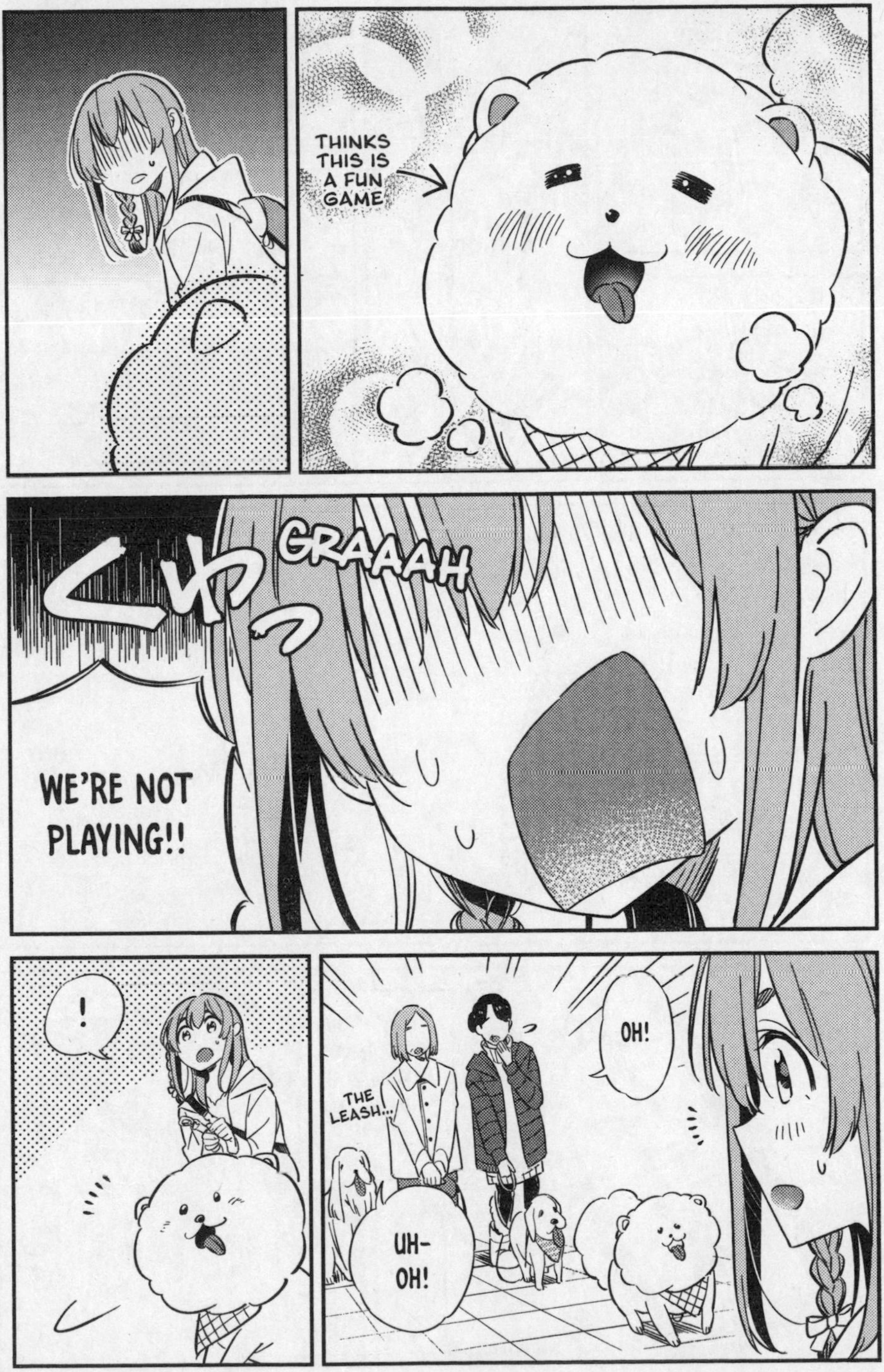
THINKS THIS IS A FUN GAME
GRAAAH
WE'RE NOT PLAYING!!
OH!
THE LEASH...
UH-OH!
!

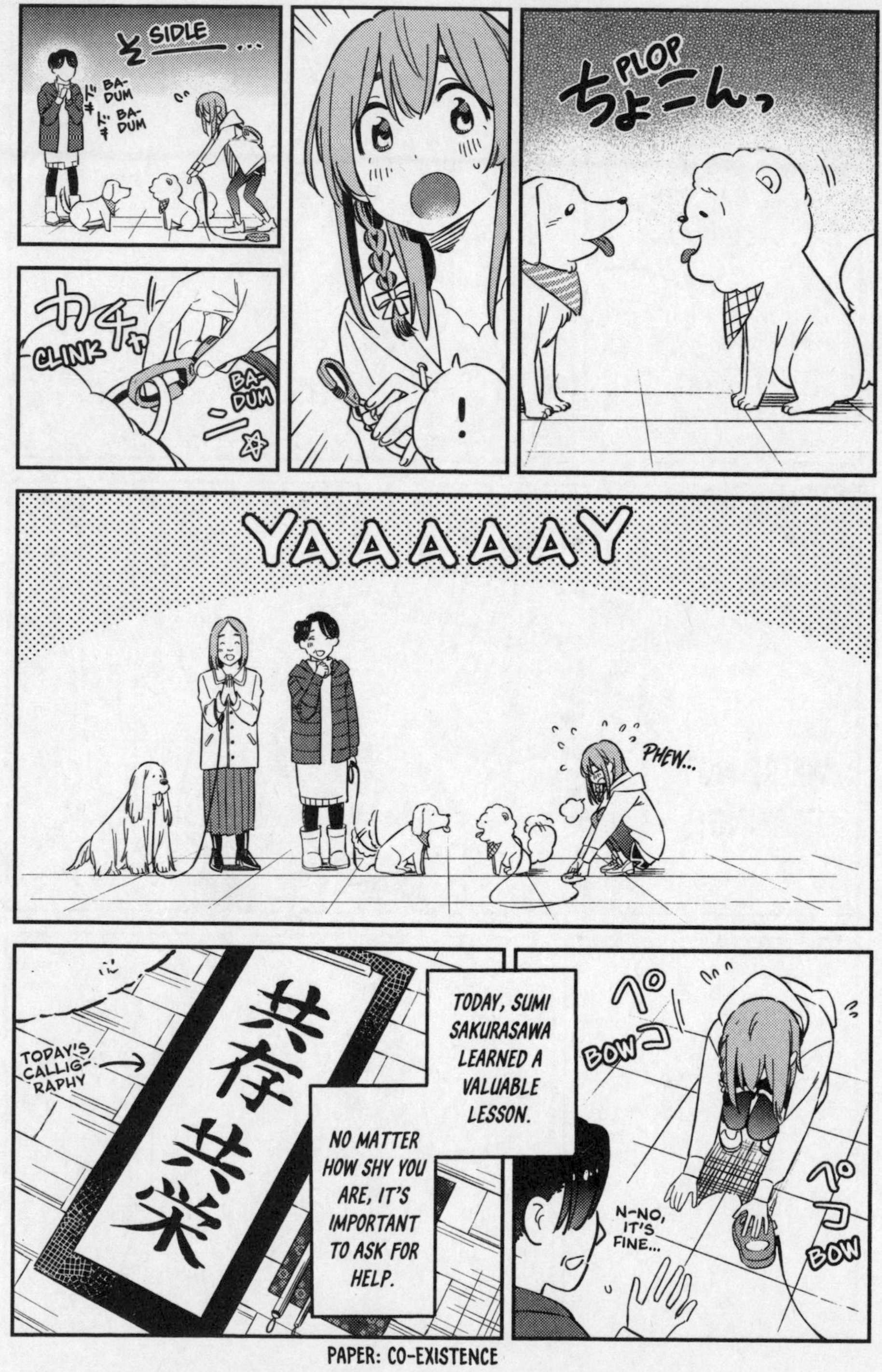
ちょこんっ
PLOP
!
と SIDLE...
ドキ BA-DUM
ドキ BA-DUM
カチャ
CLINK
BA-DUM
YAAAAAY
PHEW...
ペコ
BOW
ペコ
BOW
N-NO, IT'S FINE...
TODAY'S CALLIGRAPHY
共存共栄
TODAY, SUMI SAKURASAWA LEARNED A VALUABLE LESSON.
NO MATTER HOW SHY YOU ARE, IT'S IMPORTANT TO ASK FOR HELP.

PAPER: CO-EXISTENCE

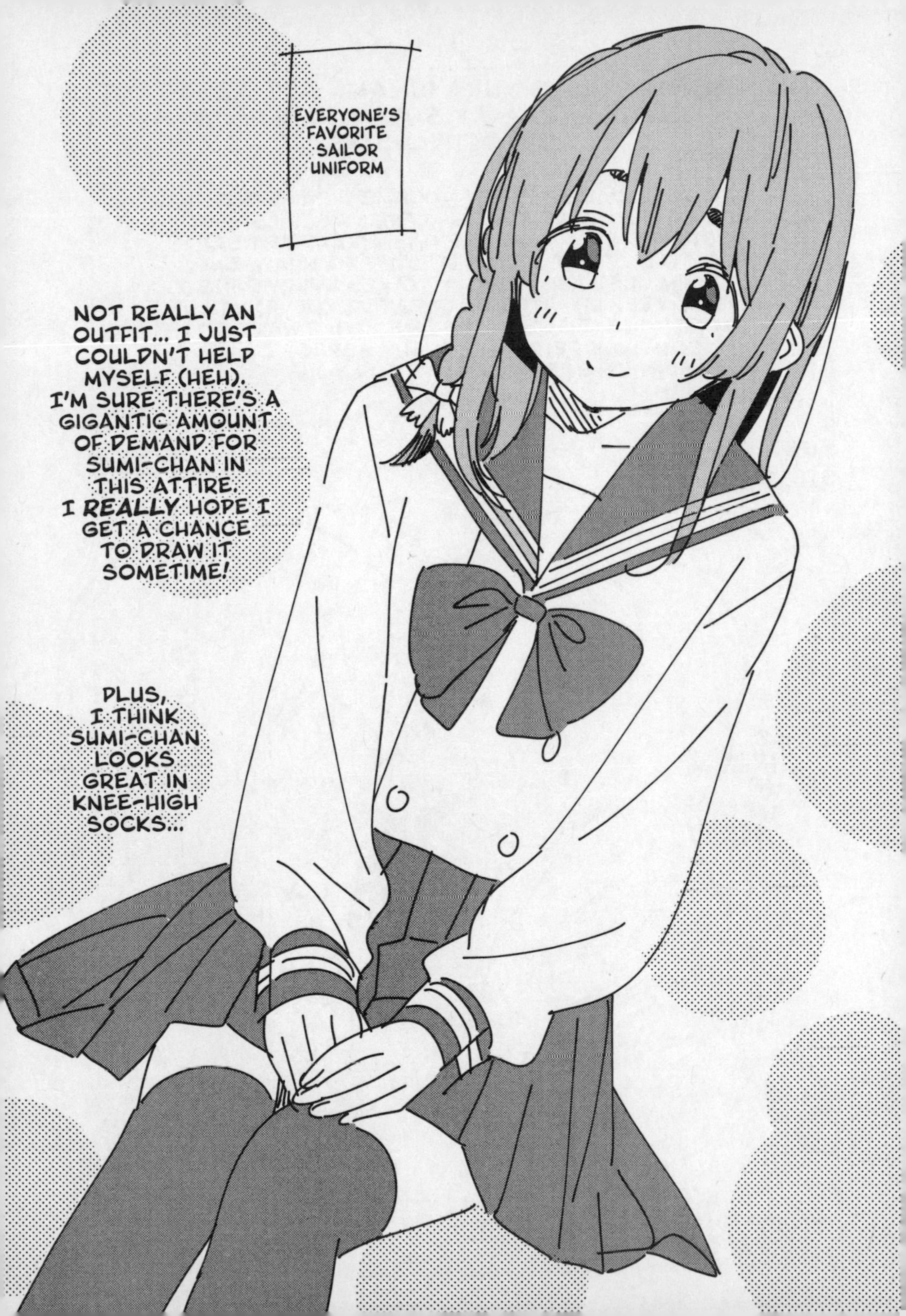
EVERYONE'S FAVORITE SAILOR UNIFORM
NOT REALLY AN OUTFIT... I JUST COULDN'T HELP MYSELF (HEH). I'M SURE THERE'S A GIGANTIC AMOUNT OF DEMAND FOR SUMI-CHAN IN THIS ATTIRE. I *REALLY* HOPE I GET A CHANCE TO DRAW IT SOMETIME!
PLUS, I THINK SUMI-CHAN LOOKS GREAT IN KNEE-HIGH SOCKS...

ONCE AGAIN, THIS IS YUKA KINAMI, ART ASSISTANT ON *RENT-A-(REALLY SHY!)-GIRLFRIEND!* (@KOTUPONN55)

I'M REALLY HAPPY THAT VOLUME 2 CAME OUT! THE ART ON THE *RENT-A-GIRLFRIEND* SERIES IS SO GOOD! IT'S CHARMING AND HAS A REAL ARTISAN FEEL TO IT... THAT MAKES IT HARD TO DRAW, AND WHILE I'M JUST ASSISTING, IT TAKES EVERYTHING I HAVE TO KEEP UP WITH THE CREATOR! (HEHE) STILL, I'M GETTING THROUGH IT SOMEHOW. I WANT TO CONTINUE DEPICTING EVERY ASPECT OF SUMI-CHAN'S CRAZY LIFE FOR YOU! ^^

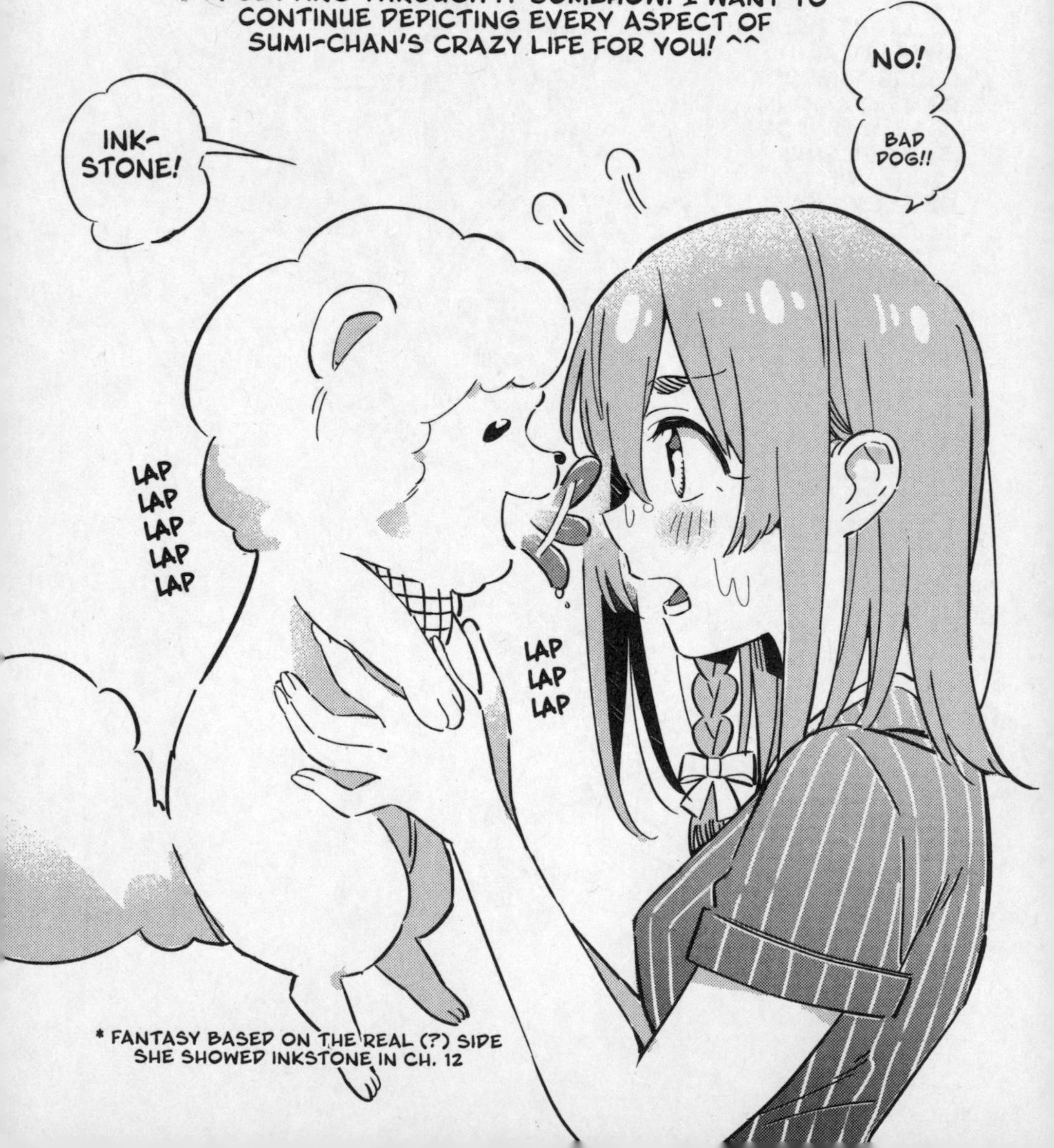
NO!
BAD DOG!!
INK-STONE!
LAP LAP LAP LAP LAP
LAP LAP LAP

* FANTASY BASED ON THE REAL (?) SIDE SHE SHOWED INKSTONE IN CH. 12

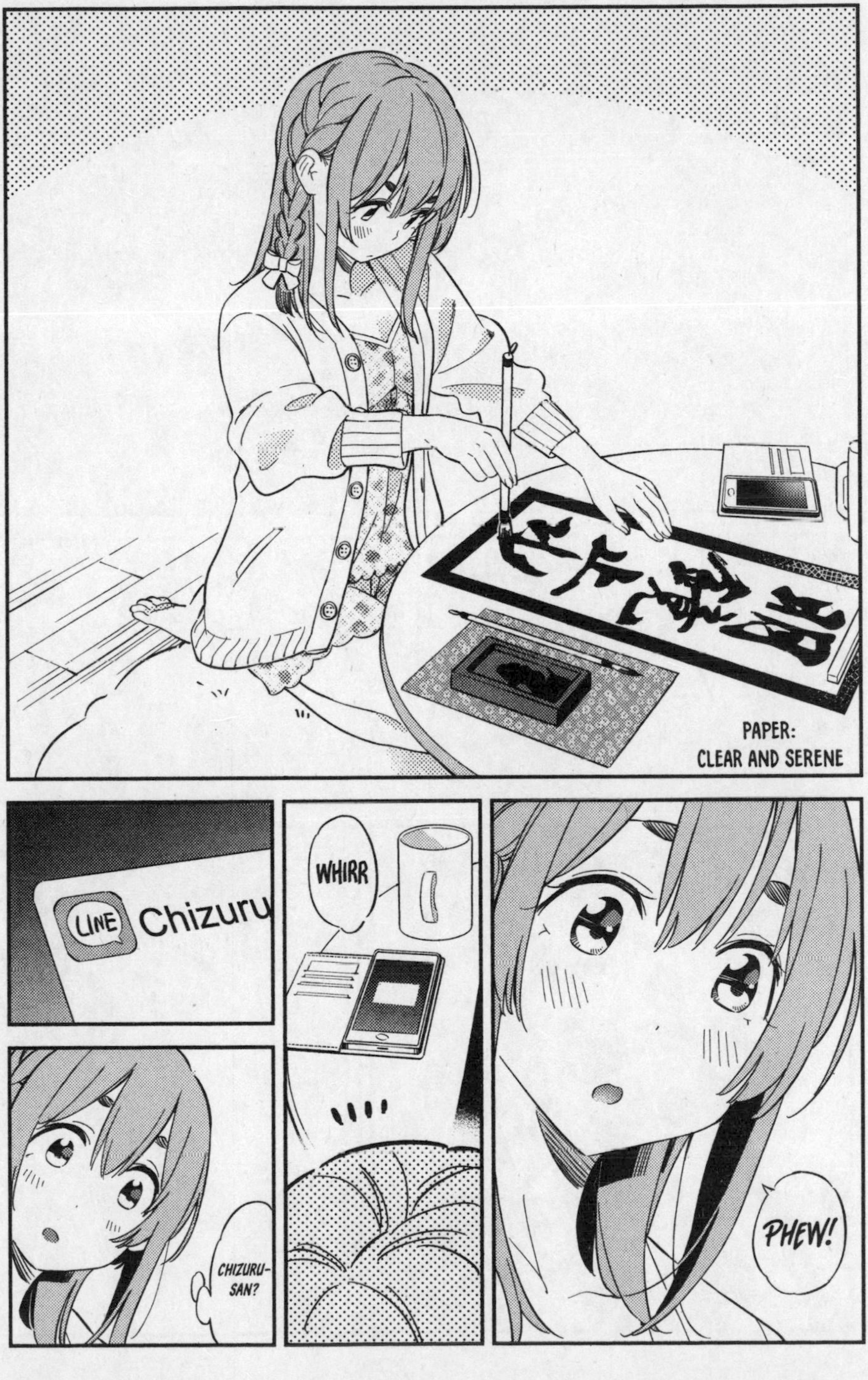
PAPER:
CLEAR AND SERENE
PHEW!
WHIRR
LINE Chizuru
CHIZURU-SAN?

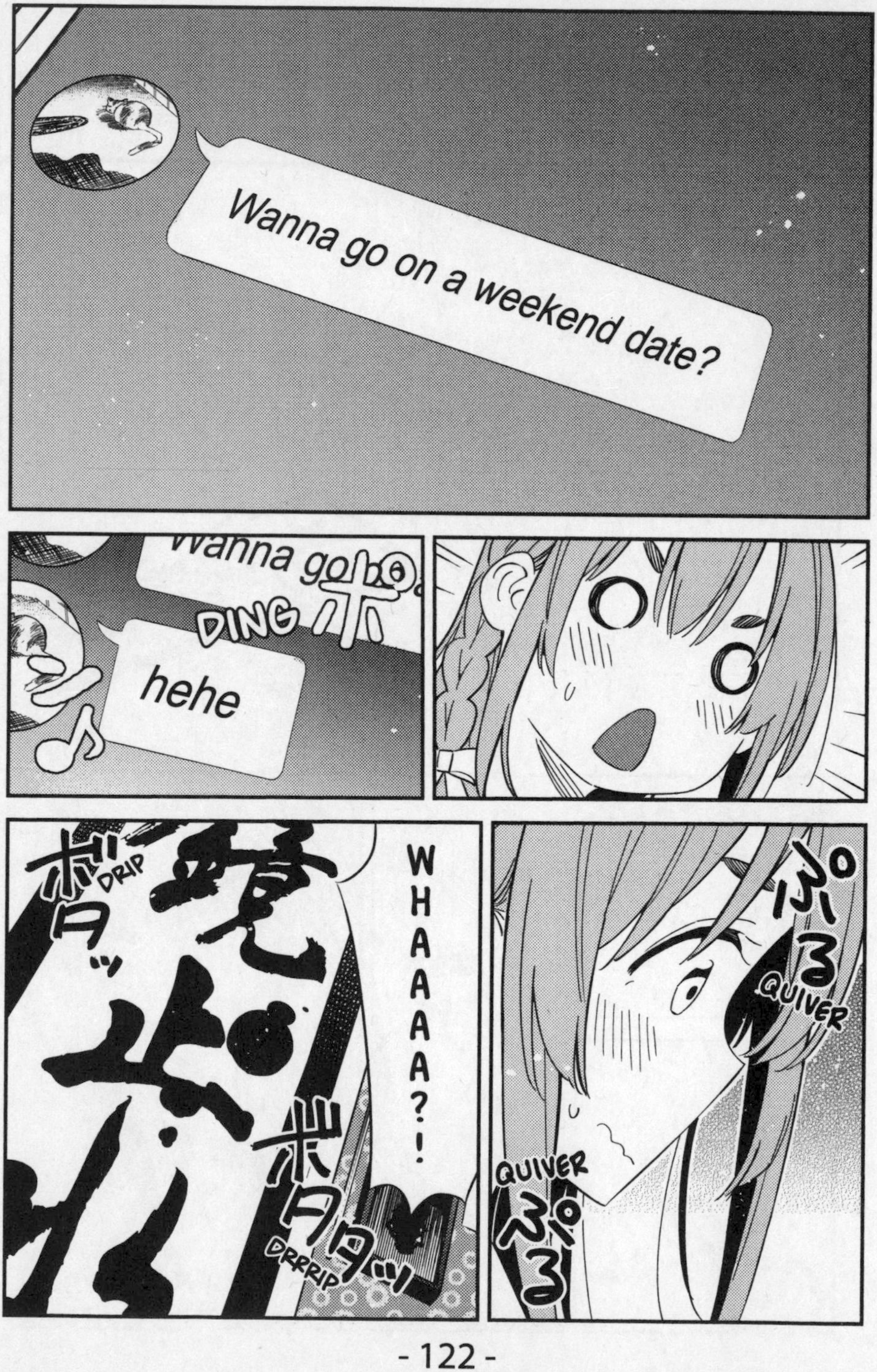
Wanna go on a weekend date?
DING
ホ
hehe
ぷるぷる
QUIVER
QUIVER
ぷるぷる
WHAAAAA?!
ポタッ
DRIP
ボタタッ
DRRRIP

RATING 13 SUMI AND THE BOYFRIEND

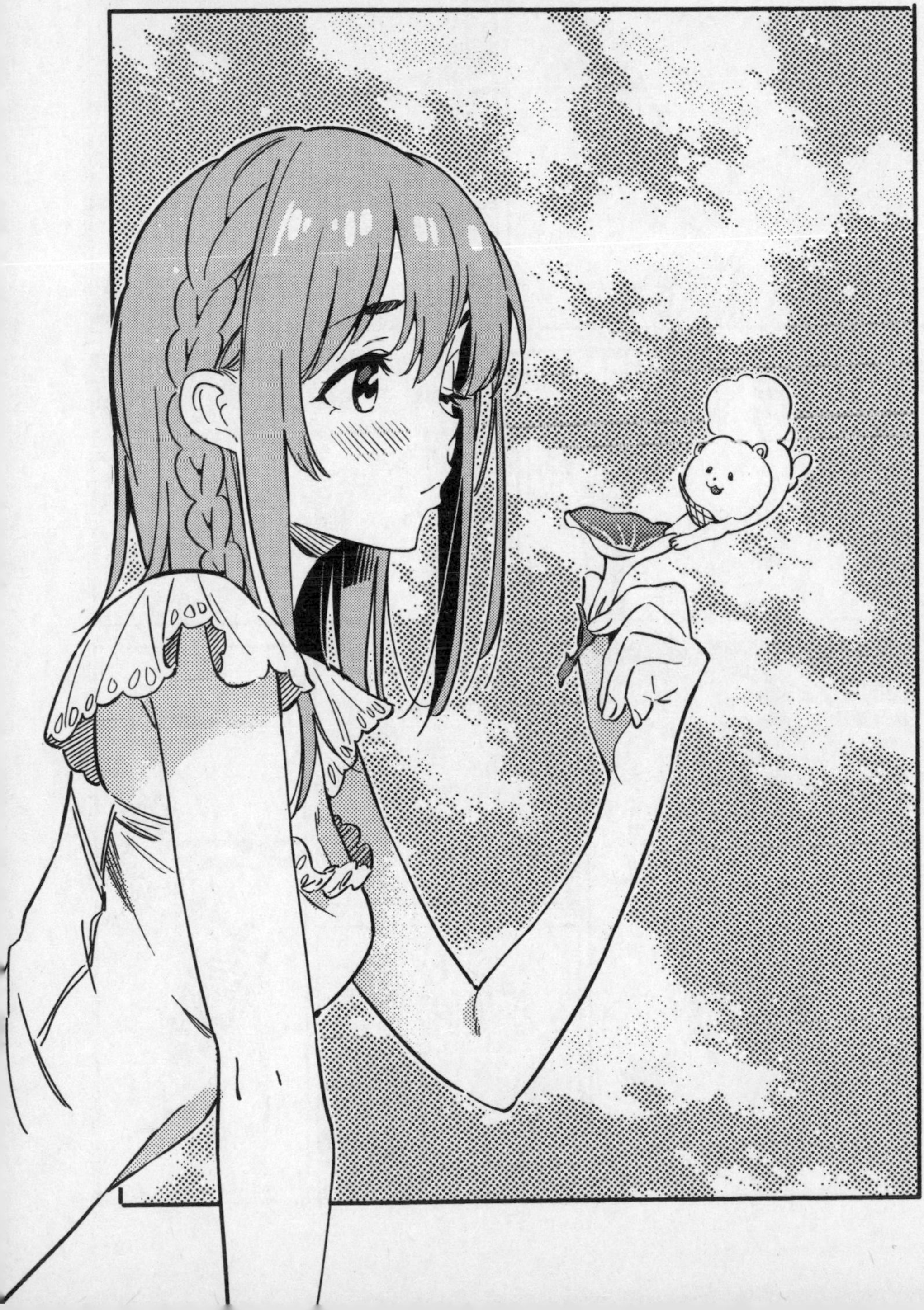

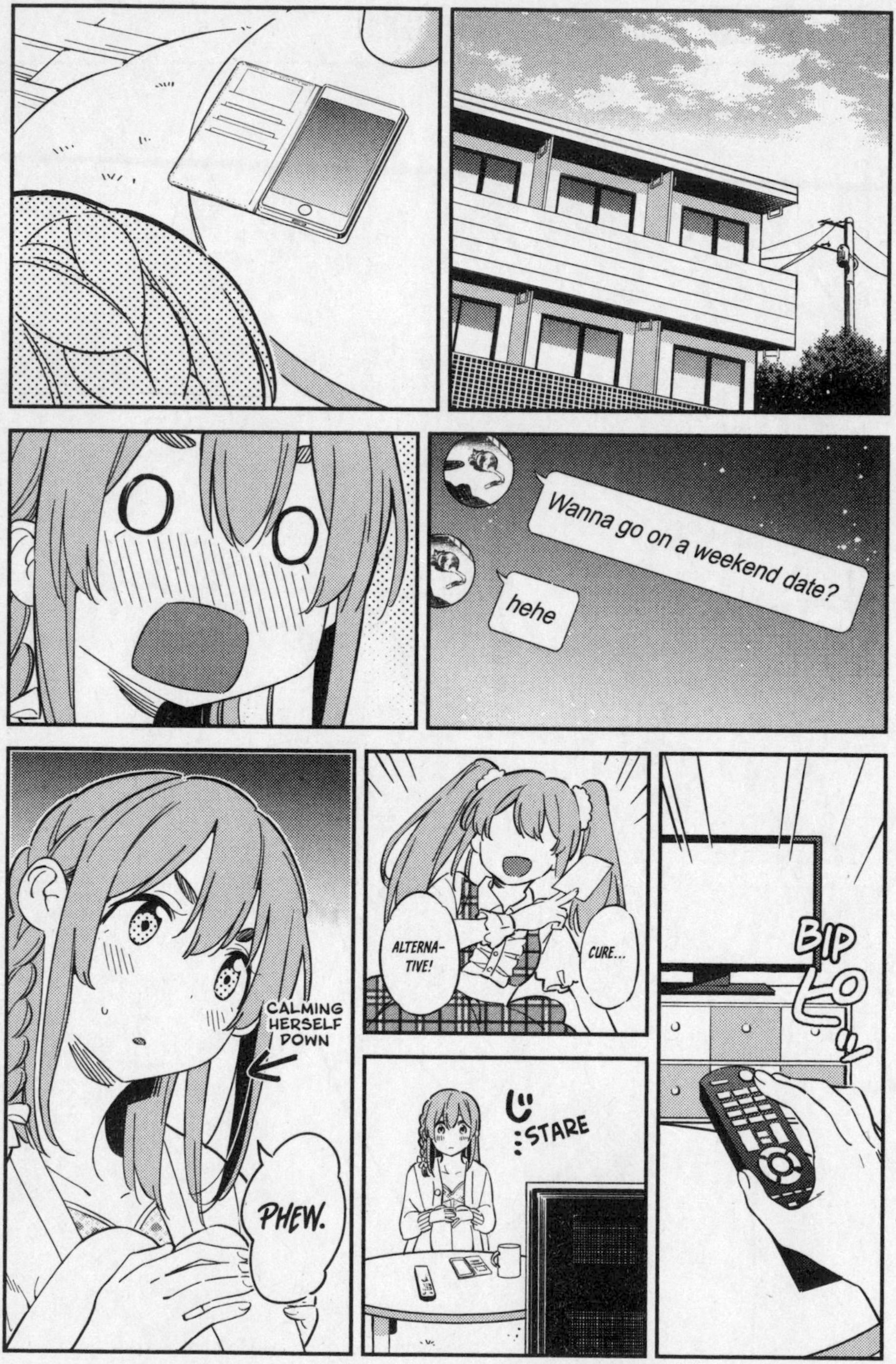
Wanna go on a weekend date?
hehe
BIP
ピッ
CURE...
ALTERNA-TIVE!
じ
STARE
CALMING HERSELF DOWN
PHEW.

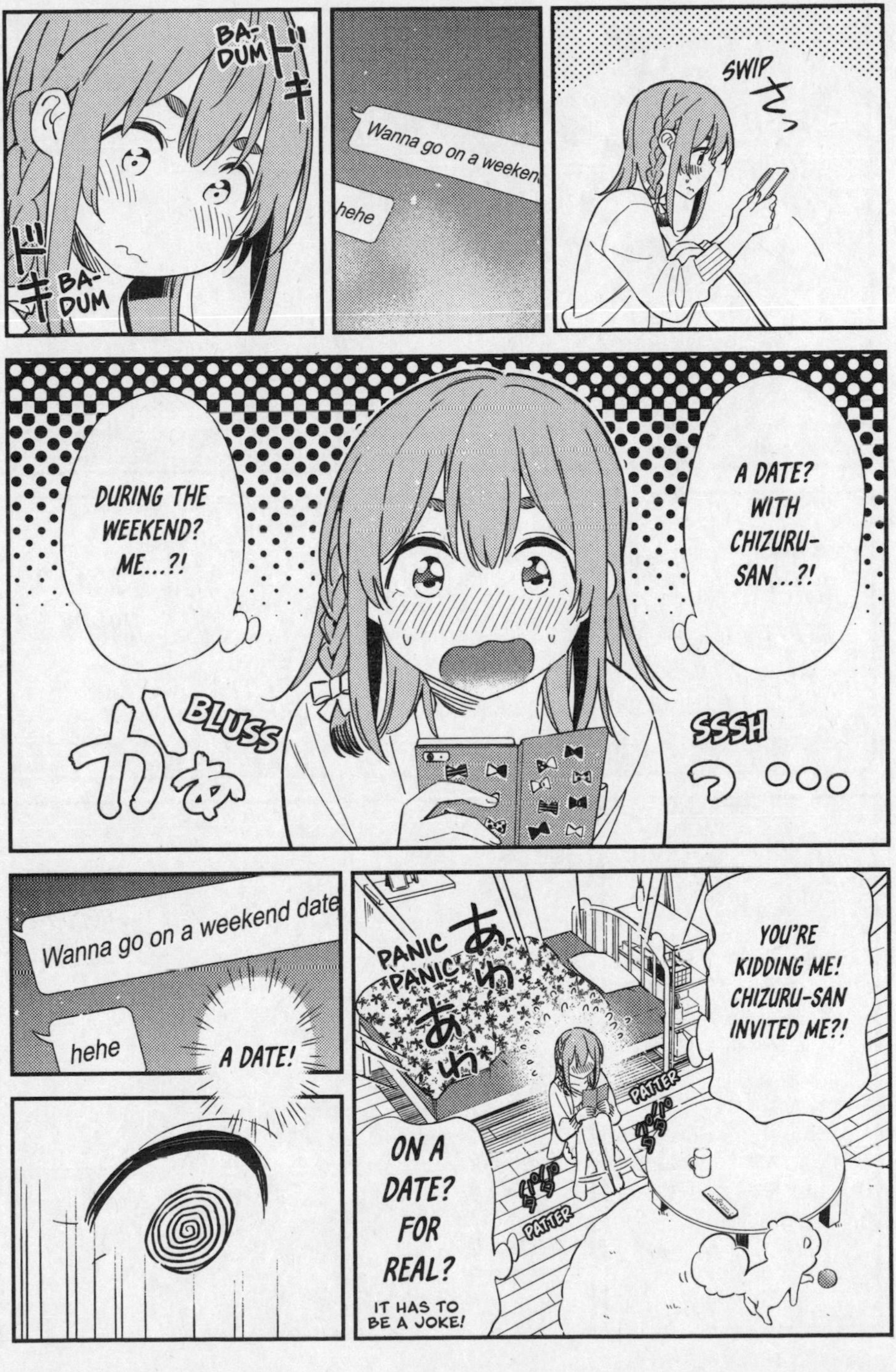
SWIP
さっ
Wanna go on a weekend
hehe
BA-DUM
ドキ
ドキ
BA-DUM
A DATE? WITH CHIZURU-SAN...?!
DURING THE WEEKEND? ME...?!
SSSH
っ...
BLUSS
かぁ
YOU'RE KIDDING ME! CHIZURU-SAN INVITED ME?!
PANIC PANIC
あわあわ
PATTER
ON A DATE? FOR REAL?
IT HAS TO BE A JOKE!
PATTER
Wanna go on a weekend date
hehe
A DATE!

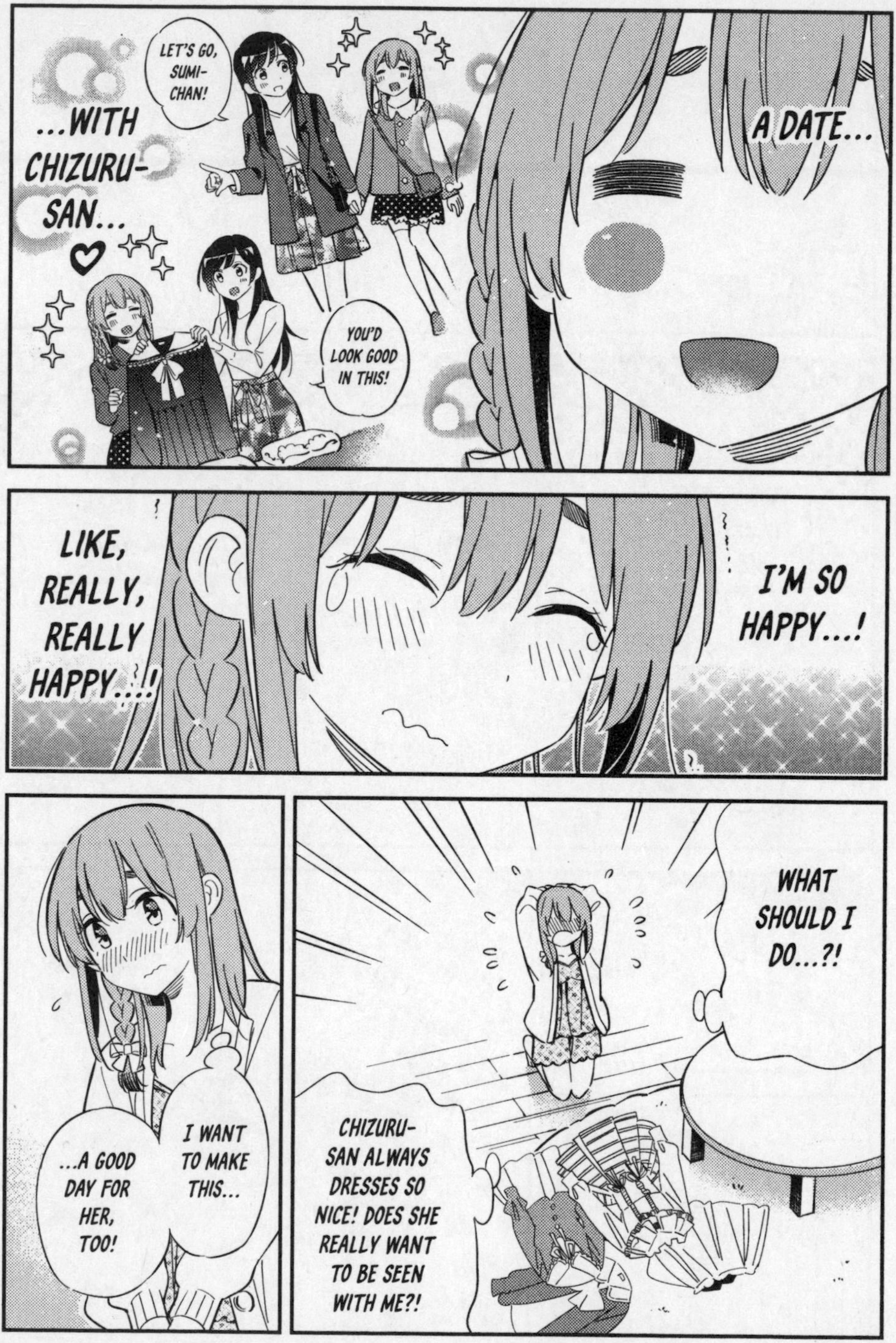
A DATE...
LET'S GO, SUMI-CHAN!
...WITH CHIZURU-SAN... ♡
YOU'D LOOK GOOD IN THIS!
I'M SO HAPPY...!
LIKE, REALLY, REALLY HAPPY...!
WHAT SHOULD I DO...?!
CHIZURU-SAN ALWAYS DRESSES SO NICE! DOES SHE REALLY WANT TO BE SEEN WITH ME?!
I WANT TO MAKE THIS...
...A GOOD DAY FOR HER, TOO!

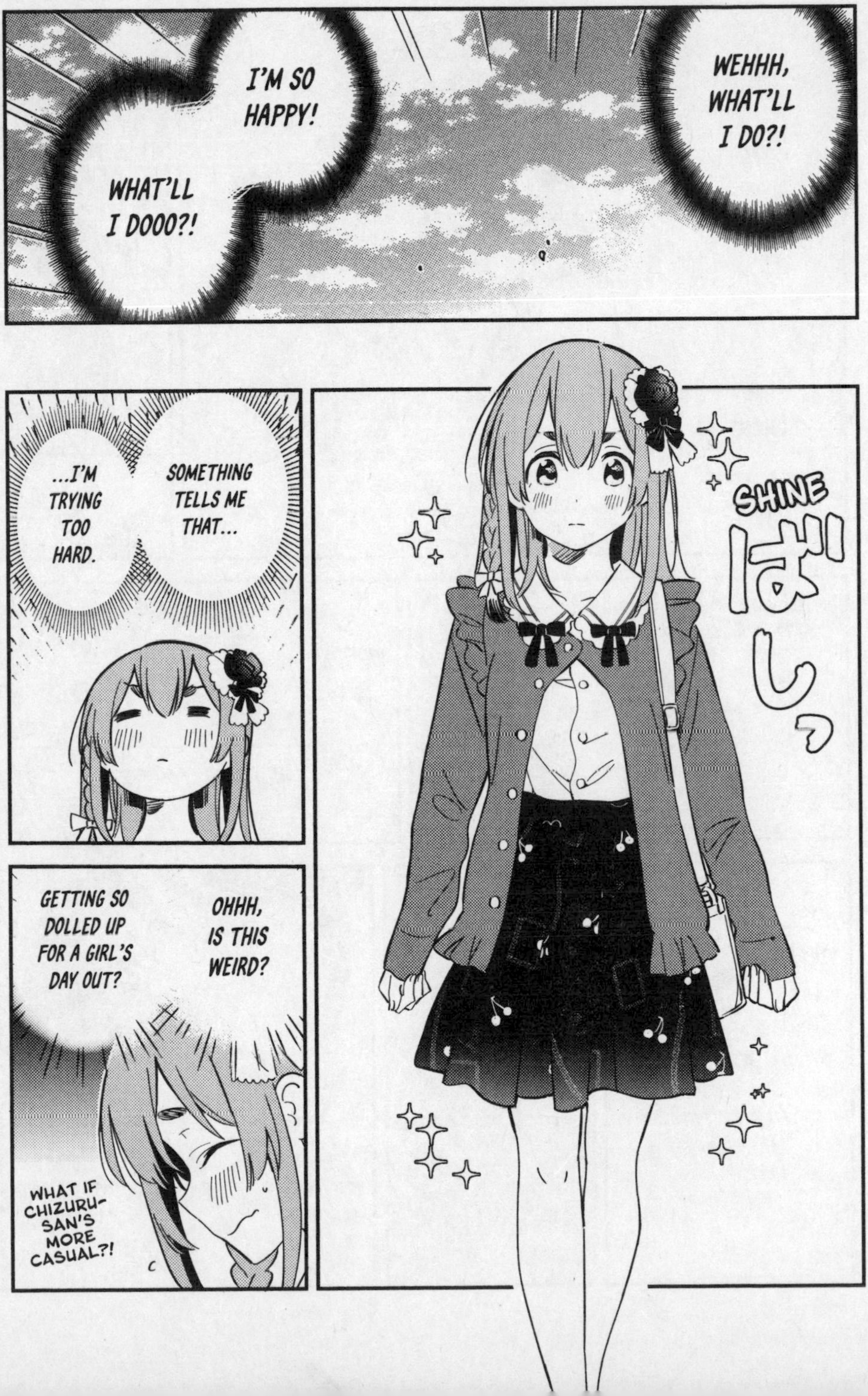
WEHHH, WHAT'LL I DO?!
I'M SO HAPPY!
WHAT'LL I DOOO?!
SHINE
ばしっ
SOMETHING TELLS ME THAT...
...I'M TRYING TOO HARD.
OHHH, IS THIS WEIRD?
GETTING SO DOLLED UP FOR A GIRL'S DAY OUT?
WHAT IF CHIZURU-SAN'S MORE CASUAL?!

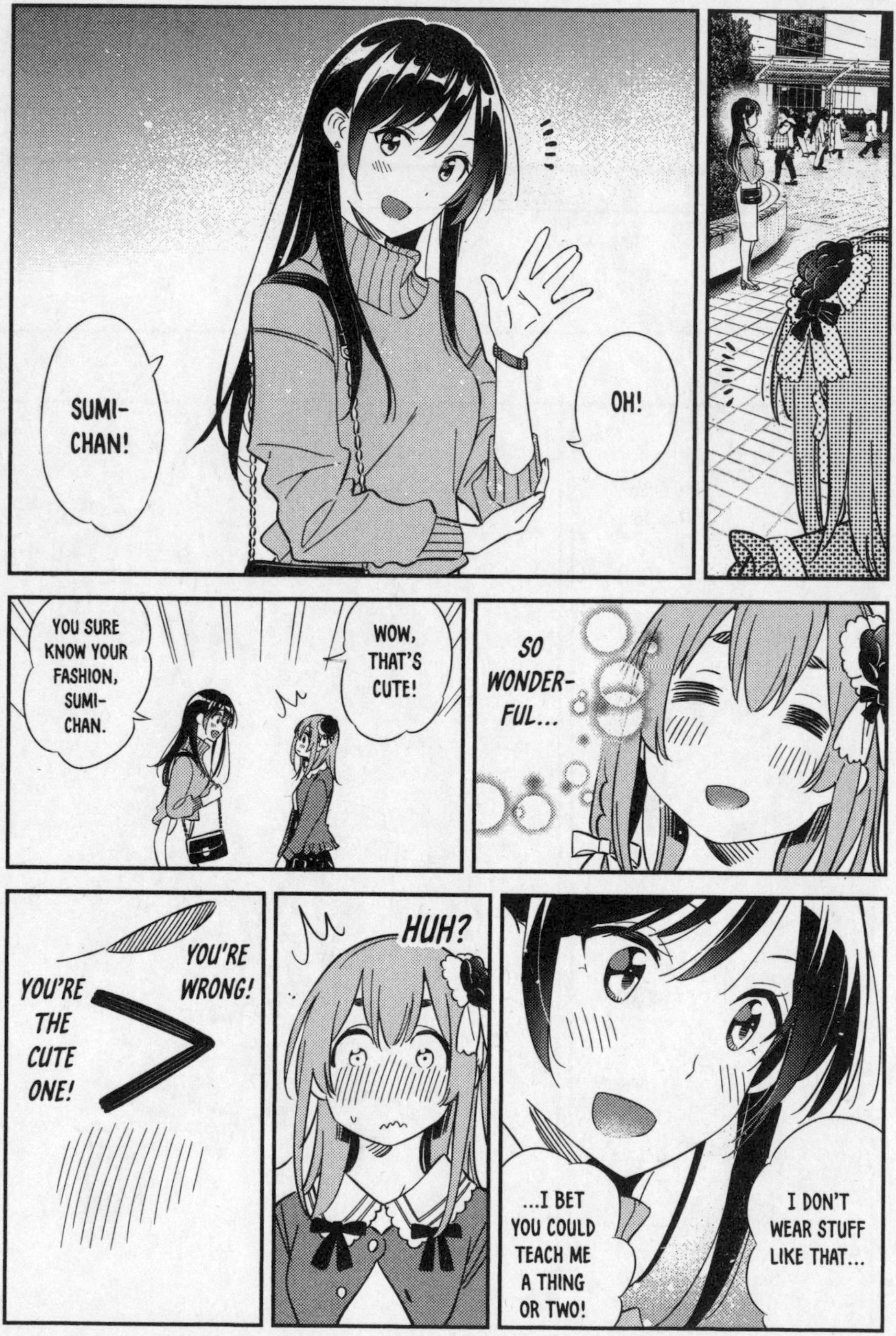
OH!
SUMI-CHAN!
SO WONDER-FUL...
WOW, THAT'S CUTE!
YOU SURE KNOW YOUR FASHION, SUMI-CHAN.
I DON'T WEAR STUFF LIKE THAT...
...I BET YOU COULD TEACH ME A THING OR TWO!
HUH?
YOU'RE WRONG!
YOU'RE THE CUTE ONE!

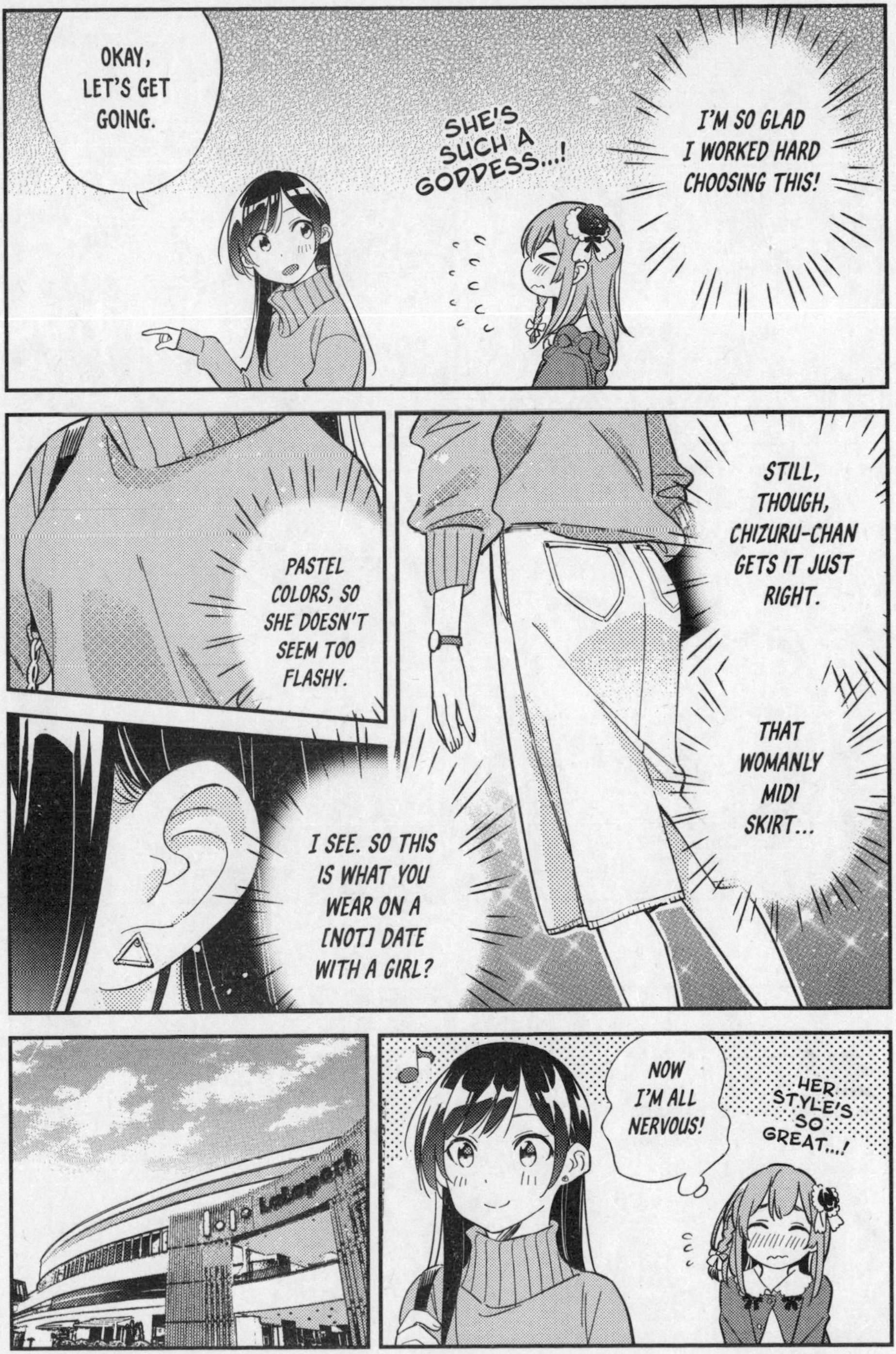
I'M SO GLAD I WORKED HARD CHOOSING THIS!
SHE'S SUCH A GODDESS...!
OKAY, LET'S GET GOING.
STILL, THOUGH, CHIZURU-CHAN GETS IT JUST RIGHT.
THAT WOMANLY MIDI SKIRT...
PASTEL COLORS, SO SHE DOESN'T SEEM TOO FLASHY.
I SEE. SO THIS IS WHAT YOU WEAR ON A [NOT] DATE WITH A GIRL?
HER STYLE'S SO GREAT...!
NOW I'M ALL NERVOUS!

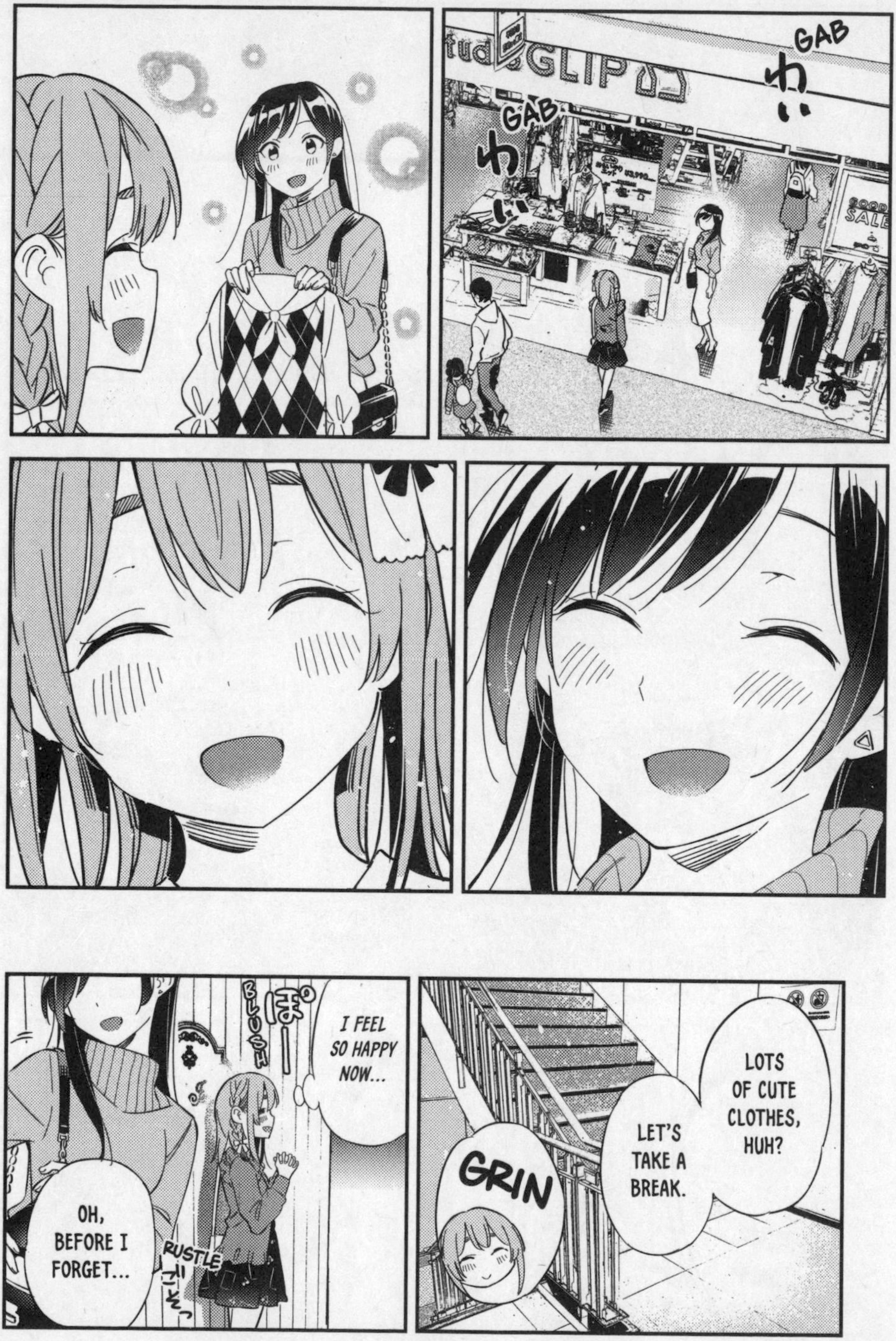

GAB
わい
GAB
わい
LOTS OF CUTE CLOTHES, HUH?
LET'S TAKE A BREAK.
GRIN
I FEEL SO HAPPY NOW...
ぽー
BLUSH
OH, BEFORE I FORGET...
RUSTLE
ごそっ

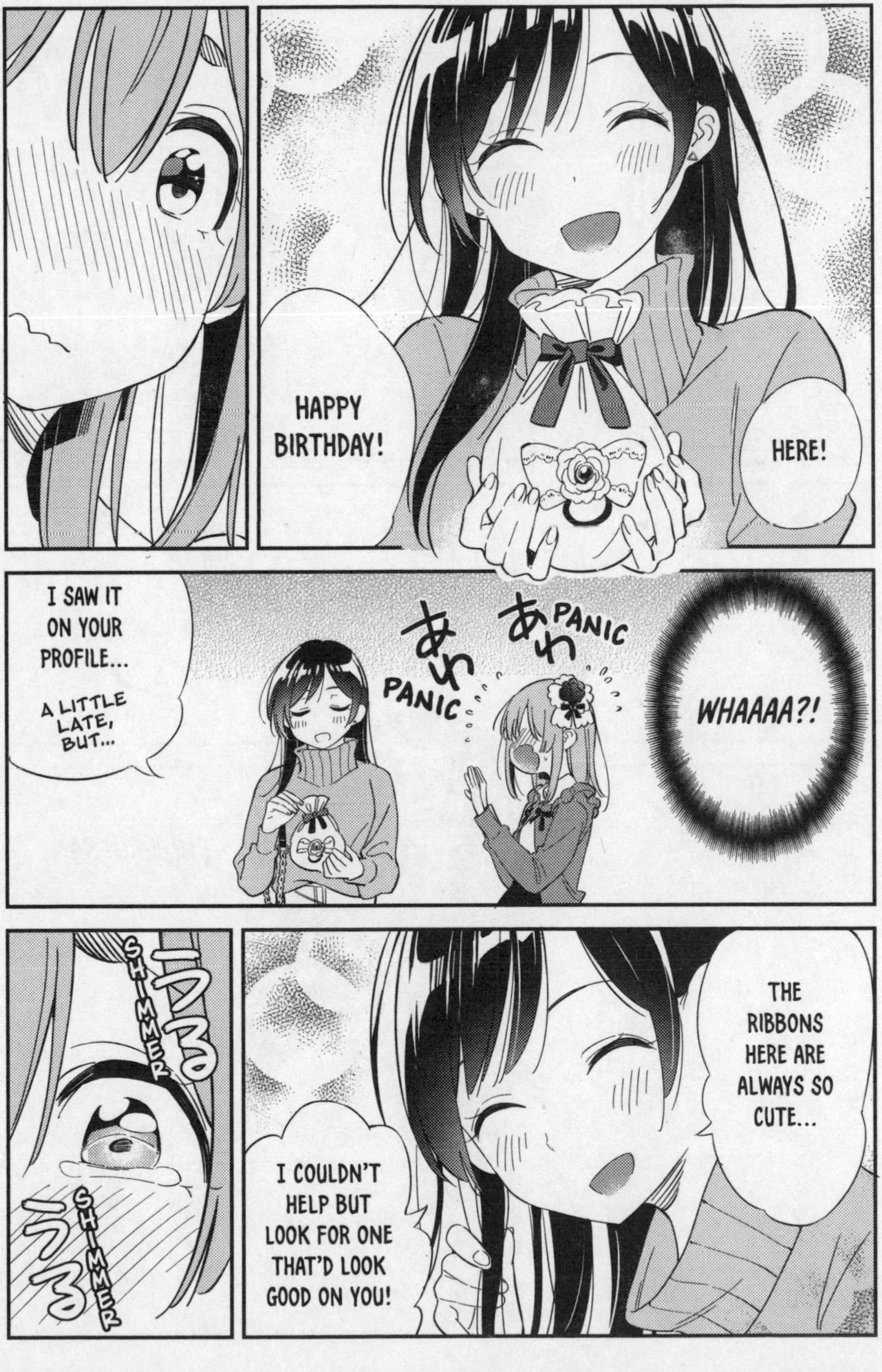
HERE!
HAPPY BIRTHDAY!
WHAAAA?!
あわ PANIC
あわ PANIC
I SAW IT ON YOUR PROFILE...
A LITTLE LATE, BUT...
THE RIBBONS HERE ARE ALWAYS SO CUTE...
I COULDN'T HELP BUT LOOK FOR ONE THAT'D LOOK GOOD ON YOU!
うる SHIMMER
うる SHIMMER

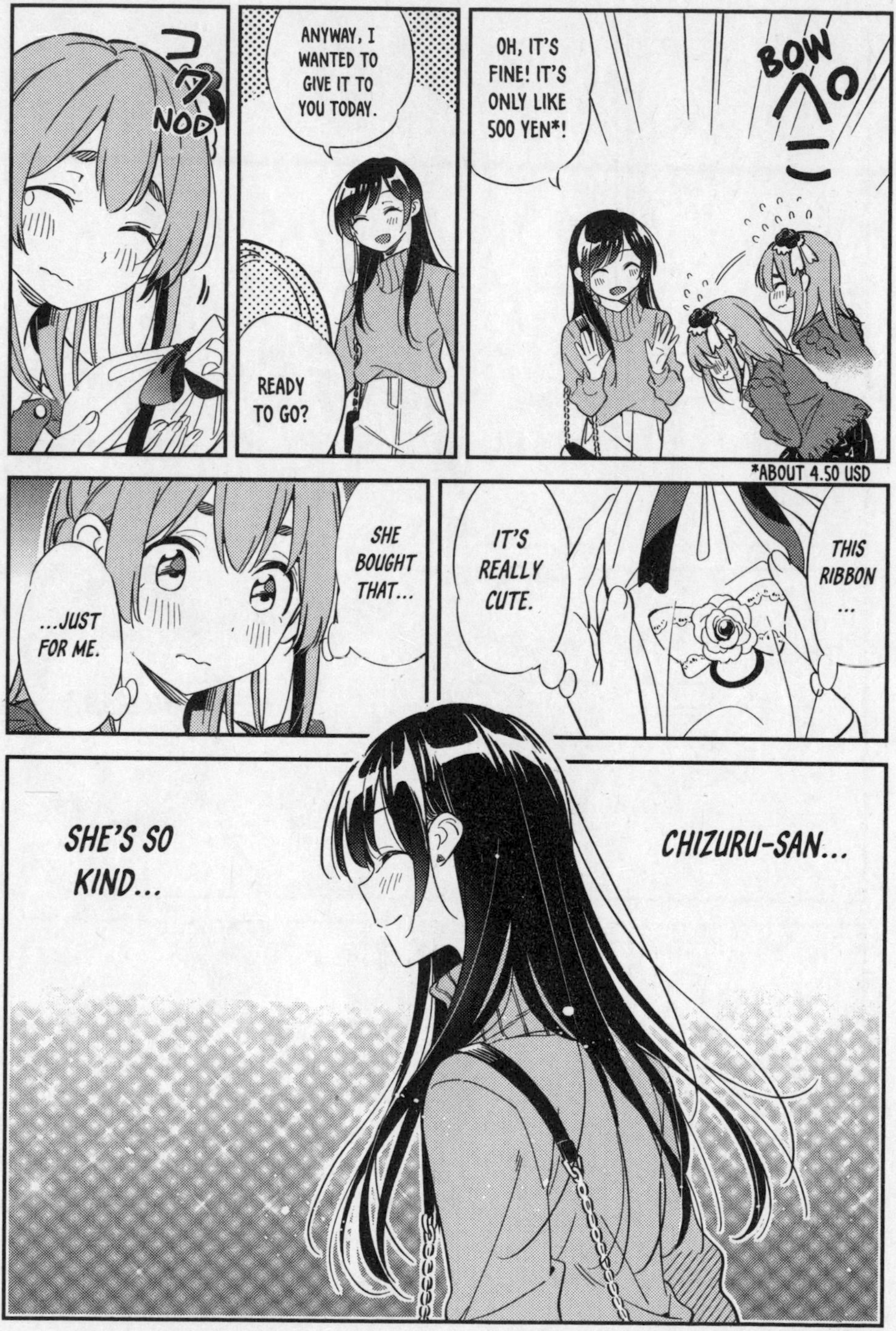
BOW
へこ
OH, IT'S FINE! IT'S ONLY LIKE 500 YEN*!
ANYWAY, I WANTED TO GIVE IT TO YOU TODAY.
READY TO GO?
コク
NOD
THIS RIBBON ...
IT'S REALLY CUTE.
SHE BOUGHT THAT...
...JUST FOR ME.
CHIZURU-SAN...
SHE'S SO KIND...

*ABOUT 4.50 USD

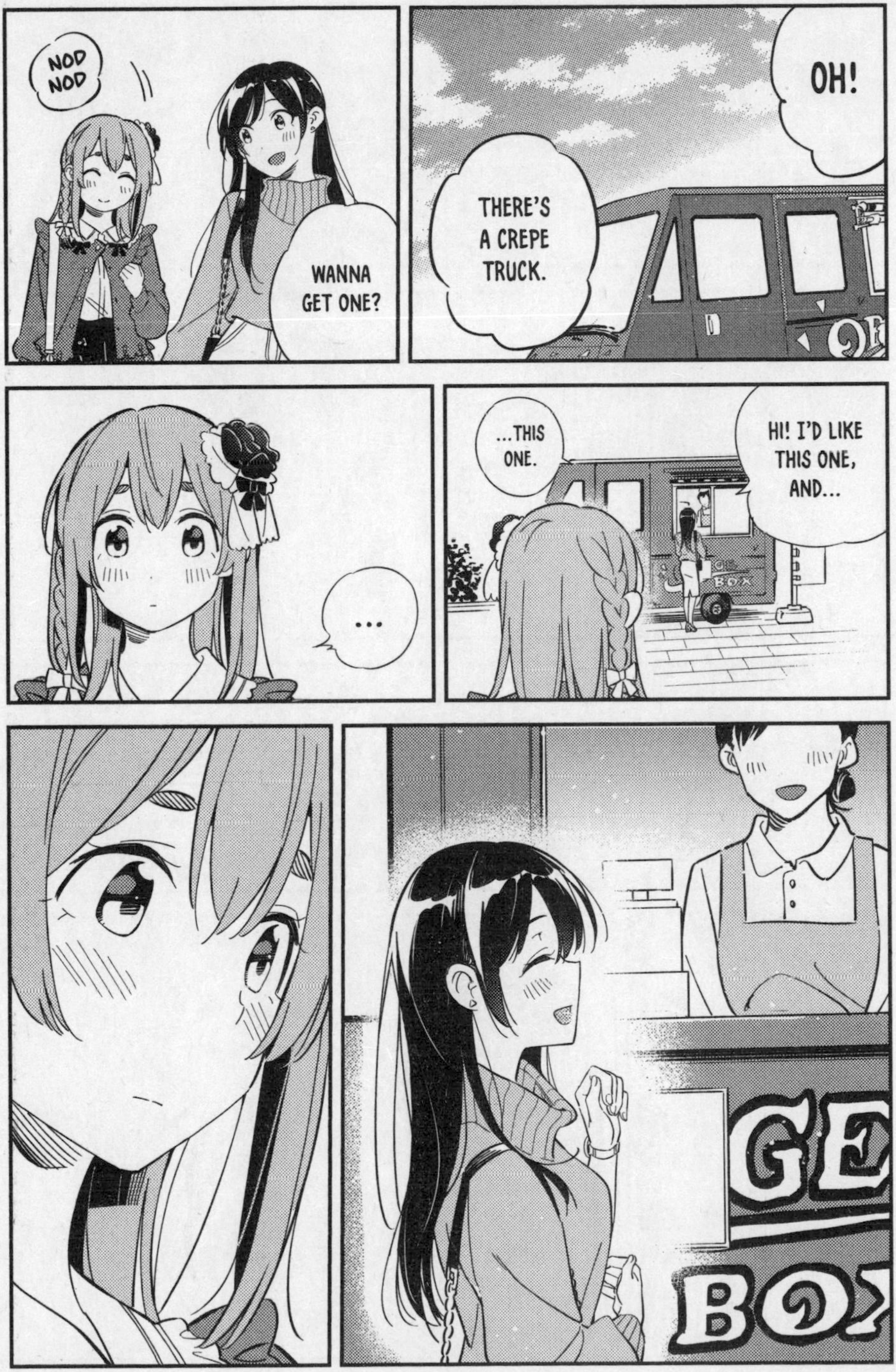
OH!
THERE'S A CREPE TRUCK.
WANNA GET ONE?
NOD NOD
HI! I'D LIKE THIS ONE, AND...
...THIS ONE.
...

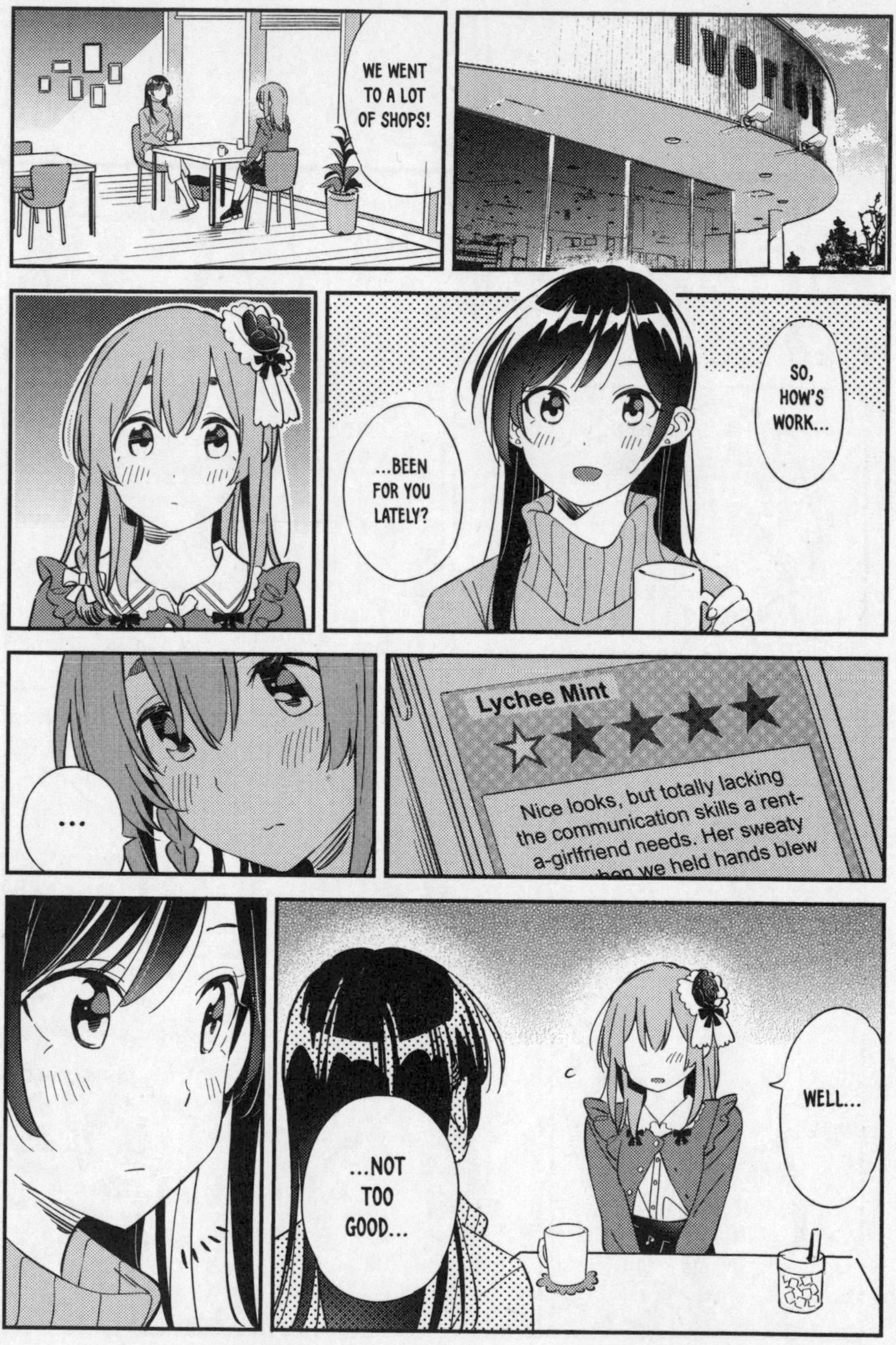
WE WENT TO A LOT OF SHOPS!
SO, HOW'S WORK...
...BEEN FOR YOU LATELY?
Lychee Mint
Nice looks, but totally lacking the communication skills a rent-a-girlfriend needs. Her sweaty
when we held hands blew
...
WELL...
...NOT TOO GOOD...

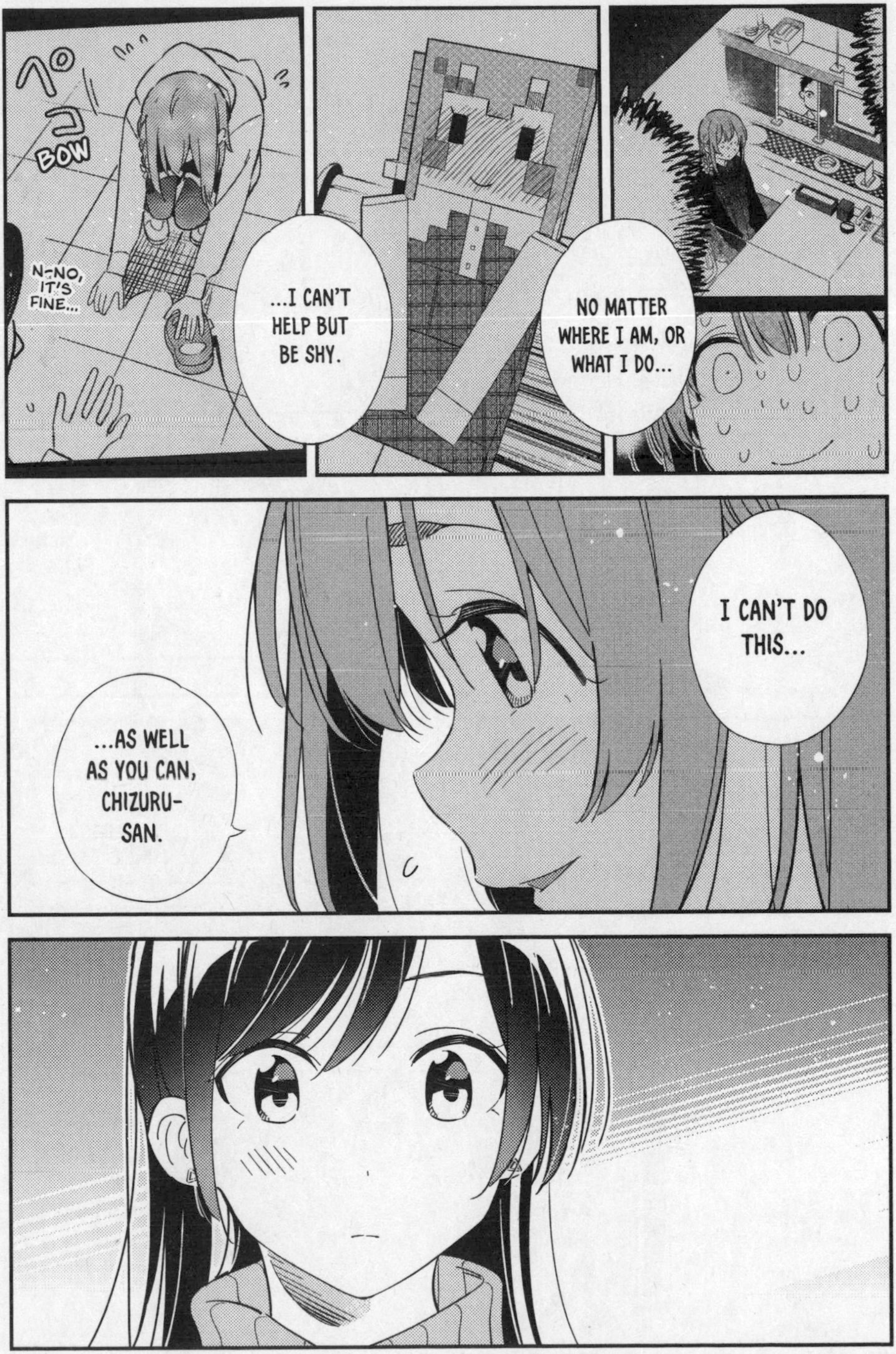
NO MATTER WHERE I AM, OR WHAT I DO...
...I CAN'T HELP BUT BE SHY.
ヘコ
BOW
N-NO, IT'S FINE...
I CAN'T DO THIS...
...AS WELL AS YOU CAN, CHIZURU-SAN.

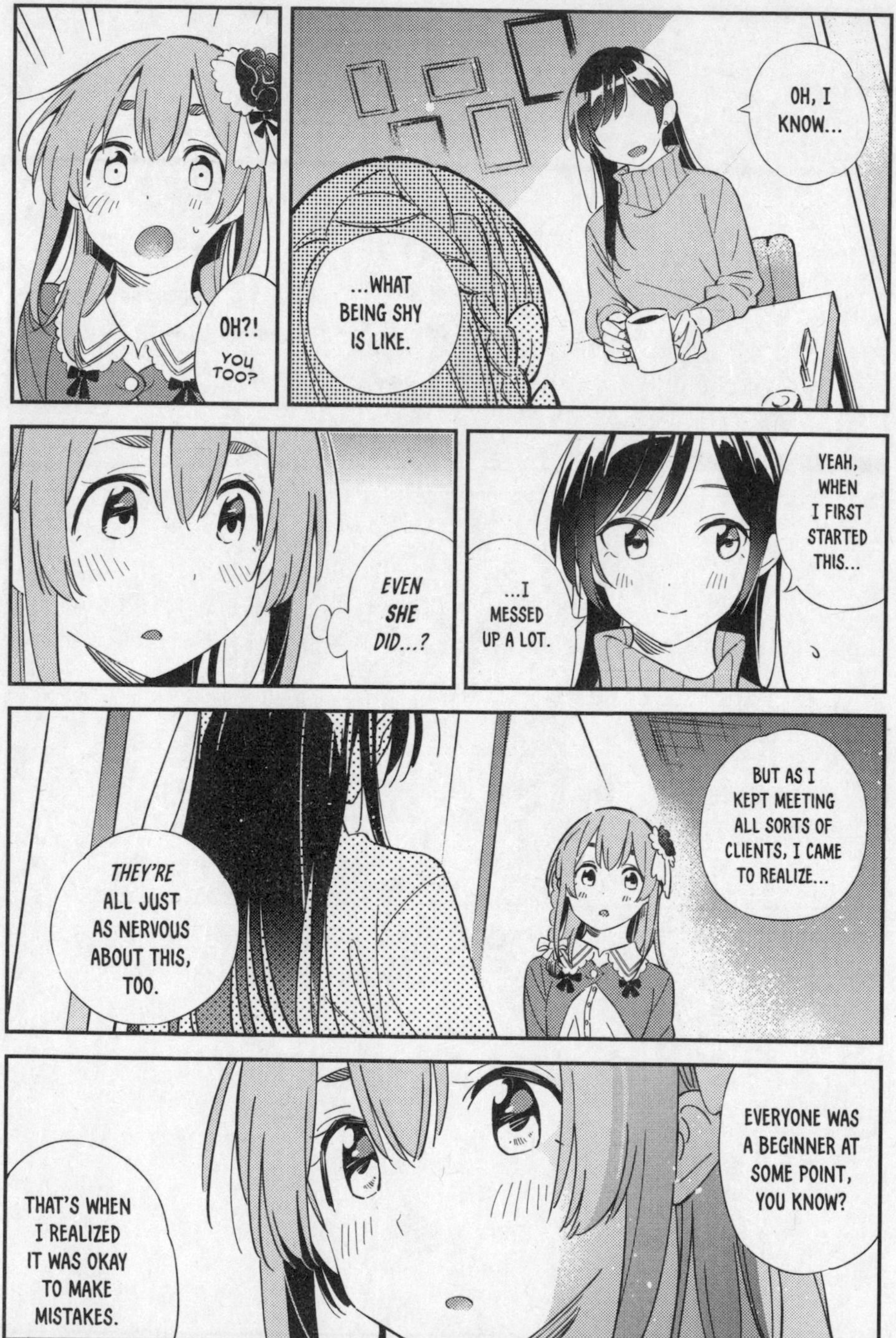
OH, I KNOW...
...WHAT BEING SHY IS LIKE.
OH?! YOU TOO?
YEAH, WHEN I FIRST STARTED THIS...
...I MESSED UP A LOT.
EVEN SHE DID...?
BUT AS I KEPT MEETING ALL SORTS OF CLIENTS, I CAME TO REALIZE...
THEY'RE ALL JUST AS NERVOUS ABOUT THIS, TOO.
EVERYONE WAS A BEGINNER AT SOME POINT, YOU KNOW?
THAT'S WHEN I REALIZED IT WAS OKAY TO MAKE MISTAKES.

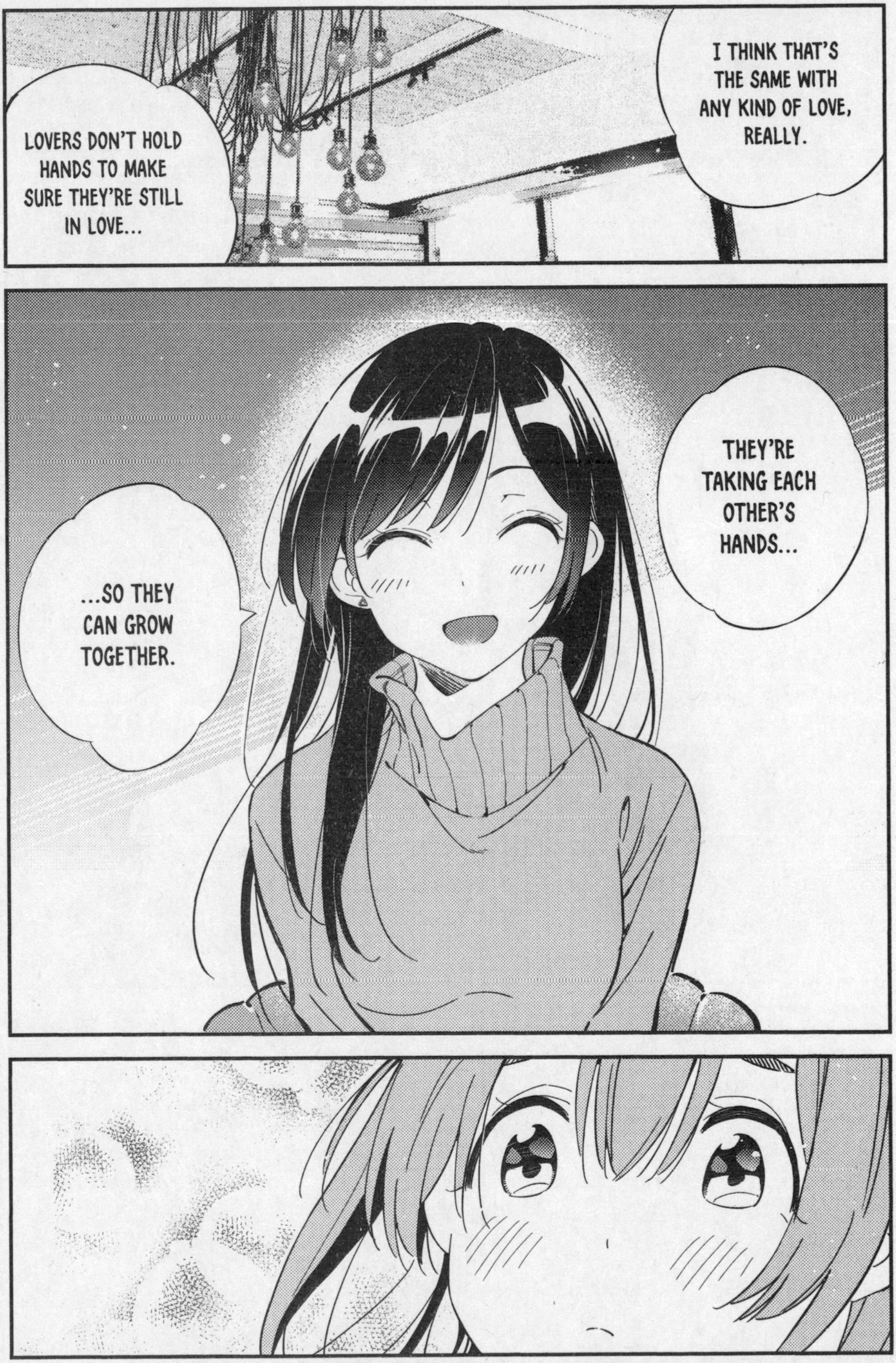
I THINK THAT'S THE SAME WITH ANY KIND OF LOVE, REALLY.
LOVERS DON'T HOLD HANDS TO MAKE SURE THEY'RE STILL IN LOVE...
THEY'RE TAKING EACH OTHER'S HANDS...
...SO THEY CAN GROW TOGETHER.

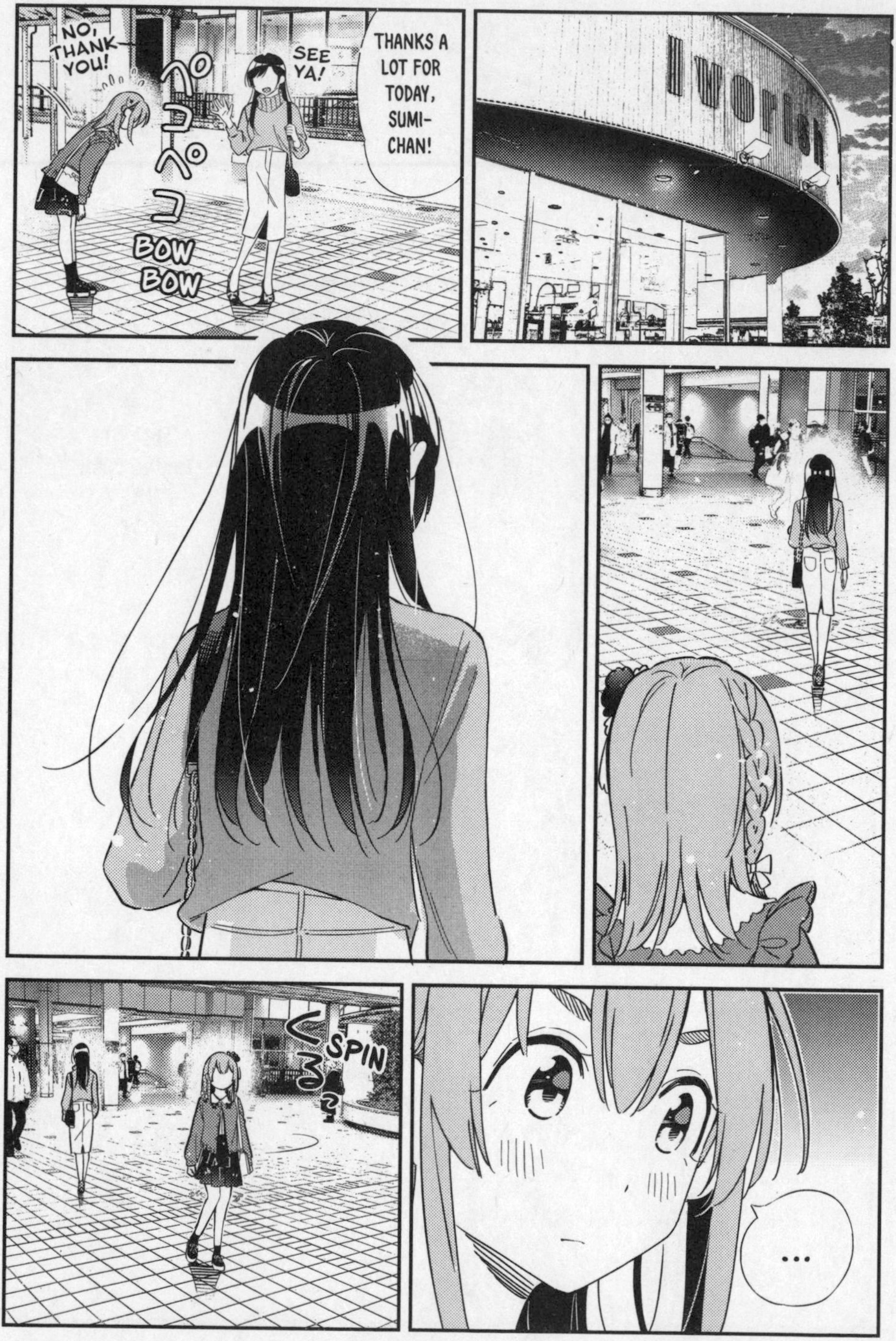
THANKS A LOT FOR TODAY, SUMI-CHAN!
SEE YA!
ペコペコ
BOW BOW
NO, THANK YOU!
...
くる
SPIN

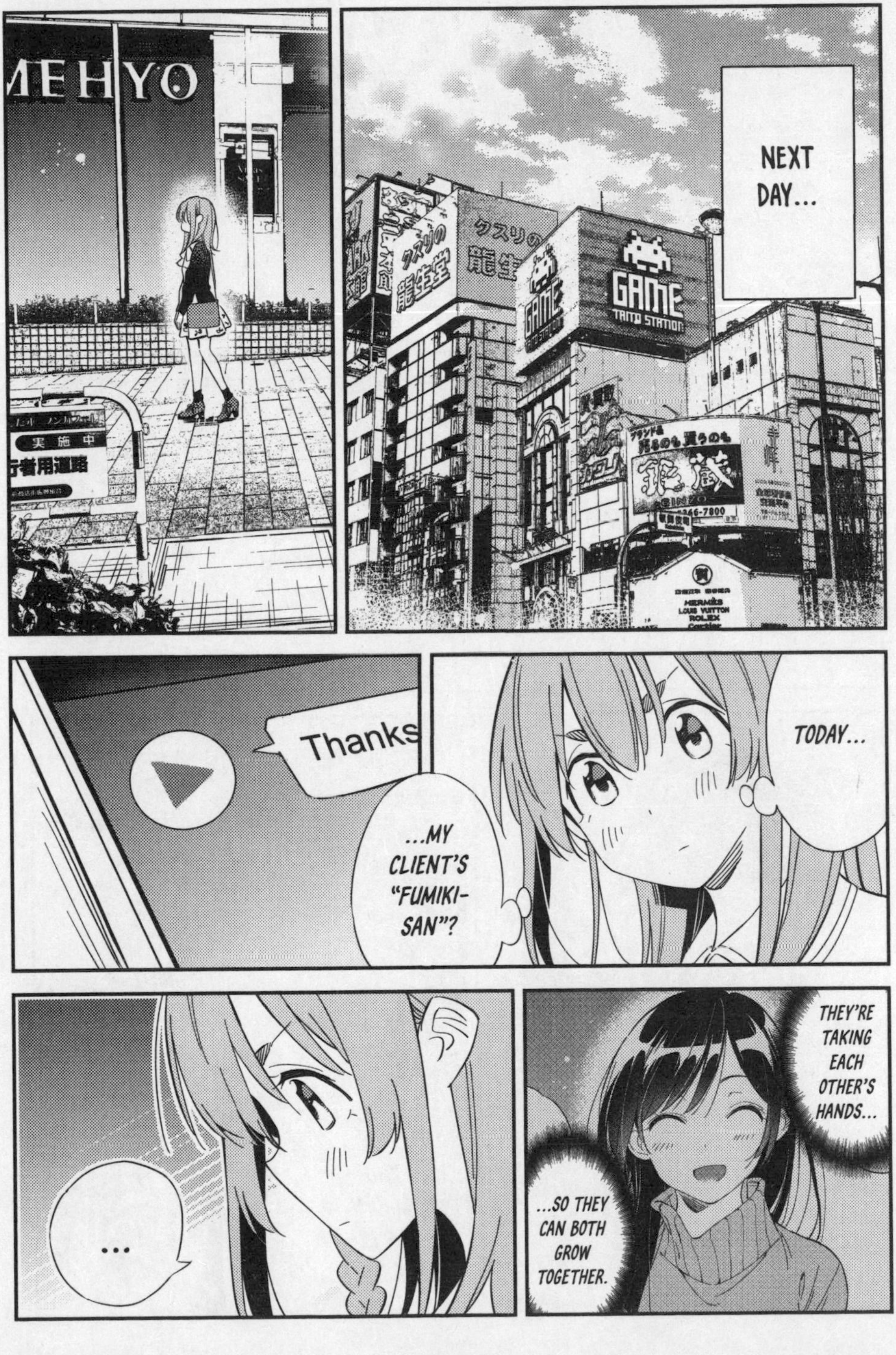
NEXT DAY...
GAME
TAITO STATION
クスリの
能生堂
HERMÈS
LOUIS VUITTON
ROLEX
MEHYO
実施中
TODAY...
...MY CLIENT'S "FUMIKI-SAN"?
Thanks
THEY'RE TAKING EACH OTHER'S HANDS...
...SO THEY CAN BOTH GROW TOGETHER.
...

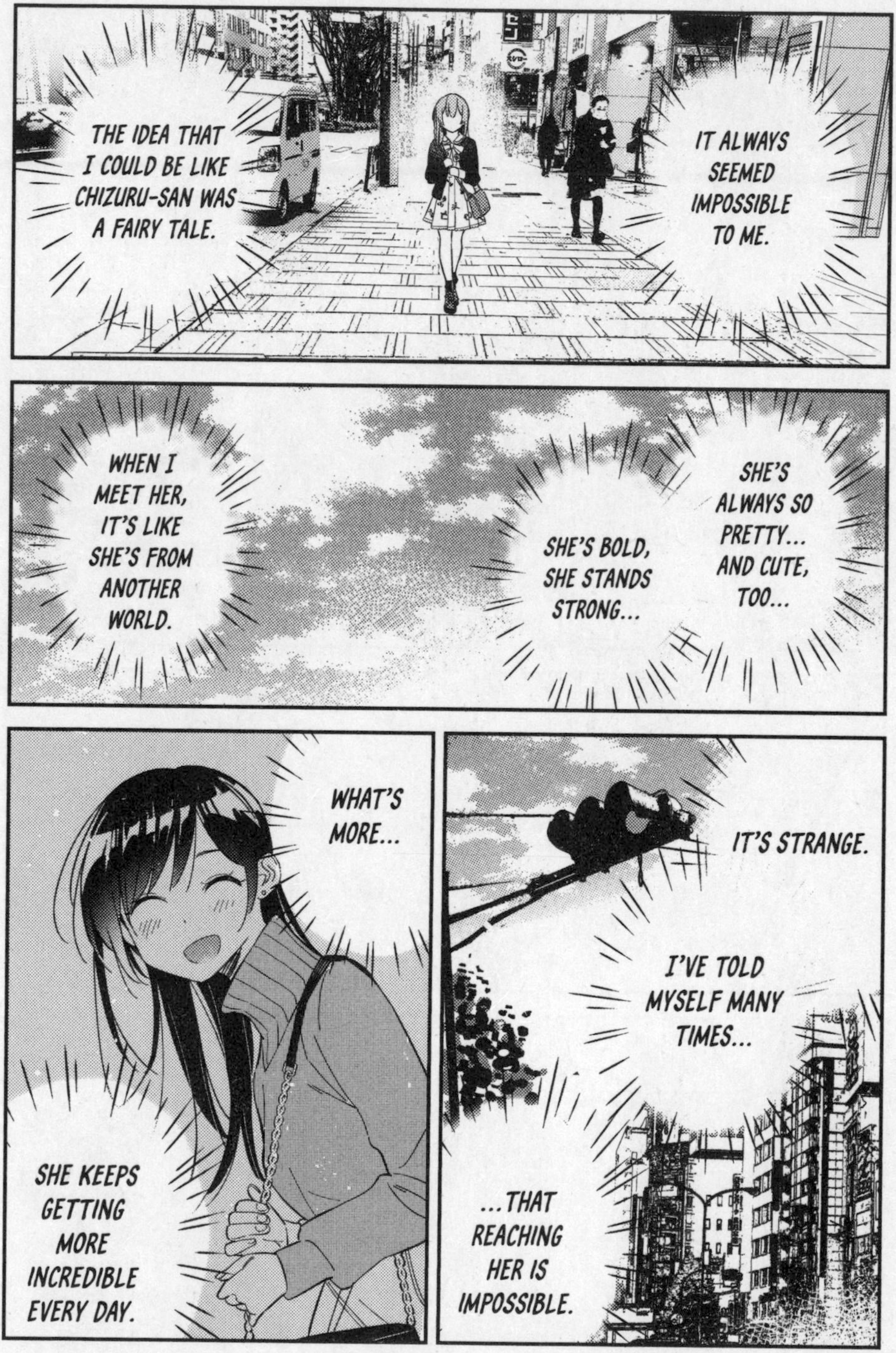
IT ALWAYS SEEMED IMPOSSIBLE TO ME.
THE IDEA THAT I COULD BE LIKE CHIZURU-SAN WAS A FAIRY TALE.
SHE'S ALWAYS SO PRETTY... AND CUTE, TOO...
SHE'S BOLD, SHE STANDS STRONG...
WHEN I MEET HER, IT'S LIKE SHE'S FROM ANOTHER WORLD.
IT'S STRANGE.
I'VE TOLD MYSELF MANY TIMES...
...THAT REACHING HER IS IMPOSSIBLE.
WHAT'S MORE...
SHE KEEPS GETTING MORE INCREDIBLE EVERY DAY.

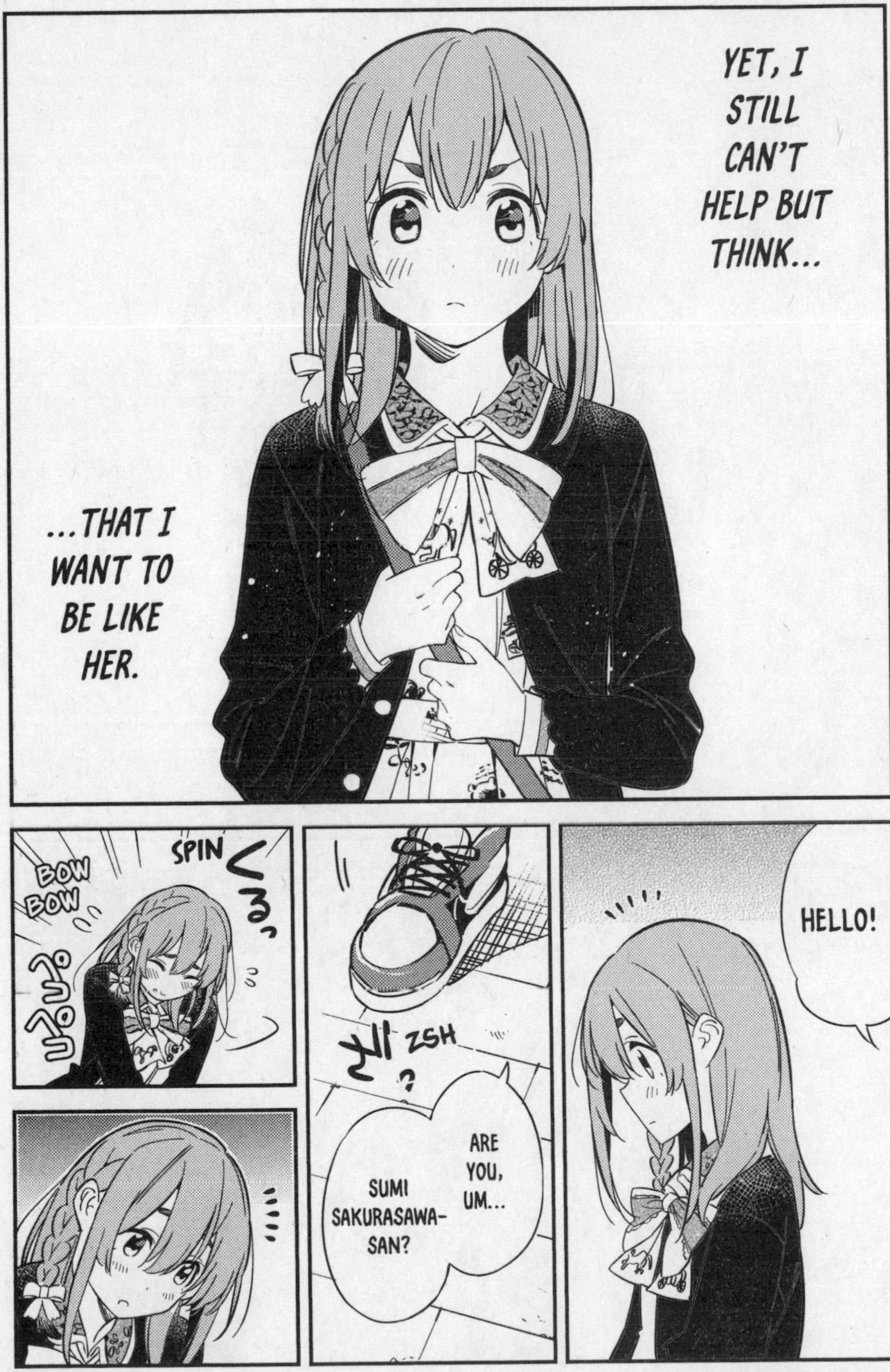
YET, I STILL CAN'T HELP BUT THINK...
...THAT I WANT TO BE LIKE HER.
HELLO!
ZSH
ARE YOU, UM... SUMI SAKURASAWA-SAN?
SPIN
BOW BOW

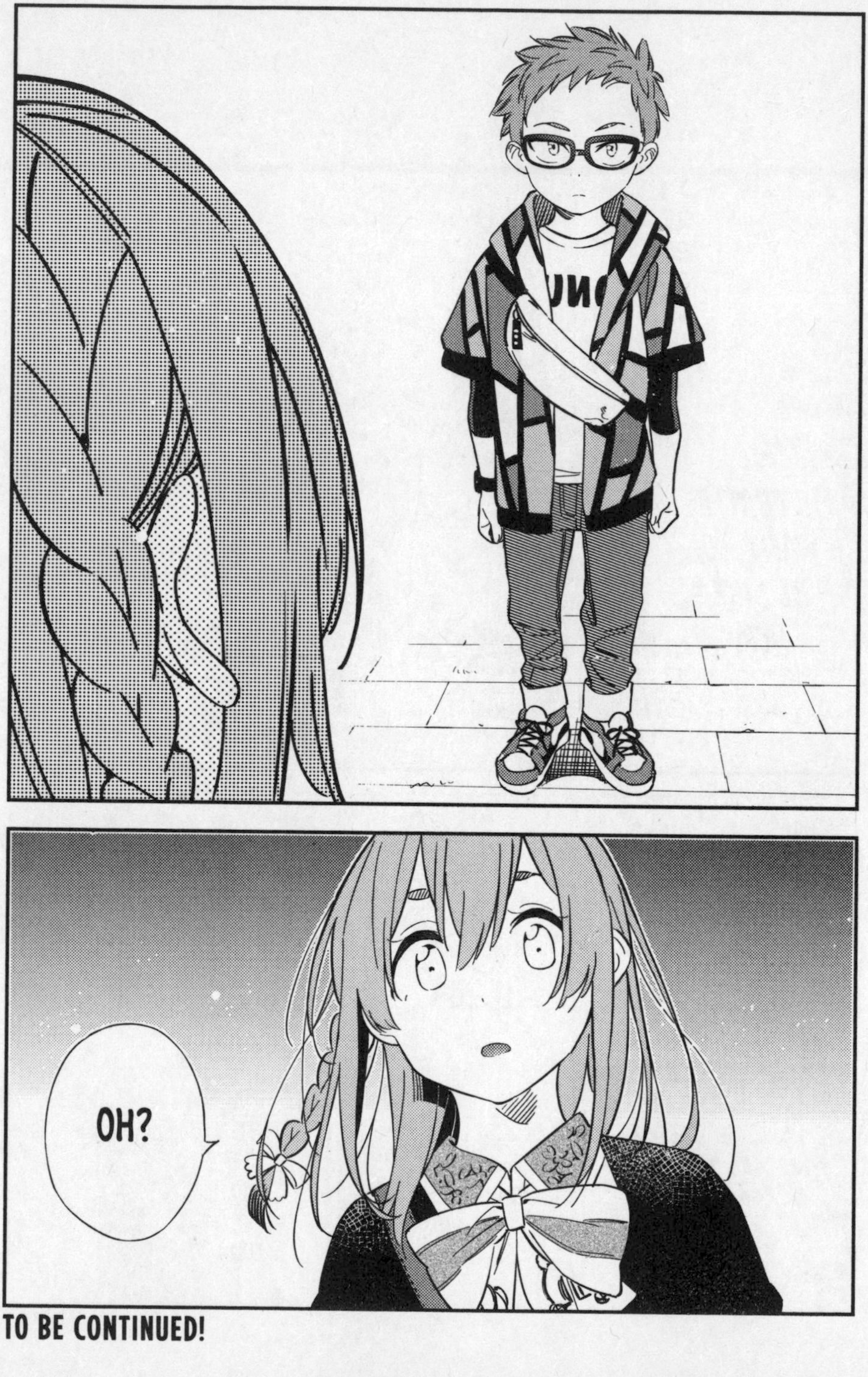
OH?

TO BE CONTINUED!

I'M WRITING THIS BONUS PAGE RIGHT AFTER THE ONE FOR *RENT-A-GIRLFRIEND* VOLUME 19. THANK YOU FOR PURCHASING VOLUME 2 OF *RENT-A-(REALLY SHY!)-GIRLFRIEND!!* I TRULY APPRECIATE EVERYONE WHO'S MAKING THE EFFORT TO READ THE SPIN-OFF AS WELL. I POUR ALL OF MY REAL-LIFE COMMUNICATION ISSUES INTO SUMI-CHAN. GETTING TO EXPRESS SOMETHING THAT I CAN'T OFTEN DESCRIBE IS INCREDIBLY REFRESHING. I FEEL LIKE I'M SHOUTING, "I'M A DARK MAN!!" AT THE TOP OF MY LUNGS. NOW, LET ME TALK A LITTLE ABOUT KINAMI-SAN, WHO HELPS ME OUT WITH THIS SERIES. KINAMI-SAN WAS ONE OF THE ORIGINAL MEMBERS OF THE STAFF ASSISSTING ME WITH *RENT-A-GIRLFRIEND*. WE FIRST MET DURING THEIR INTERVIEW, WHEN I WAS FIELDING STAFF FOR THE NEW SERIES. I WAS SPEAKING WITH TWO OTHER PEOPLE THAT DAY, AND I KIND OF REMEMBER KINAMI-SAN SIDLING UP TO THE MEETING POINT AFTER BOTH OF THEM. KINAMI-SAN HAD THIS DOWNCAST LOOK ON THEIR FACE, LIKE THEY WERE GOING TO AN INTERVIEW BUT DIDN'T REALLY WANT TO BE FOUND. I DON'T THINK THEY TALKED MUCH AT ALL THROUGHOUT THE WHOLE THING. (I'M WRITING ALL THIS WITHOUT CONFIRMING IT WITH, THOUGH...) READING THIS, YOU MIGHT THINK KINAMI-SAN SHARES A FEW THINGS IN COMMON WITH SUMI-CHAN, RIGHT? I'M SURE KINAMI-SAN WAS LATE TO THE MEETING SITE BECAUSE THEY DIDN'T WANT TO RUN INTO THE OTHER INTERVIEWEES BY ACCIDENT. STILL, KINAMI-SAN'S ART WAS REALLY NEAT, WITH SUPER CLEAN LINES AND ALL, SO I TOOK THEM OFF THE *RENT-A-GIRLFRIEND* STAFF AND HAD THEM HELP WITH THE PAGES FOR SUMI-CHAN'S STORY INSTEAD. I KNOW KINAMI-SAN'S THE TYPE TO PROCRASTINATE ON THEIR SUMMER VACATION HOMEWORK UNTIL THE DAY BEFORE SCHOOL (THAT I *HAVE* CONFIRMED), BUT THROUGH DEADLINES KEPT AND NOT-SO-KEPT, THEY'VE WORKED INCREDIBLY HARD FOR ME! VOLUME 2 ENDS ON A NICE CLIFFHANGER, SO HOW ABOUT WE ALL SEND FAN LETTERS TO KINAMI-SAN VIA KODANSHA AND HELP TO BOOST THEIR (AND MY) MOTIVATION, HUH?! LET'S DO IT! I'LL BE WAITING!!

REIJI MIYAJIMA

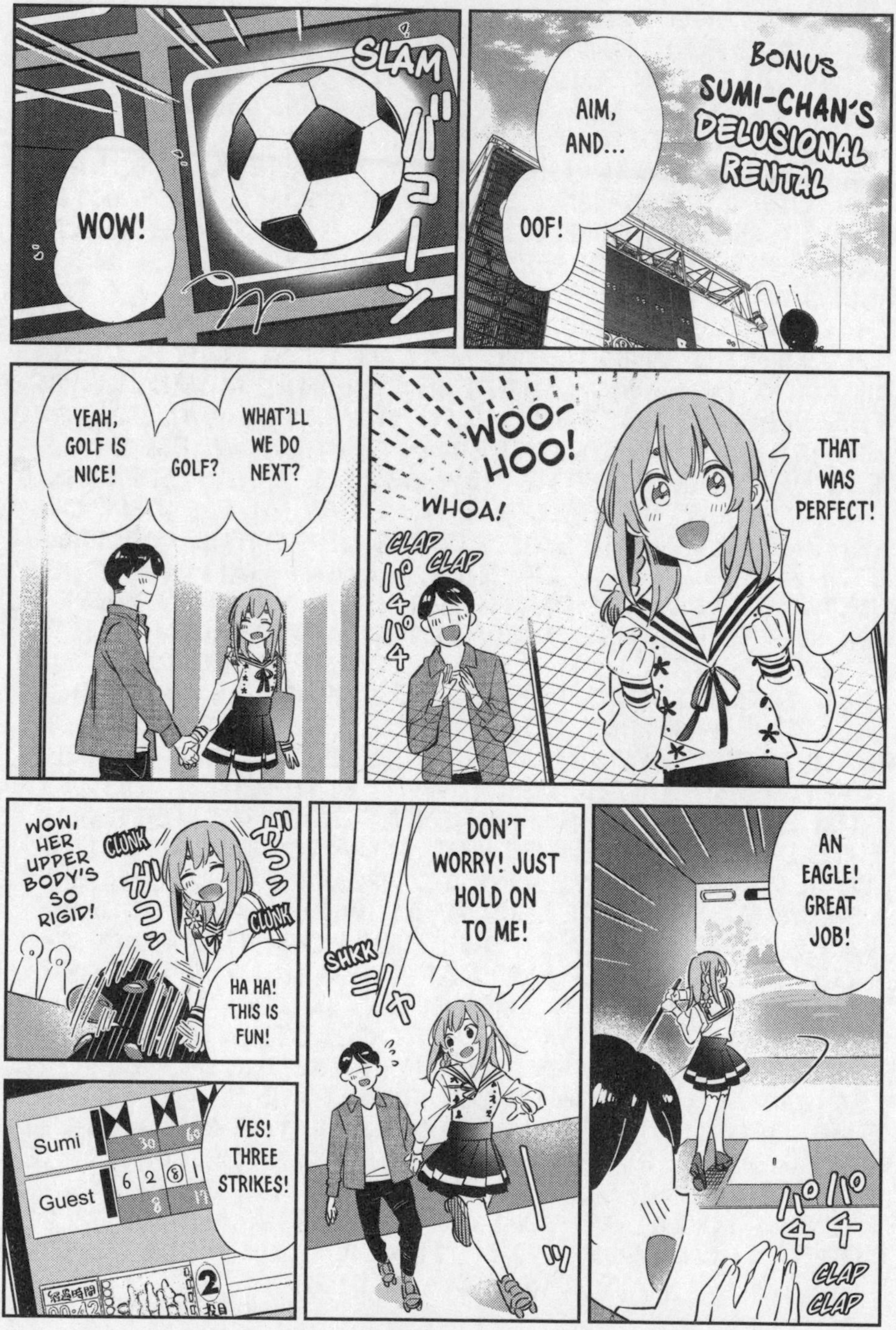
BONUS
SUMI-CHAN'S DELUSIONAL RENTAL
AIM, AND...
OOF!
SLAM
WOW!
THAT WAS PERFECT!
WOO-HOO!
WHOA!
CLAP CLAP
WHAT'LL WE DO NEXT?
GOLF?
YEAH, GOLF IS NICE!
AN EAGLE! GREAT JOB!
CLAP CLAP
DON'T WORRY! JUST HOLD ON TO ME!
SHKK
WOW, HER UPPER BODY'S SO RIGID!
CLUNK
CLUNK
HA HA! THIS IS FUN!
YES! THREE STRIKES!
Sumi
Guest

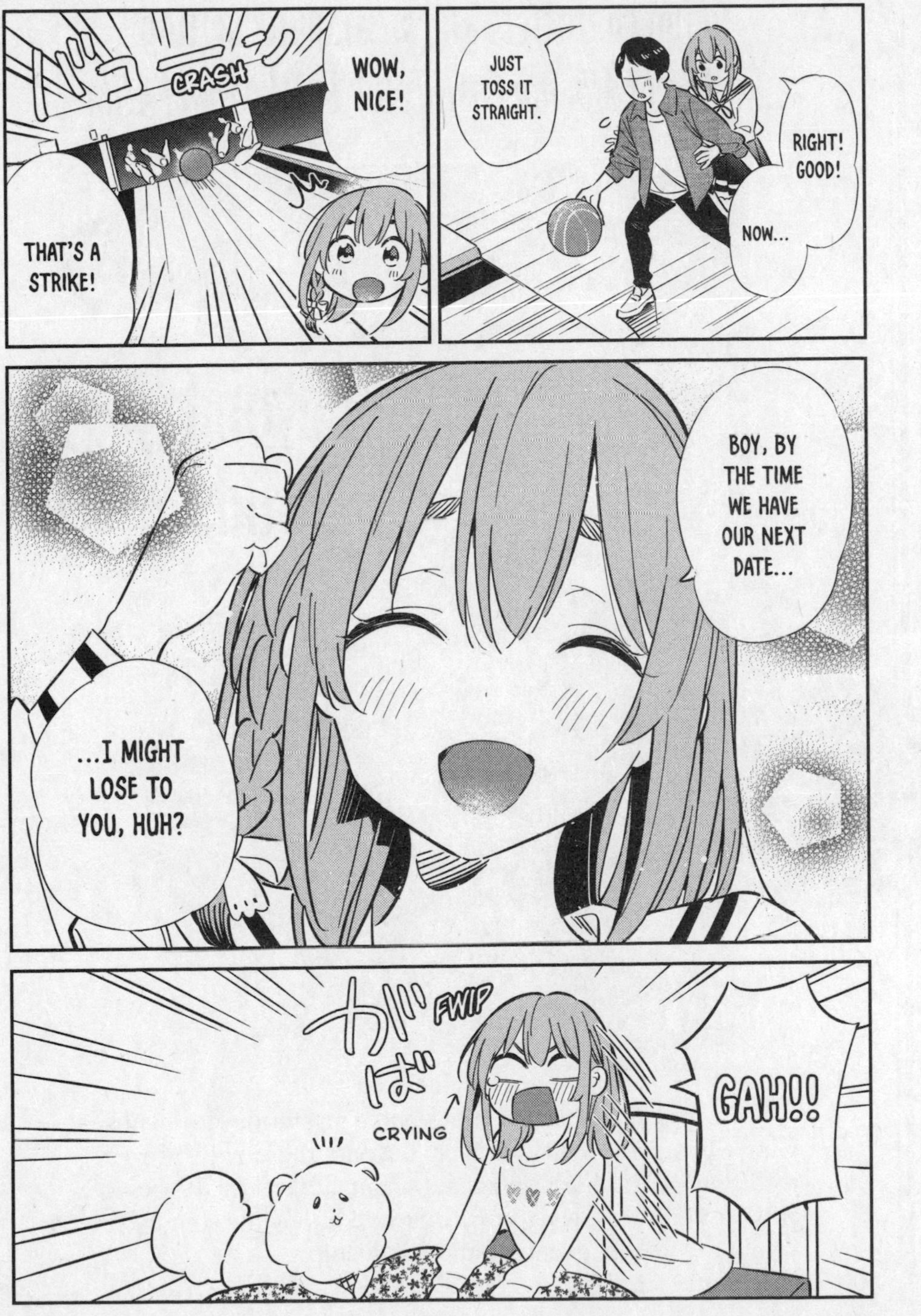
JUST TOSS IT STRAIGHT.
RIGHT! GOOD!
NOW...
WOW, NICE!
CRASH
THAT'S A STRIKE!
BOY, BY THE TIME WE HAVE OUR NEXT DATE...
...I MIGHT LOSE TO YOU, HUH?
GAH!!
FWIP
CRYING

Young characters and steampunk setting, like *Howl's Moving Castle* and *Battle Angel Alita*

Beyond the Clouds © 2018 Nicke / Ki-oon

A boy with a talent for machines and a mysterious girl whose wings he's fixed will take you beyond the clouds! In the tradition of the high-flying, resonant adventure stories of Studio Ghibli comes a gorgeous tale about the longing of young hearts for adventure and friendship!

Knight of the ICE

Knight of the Ice ©Yayoi Ogawa/Kodansha Ltd.

Yayoi Ogawa

SKATING THRILLS AND ICY CHILLS WITH THIS NEW TINGLY ROMANCE SERIES!

A rom-com on ice, perfect for fans of *Princess Jellyfish* and *Wotakoi*. Kokoro is the talk of the figure-skating world, winning trophies and hearts. But little do they know... he's actually a huge nerd! From the beloved creator of *You're My Pet* (*Tramps Like Us*).

Chitose is a serious young woman, working for the health magazine *SASSO*. Or at least, she would be, if she wasn't constantly getting distracted by her childhood friend, international figure skating star Kokoro Kijinami! In the public eye and on the ice, Kokoro is a gallant, flawless knight, but behind his glittery costumes and breathtaking spins lies a secret: He's actually a hopelessly romantic otaku, who can only land his quad jumps when Chitose is on hand to recite a spell from his favorite magical girl anime!

KC
KODANSHA
COMICS

A SMART, NEW ROMANTIC COMEDY FOR FANS OF *SHORTCAKE CAKE* AND *TERRACE HOUSE*!

Living-Room Matsunaga-san © Keiko Iwashita / Kodansha Ltd.

A romance manga starring high school girl Meeko, who learns to live on her own in a boarding house whose living room is home to the odd (but handsome) Matsunaga-san. She begins to adjust to her new life away from her parents, but Meeko soon learns that no matter how far away from home she is, she's still a young girl at heart — especially when she finds herself falling for Matsunaga-san.

PERFECT WORLD

Rie Aruga

A TOUCHING NEW SERIES ABOUT LOVE AND COPING WITH DISABILITY

An office party reunites Tsugumi with her high school crush Itsuki. He's realized his dream of becoming an architect, but along the way, he experienced a spinal injury that put him in a wheelchair. Now Tsugumi's rekindled feelings will butt up against prejudices she never considered — and Itsuki will have to decide if he's ready to let someone into his heart...

"Depicts with great delicacy and courage the difficulties some with disabilities experience getting involved in romantic relationships... Rie Aruga refuses to romanticize, pushing her heroine to face the reality of disability. She invites her readers to the same tasks of empathy, knowledge and recognition."
—Slate.fr

"An important entry [in manga romance]... The emotional core of both plot and characters indicates thoughtfulness... [Aruga's] research is readily apparent in the text and artwork, making this feel like a real story."
—Anime News Network

KC KODANSHA COMICS

Perfect World © Rie Aruga/Kodansha Ltd.

The boys are back, in 400-page hardcovers that are as pretty and badass as they are!

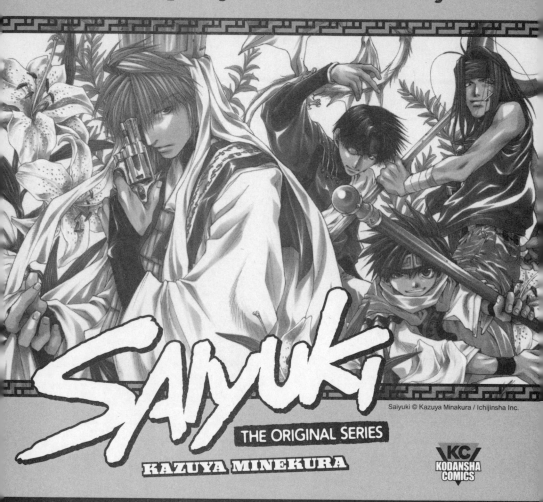

Saiyuki © Kazuya Minakura / Ichijinsha Inc.

SAIYUKI
THE ORIGINAL SERIES
KAZUYA MINEKURA

KC
KODANSHA
COMICS

"AN EDGY COMIC LOOK AT AN ANCIENT CHINESE TALE." —YALSA

Genjo Sanzo is a Buddhist priest in the city of Togenkyo, which is being ravaged by yokai spirits that have fallen out of balance with the natural order. His superiors send him on a journey far to the west to discover why this is happening and how to stop it. His companions are three yokai with human souls. But this is no day trip — the four will encounter many discoveries and horrors on the way.

FEATURES NEW TRANSLATION, COLOR PAGES, AND BEAUTIFUL WRAPAROUND COVER ART!

Something's Wrong With Us

NATSUMI ANDO

The dark, psychological, sexy shojo series readers have been waiting for!

A spine-chilling and steamy romance between a Japanese sweets maker and the man who framed her mother for murder!

Following in her mother's footsteps, Nao became a traditional Japanese sweets maker, and with unparalleled artistry and a bright attitude, she gets an offer to work at a world-class confectionary company. But when she meets the young, handsome owner, she recognizes his cold stare...

KC
KODANSHA COMICS

Something's Wrong With Us © Natsumi Ando / Kodansha Ltd.

The adorable new odd-couple cat comedy manga from the creator of the beloved *Chi's Sweet Home*, in full color!

Praise for Chi's Sweet Home

"Nearly impossible to turn away... a true all-ages title that anyone, young or old, cat lover or not, will enjoy. The stories will bring a smile to your face and warm your heart."

—School Library Journal

Sue & Tai-chan

Konami Kanata

Sue is an aging housecat who's looking forward to living out her life in peace... but her plans change when the mischievous black tomcat Tai-chan enters the picture! Hey! Sue never signed up to be a catsitter! *Sue & Tai-chan* is the latest from the reigning meow-narch of cute kitty comics, Konami Kanata.

Sue & Tai-chan © Konami Kanata/Kodansha Ltd.

KC
KODANSHA
COMICS

THE SWEET SCENT OF LOVE IS IN THE AIR! FOR FANS OF OFFBEAT ROMANCES LIKE *WOTAKOI*

Sweat and Soap © Kintetsu Yamada / Kodansha Ltd.

In an office romance, there's a fine line between sexy and awkward... and that line is where Asako — a woman who sweats copiously — meets Koutarou — a perfume developer who can't get enough of Asako's, er, scent. Don't miss a romcom manga like no other!

CUTE ANIMALS AND LIFE LESSONS, PERFECT FOR ASPIRING PET VETS OF ALL AGES!

KODANSHA COMICS

Yuzu the Pet Vet © Mingo Ito / NIPPON COLUMBIA CO., LTD. / Kodansha Ltd.

YUZU THE PET VET

1

BY
MINGO ITO
In collaboration with
NIPPON COLUMBIA CO., LTD.

For an 11-year-old, Yuzu has a lot on her plate. When her mom gets sick and has to be hospitalized, Yuzu goes to live with her uncle who runs the local veterinary clinic. Yuzu's always been scared of animals, but she tries to help out. Through all the tough moments in her life, Yuzu realizes that she can help make things all right with a little help from her animal pals, peers, and kind grown-ups.

Every new patient is a furry friend in the making!

One of CLAMP's biggest hits returns in this definitive, premium, hardcover 20th anniversary collector's edition!

"A wonderfully entertaining story that would be a great installment in anybody's manga collection."
— Anime News Network

"CLAMP is an all-female manga-creating team whose feminine touch shows in this entertaining, sci-fi soap opera."
— Publishers Weekly

Chobits © CLAMP·ShigatsuTsuitachi CO.,LTD./Kodansha Ltd.

Poor college student Hideki is down on his luck. All he wants is a good job, a girlfriend, and his very own "persocom"—the latest and greatest in humanoid computer technology. Hideki's luck changes one night when he finds Chi—a persocom thrown out in a pile of trash. But Hideki soon discovers that there's much more to his cute new persocom than meets the eye.

KC
KODANSHA COMICS

The art-deco cyberpunk classic from the creators of *xxxHOLiC* and *Cardcaptor Sakura*!

"Starred Review.
This experimental
sci-fi work from
CLAMP reads like a
romantic version of
AKIRA."
—Publishers Weekly

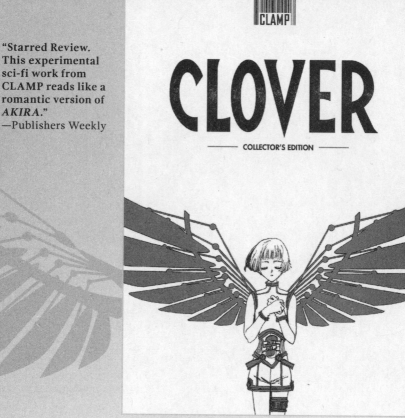

CLOVER © CLAMP ShigatsuTsuitachi CO.,LTD./Kodansha Ltd.

Su was born into a bleak future, where the government keeps tight control over children with magical powers—codenamed "Clovers." With Su being the only "four-leaf" Clover in the world, she has been kept isolated nearly her whole life. Can ex-military agent Kazuhiko deliver her to the happiness she seeks? Experience the complete series in this hardcover edition, which also includes over twenty pages of ravishing color art!

KC
KODANSHA
COMICS

The beloved characters from
Cardcaptor Sakura return in a brand new, reimagined fantasy adventure!

"[*Tsubasa*] takes readers on a fantastic ride that only gets more exhilarating with each successive chapter." —Anime News Network

In the Kingdom of Clow, an archaeological dig unleashes an incredible power, causing Princess Sakura to lose her memories. To save her, her childhood friend Syaoran must follow the orders of the Dimension Witch and travel alongside Kurogane, an unrivaled warrior; Fai, a powerful magician; and Mokona, a curiously strange creature, to retrieve Sakura's dispersed memories!

Tsubasa Omnibus © CLAMP © CLAMP·ShigatsuTsuitachi CO.,LTD./Kodansha Ltd.   Tsubasa: WoRLD CHRoNiCLE © CLAMP·ShigatsuTsuitachi CO.,LTD./Kodansha Ltd.

"Clever, sassy, and original....*xxxHOLiC* has the inherent hallmarks of a runaway hit."
—NewType magazine

Beautifully seductive artwork and uniquely Japanese depictions of the supernatural will hypnotize CLAMP fans!

xxxHOLiC © CLAMP·ShigatsuTsuitachi CO.,LTD./Kodansha Ltd.
xxxHOLiC Rei © CLAMP·ShigatsuTsuitachi CO.,LTD./Kodansha Ltd.

Kimihiro Watanuki is haunted by visions of ghosts and spirits. He seeks help from a mysterious woman named Yuko, who claims she can help. However, Watanuki must work for Yuko in order to pay for her aid. Soon Watanuki finds himself employed in Yuko's shop, where he sees things and meets customers that are stranger than anything he could have ever imagined.

KC
KODANSHA
COMICS

THE WORLD OF CLAMP!

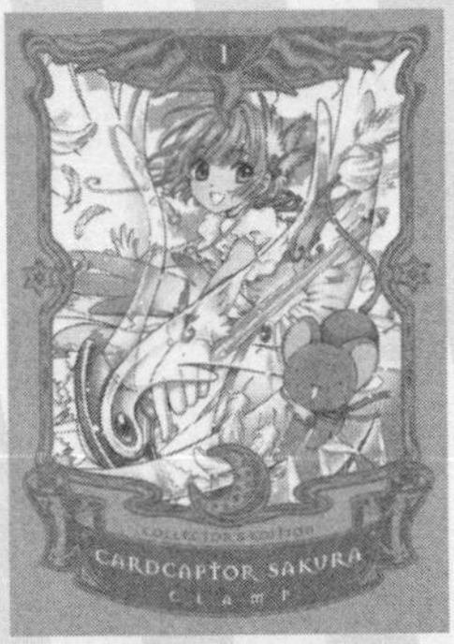
CARDCAPTOR SAKURA
CLAMP

Cardcaptor Sakura
Collector's Edition

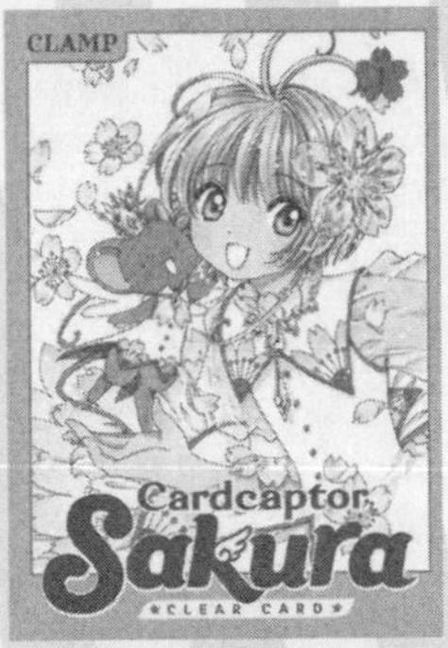
CLAMP
Cardcaptor
Sakura
CLEAR CARD

Cardcaptor Sakura:
Clear Card

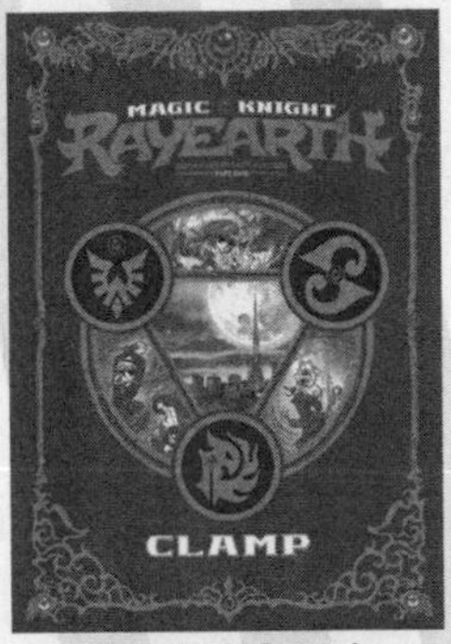
MAGIC KNIGHT
RAYEARTH
CLAMP

Magic Knight Rayearth
25th Anniversary Box Set

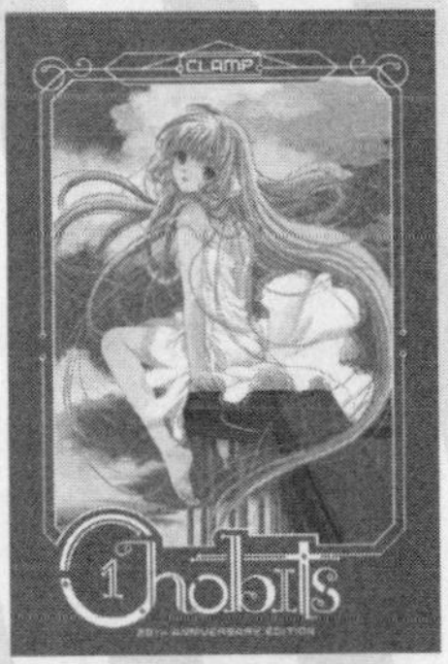
CLAMP
1
Chobits

Chobits

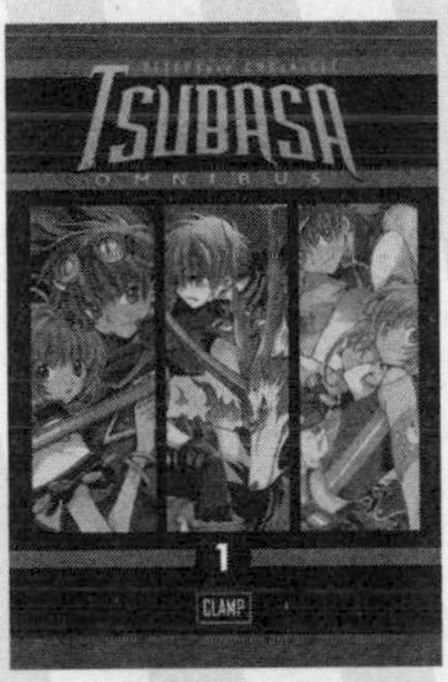
TSUBASA
OMNIBUS
1
CLAMP

TSUBASA Omnibus

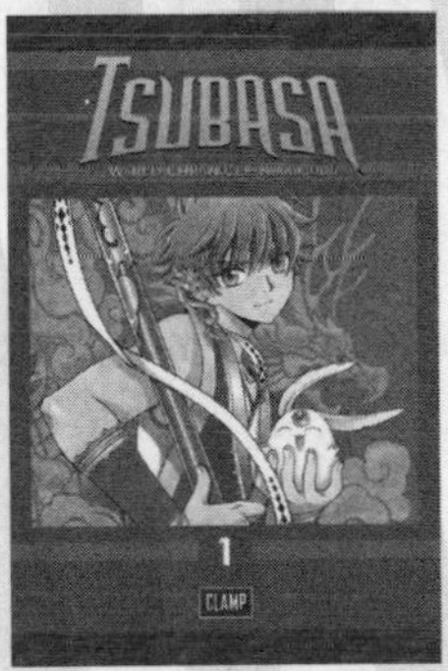
TSUBASA
1
CLAMP

TSUBASA WoRLD CHRoNiCLE

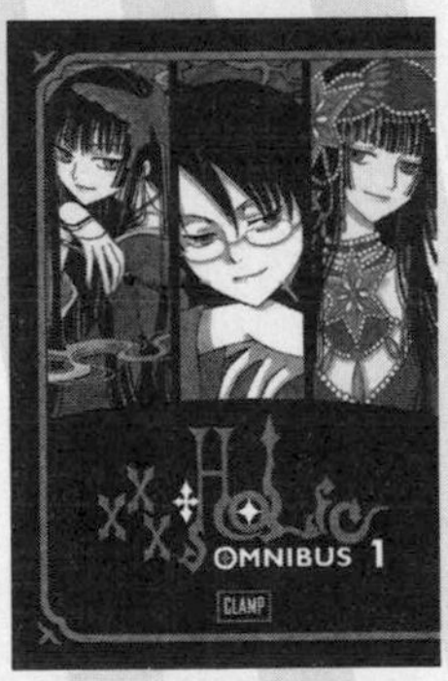
xxxHOLiC
OMNIBUS 1
CLAMP

xxxHOLiC Omnibus

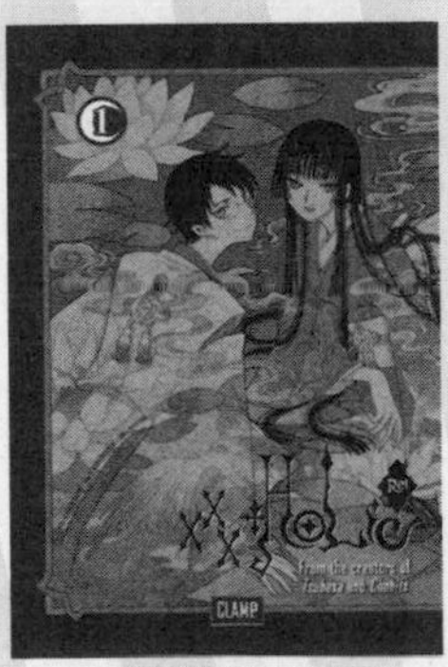
1
xxxHOLiC
CLAMP

xxxHOLiC Rei

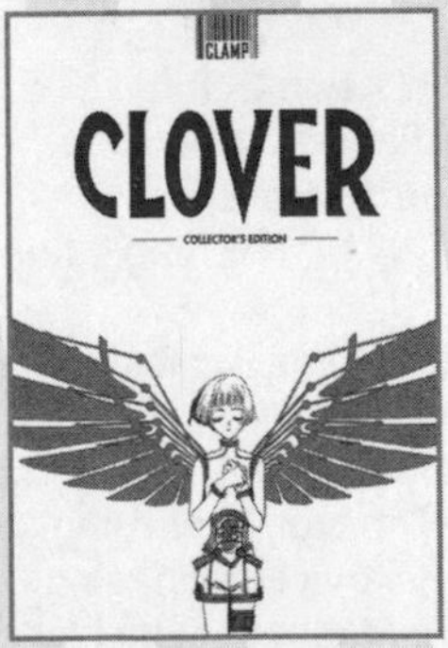
CLAMP
CLOVER
COLLECTOR'S EDITION

CLOVER Collector's Edition

KC KODANSHA COMICS

Kodansha Comics welcomes you to explore the expansive world of CLAMP, the all-female artist collective that has produced some of the most acclaimed manga of the century. Our growing catalog includes icons like *Cardcaptor Sakura* and *Magic Knight Rayearth*, each crafted with CLAMP's one-of-a-kind style and characters!

Rent-A-(Really Shy!)-Girlfriend 2 is a work of fiction. Names, characters, places, and incidents are the products of the author's imagination or are used fictitiously. Any resemblance to actual events, locales, or persons, living or dead, is entirely coincidental.

A Kodansha Trade Paperback Original

Rent-A-(Really Shy!)-Girlfriend 2 copyright © 2021 Reiji Miyajima
English translation copyright © 2021 Reiji Miyajima

All rights reserved.

Published in the United States by
Kodansha USA Publishing, LLC, New York.

Publication rights for this English edition arranged through
Kodansha Ltd., Tokyo.

First published in Japan in 2021 by Kodansha Ltd., Tokyo
as *Kanojo, hitomishirimasu,* volume 2.

ISBN 978-1-64651-385-7

Printed in the United States of America.

1st Printing

Translation: Kevin Gifford
Lettering: Paige Pumphrey
Editing: Jordan Blanco
Kodansha USA Publishing edition cover design by Phil Balsman

Publisher: Kiichiro Sugawara

Director of Publishing Services: Ben Applegate
Associate Director, Publishing Operations: Stephen Pakula
Publishing Services Managing Editors: Madison Salters, Alanna Ruse
Production Managers: Emi Lotto, Angela Zurlo

KODANSHA.US

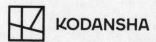